ETHICAL AND LEGAL ISSUES IN STUDENT AFFAIRS AND HIGHER EDUCATION

Publication Number 5

AMERICAN SERIES IN STUDENT AFFAIRS PRACTICE AND PROFESSIONAL IDENTITY

Edited by

NAIJIAN ZHANG, Ph.D.

West Chester University
Department of Counselor Education
West Chester, Pennsylvania

ETHICAL AND LEGAL ISSUES IN STUDENT

AFFAIRS AND HIGHER EDUCATION

Edited by

ANNE M. HORNAK

(With 13 Other Contributors)

CHARLES C THOMAS · PUBLISHER · LTD.
Springfield · Illinois · U.S.A.

Published and Distributed Throughout the World by

CHARLES C THOMAS • PUBLISHER, LTD.
2600 South First Street
Springfield, Illinois 62704

© 2020 by CHARLES C THOMAS • PUBLISHER, LTD.

ISBN 978-0-398-09310-5 (paper)
ISBN 978-0-398-09311-2 (ebook)

Library of Congress Catalog Card Number: 2019033817 (print)

With THOMAS BOOKS c*areful attention is given to all details of manufacturing
and design. It is the Publisher's desire to present books that are satisfactory as to their
physical qualities and artistic possibilities and appropriate for their particular use.*
THOMAS BOOKS *will be true to those laws of quality that assure a good name
and good will.*

Printed in the United States of America
MM-C-1

Library of Congress Cataloging-in-Publication Data

Names: Hornak, Anne M., 1972- editor.
Title: Ethical and legal issues in student affairs and higher education /
  edited by Anne M. Hornak (with 13 contributors).
Description: Springfield, Illinois, USA: CHARLES C THOMAS PUBLISHER, LTD.,
  2019. | Series: American series in student affairs practice and
  professional identity; 5 | Includes bibliographical references and
  index.
Identifiers: LCCN 2019033817   ISBN 9780398093105 (Paperback) | ISBN
  9780398093112 (eBook)
Subjects: LCSH: Student affairs services--Moral and ethical aspects--United
  States. | Student affairs services--United States--Administration. |
  Student affairs administrators--Professional ethics--United States.
Classification: LCC LB2342.92 .E74 2019 | DDC 371.4--dc23
LC record available at https://lccn.loc.gov/2019033817

CONTRIBUTORS

V. Barbara Bush, Ph.D. is an Associate Professor and Master's Degree Coordinator in the Higher Education Program at the University of North Texas. She teaches classes in student development theory, higher education administration, and cultural pluralism. She worked for several years as a student affairs professional, including the role of senior student affairs officer, in public and private colleges and universities. Her student affairs publications have been in the areas of community college student affairs, and student services such as financial aid and learning support. Other publications have addressed collaboration efforts involving K-12, community colleges, and universities.

Tricia Bertram Gallant, Ph.D. directs the Academic integrity Office at the University of California San Diego which serves to promote and support a culture of integrity in order to reinforce quality teaching and learning at UCSD. Dr. Bertram Gallant is an internationally known expert on integrity and ethics in education, having authored or edited numerous publications as well as consulted with high schools, colleges, and universities and spoken at conferences around the U.S. as well as in Australia, Canada, Egypt, England, Jamaica, Mexico, and Singapore. She is the author of "Academic Integrity in the Twenty-First Century" (Jossey-Bass, 2008), co-author of "Cheating in School" (Wiley-Blackwell, 2009), editor of "Creating the Ethical Academy" (Routledge, 2011), and section editor for the International Handbook of Academic Integrity (Springer, 2016). Tricia serves on the Executive Board of the International Center for Academic Integrity (ICAI), of which UCSD is an institutional member.

José A. Cabrales, Ph.D. works as a senior director of student success programs and operations, where he provides strategic vision, leadership, and support for developing and building a plan for the launch of a Center for Student Success. José also provides direction for developing programmatic capacity for Student Success Academies that support AASCU's student success agenda and prioritizes institutional change toward equity and credential completion. Prior to AASCU, José worked as a senior associate for higher education practice. José worked with and through a network of regional comprehensive institutions that serve significant numbers of low-income students and students of color to improve student success and close completion gaps. José has also worked as a program manager for community engagement at *Excelencia* in Education. While at *Excelencia,* José managed the outreach and technical assistance to support 13 communities working to increase Latino postsecondary achievement and degree completion. José brings to this work over 10 years of experience as an administrator in higher education, including residence life, admissions, Greek life, career services, and research on Latina/o philanthropy in higher education and student success. As a first-generation college student and a native of Watsonville, California, José earned a Ph.D. from Iowa State University in educational leadership and policy studies, a master's degree from Michigan State University in student affairs administration, and a bachelor's degree in marketing from Santa Clara University.

Patricia L. Farrell-Cole, Ph.D. specializes in organizational development, change, and leadership. She currently works at the Van Andel Biomedical Research Institute as the Organization Innovation and Learning Manager. She holds a master's degree in organizational and adult learning from the University of New Mexico and a Ph.D. in Higher, Adult, and Lifelong Education from Michigan State University. Her work in academia has included evaluating programs and organizational effectiveness and impact, directing associations, serving as a collaborator and leader on statewide initiatives, and advising and teaching students. Her work, specifically on college readiness and success for Michigan's public universities, and knowledge of organizational theories, guides the writing of the chapter on ethics and organizational culture.

P. Daniel Chen, Ph.D. is an associate professor in the Higher Education Program at George Mason University. Previously, he was an associate professor and higher education program coordinator at University of North Texas. His research and teaching focus on spirituality and ethics in higher education, higher education policy and accountability, institutional effectiveness, and science, technology, engineering, and mathematics (STEM) education.

Brian T. Dietz, M.A. is an Associate Dean of Students at Kalamazoo College. He is also a doctoral student in the Educational Leadership, Research and Technology Department at Western Michigan University. He has experience in several functional areas including student unions, new student orientation, alcohol education, residence life, and student activities. Dietz has taught graduate classes on higher education law, the foundations of student affairs, higher education organization and administration, and systems thinking. His research interests include institutional governance, student alcohol use, and higher education finance.

Regina L. Garza Mitchell, Ed.D. is an associate professor of higher education leadership in the Department of Educational Leadership, Research, and Technology at Western Michigan University. She teaches courses on governance and organization, foundations of higher education, systems thinking, and qualitative research, among others. Her research focuses on issues related to leadership, including ethical leadership, organizational change, and online education, primarily in a community college setting.

Anne M. Hornak, Ph.D. is a professor in the Educational Leadership Department at Central Michigan University. She teaches courses on ethics, social justice, and student affairs administration. She also has worked with her colleagues to continue to build a robust international study program in the department, which is focused on social justice in international contexts. Her research focuses on ethics and leadership, community colleges, and intercultural development.

Tamara Hullender, Ph.D. is an Education Services Specialist with the National Guard Bureau and assists Soldiers in the Indiana National Guard pursuing higher education. Her research explores the experiences of posttraditional students, military members, and student veterans in higher education. Specifically, she is interested in the identity development of women veterans and military members concurrently enrolled in college and serving the military.

Natalie Jackson, J. D., Ph.D. currently serves as Associate General Counsel for The University of Toledo. She previously served as Legal Counsel to Owens Community College from 2008–2015. Dr. Jackson has also served as an adjunct professor of Criminal Justice at Owens Community College and an adjunct professor of Higher Education Law at Central Michigan University. She previously served the Lucas County Prosecutor's Office as an Assistant Prosecuting Attorney from 2003–2005. Dr. Jackson earned her B.A. in American Studies from Kent State University in 2000, her J.D. from The Ohio State University in 2003, and her Ph.D. in Higher Education from The University of Toledo in 2009.

Ramona Meraz Lewis, Ed.D. is the faculty coordinator in the higher education and student affairs (HESA) leadership concentration in the Department of Educational Leadership, Research and Technology and serves in the Graduate College as the Faculty Director of Graduate Student Success at Western Michigan University. Lewis teaches foundations of student affairs, college environments, intervention skills, and global perspectives in higher education among others. Lewis' research interests include: graduate education and pedagogy, adult learning with a with a special emphasis on the 50-plus learner, and teaching experiences of student affairs professionals. Prior to joining WMU, Lewis served in a variety of administrative student and academic affairs positions.

Jonathan J. O'Brien, Ed.D. is Assistant Professor of Educational Leadership at California State University, Long Beach, where he teaches courses in law and ethics, leadership, and management in the education doctorate and master's program in Student Development in Higher Education. Jonathan has provided leadership in areas ranging from advising, campus media, health center, and student conduct. He co-chaired the ACPA/NASPA Task Force to develop rubrics for student affairs competencies and he is a regular contributor to the ethics column for ACPA Developments. His research interests focus on ethical practice in student affairs and critical approaches to moral maturity in college students.

Margaret Partlo, Ph.D. earned her degree in Higher Educational Leadership from Central Michigan University in 2015. As the evaluator/grant writer for the College of Education and Human Services at Central Michigan University, she researches, writes, and presents widely on program development and issues related to student success in K–12 and higher education.

Janelle Schaller, J.D. currently serves as Associate General Counsel for The University of Toledo, a position she has held since 2008. Prior to that, Ms. Schaller was in private practice at a Toledo litigation firm from 2003 to 2008. Ms. Schaller earned her B.A. in Political Science from Bowling Green State University in 2000 and her J.D. from The University of Cincinnati in 2003. She is licensed to practice law in Ohio and Michigan.

Without the love and support of my dear partner, David, and my kids, Olivia and Max, this would not have been possible. I thank you and hope that you always know you have a strong voice and use it to lift others up.

FOREWORD

In law a man is guilty when he violates the rights of others.
In ethics he is guilty if he only thinks of doing so.
                                                —Immanuel Kant

E *thical and Legal Issues in Student Affairs and Higher Education* edited by Dr. Anne M. Hornak is a book that helps you the reader gain knowledge on ethical and legal issues in the field of student affairs and develop competency to follow the profession's principles and standards of ethical conduct. With the knowledge and skills provided in this book, you, as student affairs educator, will develop the professional competency of self-regulating and assuring your ethical behaviors in student affairs practice. Consequently, you will know, as Potter Stewart said, "the difference between what you have a right to do and what is right to do."

Ethical and Legal Issues in Student Affairs and Higher Education is an essential volume in the *American Series in Student Affairs and Professional Identity.* The significance of this book is due to its focus on the practical value of ethics and legal issues, one of the Professional Competency Areas for Student Affairs Educators proposed by ACPA/NASPA in 2015. With that said, this book has aimed to address the knowledge, skills, and dispositions required of student affairs educators to develop and maintain integrity in their life and work as described in the Personal and Ethical Foundations Competency Area by ACPA/NASPA in 2015.

Like the editors and authors in other volumes of the series, the editor and the chapter authors of *Ethical and Legal Issues in Student Affairs and Higher Education* are very knowledgeable and experienced in the field of student affairs and higher education. Especially, their expertise on ethics has made this volume significantly valuable for graduate students in student affairs preparation programs and new student affairs educators. Dr. Anne Hornak has worked in the field of student affairs and higher education for many years and her outstanding contribution to the field and the profession has been recognized by both her own institution and the American College Personnel Association—International (ACPA). With her expertise she has identified high quality chapter authors for this book. All the insights and wisdoms on ethics and legal issues from these experts will enlighten you the readers on the development of your professional competency and identity.

Ethical and Legal Issues in Student Affairs and Higher Education provides readers with a few major unique features on ethical practice in student affairs. The first unique feature is that it offers graduate students in student affairs preparation programs and new student affairs educators with theories and frameworks which can be used to challenge student affairs educators campus wide on treating each other with respect and dignity. By doing so, student affairs educators create a culture of respect with justice and civility which makes ethical practice possible. Key concepts and terminologies are clarified and multiple foundational theories relevant to ethical practice in student affairs are integrated and applied.

Second, *Ethical and Legal Issues in Student Affairs and Higher Education* offers multiple ethical decision-making models to guide student affairs educators in their ethical decision-making process. These decision-making models represent diverse disciplinary perspectives which will help student affairs educators while addressing ethical dilemmas. Application of these decision-making models in practice is demonstrated in the book.

Third, *Ethical and Legal Issues in Student Affairs and Higher Education* proposes that ethics is not an individual but an organizational responsibility. Therefore, creating a conversation on ethics among all members of the organization is needed and recognizing ethical behaviors should be encouraged. Through this conversation on ethics, an ethical culture would be established, as a result, student affairs educators would be able to make the right decision.

Fourth, the authors of *Ethical and Legal Issues in Student Affairs and Higher Education* further suggest that ethical decision making as a professional skill that can be practiced and applied in student affairs educators' day-to-day practice. The concepts of ethics and value are distinguished and clarified. How to develop and improve ethical decision-making skills in a specific ethical dilemma is instructed and displayed.

The fifth unique feature that *Ethical and Legal Issues in Student Affairs and Higher Education* presents the reader is the knowledge on the most current legal issues in student affairs and higher education. Some of the major issues about federal law and regulation related to students' rights are on civil rights, free speech, discipline and due process, campus safety, and privacy. Issues around each subject are explained in detail and strategies on how to reduce institutional risk on legal matters are propounded.

Finally, like all other volumes in the *American Series in Student Affairs Practice and Professional Identity*, *Ethical and Legal Issues in Student Affairs and Higher Education* reflects the three themes: (1) integration of ACPA/NASPA Competency Areas for Student Affairs Educators; (2) development of professional identity; and (3) application of knowledge and theories to practice. Particularly, to reveal the theme of applying knowledge and theories to practice, this book has included numerous ethical and legal case studies to help student affairs educators to analyze complex legal and ethical issues that they may face in their daily practice. This book is a valuable tool which not only assists graduate students in student affairs preparation programs and new student affairs educators to expand their knowledge on ethical and legal issues in student affairs but also provides them with insights to develop their ethical decision-making skills.

American Series in Student Affairs Practice and Professional Identity is a unique book series that creates an integration of all ten professional competency areas for student affairs educators outlined by the College Student Educators International (ACPA) and the Student Affairs Administrators in Higher Education (NASPA) in 2015. The series reflects three major themes: professional competencies development, professional identity construction, and case illustrations for theory translation into practice. All volumes in the series are targeting graduate students in student affairs preparation programs and new student affairs educators. The series blends contemporary theories with current research and empirical support and uses case illustrations to facilitate the readers' ability to translate what they have learned into practice and decision making.

Each volume focuses on one area of professional competency except the volume *College Students and Their Environment* which addresses some major aspects of the Interaction of Competencies. As being said the series helps graduate students in student affairs preparation programs and new student affairs educators develop their professional competencies (ACPA/NASPA) by (1) constructing their personal and ethical foundations; (2) understanding the values, philosophy, and history of student affairs; (3) strengthening their ability in assessment, evaluation, and research; (4) gaining knowledge, skills, and dispositions relating to law, policy, and governance; (5) familiarizing with and learning how to effectively utilize organizational and human resources; (6) learning leadership knowledge and developing leadership skills; (7) understanding oppression, privilege, power, and then learning how to understand social justice and apply it in practice; (8) acquiring student development theories and learning how to use them to inform their practice; (9) familiarizing themselves with technologies and implementing digital means and resources into practice; and (10) gaining advising and supporting knowledge, skills and dispositions. As a result, the series helps graduate students in student affairs preparation programs and new student affairs educators foster their professional identity and ultimately achieve their goal of the whole-person education.

Naijian Zhang, Ph.D.
West Chester University of Pennsylvania

ACKNOWLEDGMENTS

This volume has come together with the hard work and dedication of multiple professionals and their perspectives on ethical and legal issues in student affairs and higher education. It is important that I acknowledge the contributions of the chapter authors in this volume; Jonathan O'Brien, Barbara Bush, Daniel Chen, Regina Garza Mitchell, Ramona Meraz Lewis, Brian Deitz, Natalie Jackson, Janelle Schaller, Tricia Bertram Gallant, Patty Farrell-Cole, José Cabrales, Tammy Hullender, and Margaret Partlo. I also wish to acknowledge the editing and manuscript preparation work of Sean Hill. Your diligence and willingness to offer insights and feedback was invaluable along the way. Additionally, I thank Naijian Zhang who shared a vision of a book that would be a tool for student affairs educators, new professionals, and senior student affairs educators as they navigate the complex ethical and legal issues they are faced with regularly. Finally, I wish to thank my colleagues, family, and friends who have been on this journey with me as I navigated this process.

Anne M. Hornak

CONTENTS

ETHICAL AND LEGAL ISSUES IN STUDENT AFFAIRS AND HIGHER EDUCATION

Chapter 1

OVERVIEW OF THE VOLUME

Anne M. Hornak

Universities should be about more than developing work skills. They must also be about producing civic-minded and critically engaged citizens—citizens who can engage in debate, dialogue and bear witness to a different and critical sense of remembering, agency, ethics and collective resistance.

—Henry Giroux

Ethical and Legal Issues in Student Affairs and Higher Education is an edited book exploring ethical and legal issues faced by student affairs educators on our college campuses. The volume will be organized around three major components: (1) professional identity; (2) professional standards and competencies (e.g., CAS, ACPA & NASPA, etc.); and (3) case studies and practical exercises. The three components will be integrated into the chapters in the volume.

The need to create meaningful learning experiences for graduate students and new professionals has long been the goal for many faculty and student affairs educators as they design courses, facilitate professional development training programs, and mentor new professionals. Meaningful learning experiences are situations where students make meaning of information and learn to process it in their own contexts. Ideally in these learning situations, students ask themselves, "How does this impact my life and work?" Baxter Magolda (2001) says "preparing students for life after college requires engaging their minds and their internal selves to work toward the complexity they will need for success" (p. 326). Providing opportunities for students to explore the legal and ethical realities they will face as they navigate student affairs and higher education is an invaluable way to engage both their minds and internal selves.

Professional ethics are a key component of the work we do every day in student affairs and higher education. As a profession we often are faced with ethical and legal issues and many times do not have the proper training or resources to address the dilemmas we face. This book begins to add to the available resources for the preparation of ethical leaders. The chapters will offer an exploration of the dynamics of developing an ethical culture from a conceptual and theoretical perspective, as well as the development of a professional identity.

This book is both critical and timely. A book that focuses on ethical and legal issues in student affairs is needed for faculty in preparation programs, new professionals navigating their identity as student affairs educators, and a resource for mid- and senior-level professionals facilitating ongoing professional development. The book begins to address what it means to have a professional identity, which is ground in the shared ethical and legal values espoused within the profession and academia. Each chapter uniquely contributes to the complexity embedded in the study of ethics and how that is applied to practice. Additionally, the volume is a balance of procedural knowledge, case illustrations, and guided practice exercises to facilitate the reader's ability to translate the theory and research discussed into professional decision making and application.

This text includes nine chapters that will address the complex nature of legal and ethical issues in higher education. This chapter (Chapter One) provides readers with an overview to the volume and orient them to the unique contributions of each chapter. The goal is to situate the importance of ethical and legal preparation in student affairs. Many times, practitioners see themselves as "doers" and overlook the complexity of the work they are doing related to relationships, identity development, behavior, and the truly gray area of what is ethical and what is unethical. The field of student affairs has shared values and standards related to work with students; however, the accountability of acting in ethical ways is often undefined in the field. The major professional organizations (ACPA and NASPA) have ethical standards and principles and a standing ethics board for consultation. However, these ethics boards do not have the power to sanction or hold accountable individual professionals.

Below you will find a brief overview of the chapters that contribute to the entirety of the volume.

Chapter 2: Theoretical Frameworks for Ethical Practice–Jonathan O'Brien

There is a long tradition of character development in U.S. higher education and student theories behind the actions they take in the best interests of students. To illustrate, this chapter focuses on *Respect Happens Here,* a campus-wide campaign that challenges us to think about how we should treat each other. Although the campaign's promotional material rightly calls for civility and justice on campus, it lacks a meaningful statement about why all members of the campus community should participate. After defining key terms, the discussion applies foundational ethical theories and frameworks to the campaign, identifying limitations and tensions and suggesting new directions in student affairs practice grounded in ethical theory. Using multiple theories and perspectives in ways that prioritize students and meet institutional obligations is essential to ethical practice.

Chapter 3: Practical Overview of Ethical Decision-Making Models—Anne M. Hornak

This chapter provides an overview of three ethical decision-making models that are often used for making ethical decisions. The models that will be included represent multiple disciplines, including but not limited to counseling and psychology, social work, sociology, and education. The three models overviewed in the chapter include differing methods for focusing the issue and then exploring potential solutions. The chapter concludes with a case study that is used as an example of how the models can be a guide to making ethical decisions.

Chapter 4: Creating a Campus Conversation About Ethics—Barbara Bush and Daniel Chen

Many researchers and educators have stated the need for ethics curriculum in undergraduate, graduate, and professional educations. However, few have discussed the need for a campus-wide conversation of ethics among administrators, faculty, staff, and students. Indeed, though most people recognize the importance of ethical culture, in practice most people assume ethics as an individual responsibility. For this chapter, we stress the importance of ethics as an organizational responsibility and that an ethical culture in crucial for individuals within the organization to make ethical decisions. We also believe that ethics must be explicitly discussed and ethical behaviors should be recognized in order to create an ethical culture. Therefore, it is extremely important for institutional leaders to create conversations on ethics among all members of the organization. In this chapter, we will first provide a theoretical framework on why campus conversation on ethics is needed. Then, we will use our institution's journey and goal of creating a campus culture of ethics and a shared language and vision for ethics among administrators, faculty, staff, and students as a replicable case study for others.

Chapter 5: Ethical Decision-Making in Practice—Regina Garza Mitchell, Ramona Meraz Lewis, and Brian Deitz

Professionals working in student affairs and higher education make countless decisions on a daily basis. Each of those decisions impacts human lives, whether students, faculty, or staff, which requires a focus on ethics in addition to rules and policies. Being aware of the ethical nature of problems, the ethical approaches you prefer, and the codes to which you adhere can lead to more effective decision-making. It is to this end that we focus on ethical decision making as a professional skill that can be practiced and applied in our day-to-day practice.

Chapter 6: Current Legal Issues in Student Affairs—Natalie Jackson and Janelle Schaller

The relationship between a higher education institution and its students is a complex one that requires student affairs educators to understand the legal rights of students and an appreciation of the legal responsibilities of the institution. A critical competency for student affairs professionals is the ability to identify legal issues arising within daily practice. This chapter introduces the reader to the legal basis for many of the rights afforded to students in the higher education context, including but not limited to federal laws and regulations related to student civil rights, privacy, safety, discipline, and free speech. The authors offer practical discussion of how to reduce institutional risk by leveraging available resources (internal and external), documenting potential issues, and considering all factors for informed decision-making.

Chapter 7: Academic Integrity and the Student Affairs Professional—Tricia Bertram Gallant

Academic integrity may not be the foremost ethical issue on the mind of the student affairs professional, given that it primarily falls under the purview of the faculty and there are a multitude of other pressing ethical issues that fall under the typical jurisdiction of student affairs. Yet, student affairs educators are often pulled into academic integrity matters whether by design or happenstance. In this chapter, the author provides a brief introduction to academic integrity, an overview of different academic integrity systems found in higher education and how the student affairs educator might be situated within such systems, and the different ethical touchpoints at which a student affairs professional might interact with academic integrity. The chapter includes a case studies and recommendations for how student affairs educators should be intentionally designed into an institutional approach to academic integrity.

Chapter 8: Designing a Collective, Ethical, and Equitable Student Success Culture in Hispanic-Serving Institutions—Patty Farrell-Cole and José Cabrales

What does it mean creating and upholding a culture of ethical practices within student affairs at public postsecondary institutions during a time when institutions are under scrutiny for college completion and success? This chapter examines this question by providing the readers a practice-based framework along with questions and potential implications to the questions. The heart of this chapter will be for student affairs professional working in institutions serving low-income students and students of color.

Chapter 9: Ethical Vignettes and Case Studies— Tammy Hullender and Margaret Partlo

This chapter includes three ethical and legal case studies/vignettes that readers may use to analyze complex issues faced within the student affairs profession. Each case study presents an ethical dilemma in higher education associated with special populations of students such as those who study abroad, have military service obligations, or who are in degree programs requiring an internship. Specific state or institutional policies or actual events from legal cases are intertwined with hypothetical concerns posed by a group of student affairs professionals to form a vignette.

Chapter 2

THEORETICAL FRAMEWORKS
FOR ETHICAL PRACTICE

Jonathan J. O'Brien

In many ways, student affairs professionals are applied ethicists, creating working theories based on insights they gather from past dilemmas and their own moral intuition. In fact, most of us use several approaches from traditional ethical theories, although we may not recall their formal names. In this chapter, I present an overview of foundational ethical theories and frameworks that apply to student affairs practice. To frame the discussion, I begin by describing a national campaign designed to promote respect on campuses and I locate it in the context of character education in student affairs. Next, I define ethical terms and concepts used in this chapter. Then, I turn to brief accounts of each theory, discussing their purposes and limitations, and I apply them to the national campaign. Finally, I present complex ethical frameworks relevant to student affairs that draw on the foundational theories.

Creating a Culture of Respect

Recently, a coalition of student affairs professional associations launched, "Where Respect Happens," a campaign to promote openness, connection, support, and civility on campus (ACPA, 2017). Members were asked to create and upload personalized videos responding to questions like, "How has respect benefited you, your students, and your career?" and "How will respect of self and respect of others as a central core cultural value benefit Higher Education?"

Certainly, it is gratifying to know that respect happens here, on our campuses; yet, the campaign materials are vague about why we should respect each other in the first place. Instead, there are references to outcomes like engagement and recommendations from professional associations outside of student affairs. Simply declaring that respect happens on campus does not make it so. In fact, *respect* is a core moral value in building community (Fried, 2011) and a professional virtue in student affairs (ACPA, 2006). No connection is drawn between the purpose of the program and why we should be creating ethical campus communities to enhance the moral character of students and professionals.

The way we think about moral development and ethics has evolved rapidly in a short time; nonetheless, this campaign is part of a legacy of student affairs educators helping students to reach their moral potential and to thrive in ethical campus communities. Throughout this chapter, when I discuss theories and frameworks, I will return to this campaign as a model for how organizers can apply these concepts in ways that promote moral development in students and professionals.

Student Affairs and Moral Development

Historically, a core purpose of U.S. higher education was to develop the moral character of students. This mission persisted well into the twentieth century, as student affairs was maturing into a distinct profession. Writing to contemporary professionals, Hawkes (1954) proclaimed: "The first obligation of any college, which professes the personnel point of view, therefore, is to see to it that its students are presented with challenging opportunities to develop their moral and spiritual potentialities as well as their academic possibilities" (p. 258). In addition to teaching and leadership, faculty and administrators shaped the character of students by setting standards of academic and moral discipline through codes that defined respect for authority and conformity to social norms aligned with the nation's white, middle-class majority.

The social and political turmoil of the 1960s and 1970s brought to the forefront new and long-standing moral concerns about war, poverty, and racism. At the same time, several court rulings and federal regulations effectively ended *in loco parentis,* a legal doctrine that had established a college's formal authority over the moral lives of college students. Henceforth, college students were adults, particularly in matters of discipline and personal responsibility. Encouraged by this freedom, students engaged in protests and other actions to express their frustration with conventional systems of authority that they believed were corrupt and out of touch with many pressing social issues, including discrimination against racial minorities and women. Student affairs professionals mediated interactions between students and campus authorities, assuming the role of moral conscience for the institution (Brown, 1985). As the profession's focus shifted from personnel management to human development, moral discipline was understood as a fairly organized developmental process, described in the cognitive structural theories of William Perry (1999, Lawrence Kohlberg (1986), and Carol Gilligan (1977; 1982).

By the 1990s, U.S. campuses were the frontlines of ideological culture wars among conservative and progressive politicians, educators, and student activists who debated hotly contested social issues like gay rights, abortion, and gun control. In their attempts to gain public support, partisans from all sides appealed to moral principles and religious values. These tensions were reflected in student affairs as well. Defending a conventional morality, Blimling (1998) argued that a "postmodernist philosophy of a value-free society" (p. 72) was contrary to the core values of higher education (e.g., honesty, self-discipline, civility) and eroded its goal of preparing students to be democratic citizens. Fried (1997) embraced this shift in thinking and heralded the dawn of a *new paradigm,* in which competing moral narratives collided in "a blend of interpretations in which no particular set of ideas about 'the good' would dominate and no resolution or course of behavior would be taken for granted" (p. 9).

Today, students continue to advocate for their rights, seek justice for the oppressed, and broadcast their views in real-time via multiple social media platforms. Professionals and students are embedded in a fluid and dynamic ethical context, in a constant state of becoming moral agents (O'Brien, 2016). Although professionals still support students, moral development seems like a charming relic and disciplining students for moral reasons borders on unlawful or immoral in itself. As Nash (1997) observed, colleges focus more effort teaching students how to abide by "laws, rules, procedures, individual and group rights, and entitlements and less on becoming 'good' human beings" (p. 43). Many professionals are left searching for guidelines to support students in a shifting landscape of ethical dilemmas and moral conflicts.

Student affairs professionals are moral mentors for students (Healy, Lancaster, Liddell, & Stewart, 2012) who must demonstrate ethical competency that includes knowledge of ethical theories and how to apply them in rapidly unfolding situations (Fried, 2011). The standards, competencies, and ethical codes published by professional associations are of little help unless we know how to use them and to evaluate their benefits and limitations. This can be confusing for professionals who come to student affairs from related but distinct fields (i.e., lawyers, clinicians, security personnel) and bring their own ethical standards that impact their ethical interactions with students and colleagues (Anderson, Harbor, & Davies, 2007). Even graduates from preparation programs may have only had one or two lectures in a single course in which they memorized codes and ethical decision-making models. For their part, faculty often feel unqualified to teach ethics or they are uncomfortable with the religious overtones of teaching students how to be good. Since there is no licensure in student affairs to enforce ethical standards, all we have is the quality of our interactions with stakeholders to confirm that what we do contributes to the greater good for students, our institutions, and society. We are always representing the student affairs profession and ethics is essential to sustaining our credibility, especially at the campus level where it really matters.

Key Concepts and Terminology

Before presenting the theories, I define the terms used in this chapter. *Ethics* refers to a branch of philosophy concerned with answering life's big questions about what constitutes a good life and the tools we use to guide our choices and actions. *Morality* relates to one's obligation to uphold the ethical values and standards of a group and how to live within this framework. Although ethics and morality are separate ideas, they do overlap in many ways. The extent to which they differ is beyond the scope of this discussion; thus, I use the terms interchangeably to avoid confusion. In a professional field like student affairs, ethics is *applied,* meaning that questions about what to do in difficult situations are focused on the realities of practice, rather than on abstract problems. Thus, for practitioners, *moral conduct* is behavior that comports with ethical codes and institutional values.

Ethical codes are generated by a community of practitioners as a formal statement of good conduct, or as Nash and Jang (2016) have said, the "inspiring story your profession is trying to tell to itself and to outsiders" (p. 57). Examples include the ACPA (2006) *Statement of Ethical Principles and Standards* and the *Statement of Shared Ethical Principles* published by the Council for the Advancement of Standards (CAS) in 2006. Since codes and standards are static, they are not very helpful in dealing with evolving dilemmas. When codes are inadequate, practitioners struggling with an ethical conflict turn to *principles,* like *beneficence, fidelity,* and *justice* (Kitchener, 199), because they help to make a murky decision less complicated. While they lack the specificity of codes, the generality of principles makes them applicable in a broader array of ethical situations and useful for pointing us in the right direction. Principles also ground our actions in accepted values and provide justification for our decisions.

Ambiguity in an ethical conflict is usually due to conflicting principles, rather than codes. An *ethical dilemma* is a situation in which at least two ethical principles are at odds, requiring an individual to make a choice that does the least amount of harm to those involved. Many people confuse dilemmas with "choices between right and wrong or choosing between two unsatisfactory alternatives" (Janosik, Creamer, & Humphrey, 2004, p. 370). Indeed, there are ethical quandaries involved in such situations, but they are not dilemmas. Often, the unpleasant decision we struggle with can be resolved using ethical codes or principles.

When principles conflict with one another, professionals turn to *ethical theories,* which are higher order frameworks that prioritize principles. Ethical theories help us to see why we should be concerned about a dilemma, rather than how we should resolve it. Most ethical decision-making models incorporate more than one theory, in order to cover the spectrum of approaches. Goodchild (2011) reviewed several models used in higher education and found they all contain at least four essential steps:

1. **Focus on the case**—conduct a thorough understanding of the case with detailed analysis of the facts, problem, and parties involved in the situation.
2. **Reflect on laws and professional codes**—use appropriate laws and professional codes of ethics to understand all aspects of the problem and case.
3. **Incorporate foundational theories**—consider the traditional foundational approach, including the ethical theories, related virtues, and theological/religious ethics, in reviewing the moral dimensions of the problem and case as well as its resolution.
4. **Collaborate and assess**—seek to implement the resolution by collaborating with all affected parties and review its outcomes. (p. 149)

This chapter focuses on the third step, in which we scrutinize dilemmas from more than one theoretical stance to achieve the best possible decision. One approach is often inadequate to resolve an ethical conflict. Instead of blindly following steps, we learn to prioritize principles and combine theoretical approaches. Ultimately, we can develop ethical models that best fit our leadership style and the situations we encounter.

Incorporating Ethical Theories in Practice

As professionals who work closely with students every day, ethical theories can seem like an abstract and tedious distraction. This belief persists until we confront an incident with ethical implications and struggle to explain why we are compelled to act. For example, the *ACPA Ethical Principles and Standards* (2006) expects professionals to:

Be aware of situations in which concepts of social justice may conflict with local moral standards and norms and may choose to point out these conflicts in ways that respect the rights and values of all who are involved. They will recognize that violations of accepted moral and legal standards may involve their clients, students, or colleagues in damaging personal conflicts and may impugn the integrity of the profession, their own reputations, and that of the employing institution. (p. 5)

We risk professional negligence and losses of credibility unless we know the values espoused by our institutions and understand the moral basis of principles like *social justice* or *respect.* It is important to ground our actions in a solid foundation of ethics and values so that we can confidently articulate our positions without surrendering to moral relativism and equivocation.

Knowledge of ethical theories also helps to identify the benefits and limitations of different models and apply those that work best for the situation. For example, professionals often use Kitchener's (1985) ethical principles to guide decisions. These were directly adapted from biomedical ethics (e.g., *beneficence* or "do no harm"), making them a good fit for the helping and advising aspects of student affairs work. Yet, Upcraft and Poole (1991) argued that principle-based reasoning may be ill-suited to administrative problems that require a different approach. As an example, they pointed to *autonomy,* a principle referring to a patient's capacity to make informed healthcare decisions; however, in higher education, *autonomy* is often used to justify prioritizing individual rights, like freedom of expression. The First Amendment is law, a baseline standard that protects political or provocative speech; conversely, *autonomy* is a moral principle that calls on us to do what is right rather than what is merely legal. When used as a policy instrument, autonomy is stripped of its moral authority. Later, Lampkin and Gibson (1999) explained that principle-based reasoning is an essential tool for ethical thinking and should not be rejected based on problems of how principles are defined. These shifting perspectives illustrate why understanding the nuance and purpose of ethical theories helps us to apply theoretical approaches appropriately.

Foundational Theories and Perspectives

In this section, I present five major ethical perspectives with important insights for student affairs educators. Just as the respect campaign asks participants to reflect on questions like, "What drives your commitment?" and, "What do YOU believe will be changed in this world with respect as a commitment for everyone?" (ACPA, 2017), it helps to consider our views about moral conduct so we can compare them with the various approaches. Lampkin and Gibson (1999) offered six prompts to help professionals clarify their values and beliefs:

1. Make a list of the values in your moral life.
2. Is there a difference between the way you conduct yourself in your professional and personal roles?

3. What do you think about rules in general?
4. What role do circumstances and consequences play in your moral decisions?
5. How do virtues, principles, and your community interact in your life?
6. How do principles and relationships connect in your life? (pp. xiii–xv)

To this list, I would add two questions of my own: "Is morality an expression of innate characteristics, cultural conditioning, or a combination of both?" and, "How far does your circle of concern extend and whom does it encompass?" Each of these questions draws out key ideas related to each theory.

Principlism

Principlism refers to making ethical judgments guided by values-based standards that are independent of the context of a dilemma or conflict. These theories are also called *deontological,* from the Greek word *deon* or duty. When we follow principles, it means that meeting an ethical standard is more important than the consequences of our actions or how a judgment might reflect on our character. Perhaps the most well-known deontological principle is the *categorical imperative,* proposed by Immanuel Kant (1785/2002). Kant argued that if we all have an obligation to follow rules and laws, then the most important command would be to treat one another with respect and never to exploit others for personal gain or violate their dignity. As the name declares, the categorical imperative is a clear-cut rule that is not negotiable. In addition, it is *reversible,* meaning that we will only do something that we would be willing to have others do to us, and it is *universal,* to be applied always and in every situation. So, for example, if I believe that it is wrong to take a human life, then I would be making this vow because I would not want my life taken from me; moreover, I can never make a special exception for killing another person, even in cases of self-defense or legal execution.

Another well-known deontological theory, *justice as fairness,* was proposed by John Rawls (2001) as a remedy to what he saw as the inherent inequities in utilitarianism (see the *Consequentialism* discussion later in this section). Utilitarian methods attempt to maximize happiness for the most people, but in doing so they can neglect smaller groups or outliers who often are the least advantaged in other ways. Instead, Rawls proposed social justice through the "appropriate distribution of the benefits and burdens of social cooperation" (p. 4). Although this sometimes meant treating privileged individuals differently, he argued that it would be morally defensible if it improves the lives of the least advantaged. Rawls made this assertion based on the observation that if we were all equal and free to choose social and economic arrangements, then we would want to live in a world in which our rights and duties were equally distributed. To illustrate this idea, he described an imaginary, "original position" (p. 11), in which equal members could design the rules for a new society. The only limitation was that the members could not know what their status (e.g., class, race, gender) in the new society would be until after they entered it. Given these conditions, Rawls believed it was unlikely that anyone would want to be disadvantaged. Since we cannot create a new moral order, we must balance the discrepancies between our ethical judgments and our moral intuitions through *reflective equilibrium,* a process of discernment that produces a working theory of justice and brings us closer to an original position (p. 18). This state is never permanent, since we encounter new ethical challenges that disrupt the status quo and restart the discernment process.

The prescriptive nature of principles is both a benefit and a limitation. On one hand, they are relatively easy to describe and can be applied consistently across all ethical conflicts. This is useful in vague situations when we need to convey what is morally acceptable and to justify our actions. Most codes of ethics published by student affairs professional associations are based on principles, such as *autonomy, nonmalfeasance, beneficence, justice, fidelity, veracity,* and *affiliation* (CAS, 2006). Justice, in particular, is a compelling moral principle for student affairs professionals who are committed to increasing access to higher education and equity for underserved student populations. On the other hand, when we limit our ethical judgments to principles, every problem starts to look like a dilemma (Fried, 1997). Indeed, those who insist that principles are permanent are often the ones who benefit most from keeping them in place (Lekan, 2003).

Returning to the campaign example at the start of this chapter, if we view respect as a shared principle, then it is applicable to everyone, across all situations, and we each have an obligation to uphold it. Professionals in orientation, conduct, or academic affairs are familiar with promoting community norms and helping others to live by them. The campaign organizers can bring together campus stakeholders and engage them in an "original position" discussion to reach consensus on what the principle of respect means for their community. Campaign organizers would explain that a principle is never so rigid that we must suppress our conscience to abide by it; they can explain how *reflective equilibrium* is used to resolve personal conflict while preserving an overarching commitment to respect.

Consequentialism

When the impact of our ethical decisions takes priority over principles, we are using a consequentialist approach. Philosophers also refer to these as *teleological* theories, evoking the Greek word *telos,* a worthy purpose. Kidder (2005) referred to these as *ends-based* theories, "focused on arriving at good outcomes rather than the motives or rules that guided us in our choices" (p. 91). A familiar consequentialist theory is *utilitarianism,* advanced by Jeremy Bentham and adapted by John Stewart Mill (1975). The core principle of utilitarianism is *utility,* any action that produces the most benefit for the greatest number of people. Utilitarian judgments begin with predictions about the possible moral consequences of our actions. After imaging multiple outcomes, we narrow them down by using an even-handed analysis of the costs and benefits associated with each, eventually selecting the best course of action. We can apply the utility principle to a specific situation or we can use the principle to determine which rules would lead to the greatest utility and then evaluate our actions (according to those rules) toward achieving utility. Not everyone will flourish by acting according to utility, but the benefits that accrue to the most people can contribute to positive outcomes for everyone.

For some, consequentialism may feel like a kinder approach than principlism, which can seem cold and formulaic. Principlists assert that they are doing the right thing by applying objective principles to problems, and they criticize consequentialists who seem to be sacrificing what is *right* to achieve a *good* (but not necessarily right) outcome. Utilitarianism, in particular, is criticized because it is impossible to predict all the possible outcomes of our decisions. People in the minority of a utilitarian outcome can become collateral damage in the pursuit of happiness for a majority. Thus, consequentialists must be vigilant about implicit biases, which can mask the needs of individuals in vulnerable or smaller groups.

In the respect campaign, a consequentialist view would define the utility principle as maximizing respect for the most people. We want to evaluate situations and rules so that respect is increased. Campaign organizers could encourage participants to reflect before they act, identifying which decisions will increase respect for all involved. Likewise, administrators would be asked to evaluate the rules and practices of their departments per the principle of respect and then monitor the impact of their operations and the degree to which they achieve the desired outcome. A classic utilitarian problem is the budget crisis, in which managers must make difficult decisions about cutting programs. The respect campaign would ask managers to incorporate respect as the utility principle into the cost-benefit analysis. In this approach, we may decide that some programs should not be cut based merely on cost savings; instead, we should consider their impact on retaining students or connecting with minoritized communities.

Care and Responsibility

An orientation to care offers another way of resolving moral dilemmas that is distinct from weighing principles like justice or calculating the potential for utility. Judgments based on care and responsibilities combine the facts of a dilemma with the value of our relationships. In other words, "morality is a matter of responsibility and accountability to particular people in particular situations given the intricate relationships among them" (Lampkin & Gibson, 1999, p. 128). Most student affairs professionals are familiar with the care-based theory of Carol Gilligan (1977; 1982). The theory has three levels, the first of which is an *orientation toward survival,* in which the individual focuses on what is practical for continued existence. Second, *goodness as self-sacrifice,* places the needs of others over the needs of self. And, third, the *morality of nonviolence,* in which one realizes that hurting anyone, including oneself, is immoral. There are transitions between these levels that reconcile what caring means to the individual from one level to another. The highest level of moral judgment is care for others and personal responsibility for making nonviolent choices.

It seems absurd to describe the drawbacks of caring; however, there are some concerns. The web of responsibility we create can also envelop those whom we will never know but are impacted by our actions. Accordingly, we must be mindful of our power and privilege and the (unintentional) harm we can inflict when making moral judgments. For professionals, this means reimagining the prevailing, top-down management paradigm so that it incorporates diverse perspectives (Shapiro & Stefkovich, 2016). Relationships are the focus of care-based ethics; however, some relationships can be toxic and exploitation or manipulation can be masked by abusers who create a false sense of loyalty to a dysfunctional family (Lampkin & Gibson, 1999). In addition, the limits of caring are often not articulated very well. Without boundaries, caregivers quickly find themselves consumed by ostensibly caring relationships. Conversely, we must know how far we will go to care for someone who has committed a reprehensible act or who has simply declined our repeated efforts to care (Tronto, 1987).

The respect campaign benefits from a care-based insight, doing the right thing means being accountable for our actions and pursuing benevolence over violence and self-interest. Although some feminist ethicists have argued that *respect* is a principle-based ethic that reproduces patriarchy, Dillon (1992) explained that caring for other people can lead to respect when first we attempt to know their lived experience through their eyes. Thus, campaign organizers must explain that bestowing respect on someone from a position of power or principle is oppressive. Instead, we should care for others first, as a foundation for respect, which will ultimately reinforce our care for them.

Finally, it reminds organizers that the campaign cannot be imposed on community members by a select group; everyone with a stake in the outcome must be invited to contribute.

Cosmopolitanism

In some ways, cosmopolitanism extends an ethic of care to a global scale, bringing all of humanity into our circle of concern. The term *cosmopolitan* is traced to Diogenes of Sinope, a Greek philosopher, who considered himself a citizen of the world and aligned himself with fellow humans rather than swear allegiance to any city-state or nation. Today, one who claims to be a cosmopolite will accept that "we all have obligations to strangers" (Appiah, 2006, p. 153) and will pledge "ultimate moral responsibility to the whole of humanity, rather than absolutizing a presumably exceptional part" (Khan, 2015). As Nash and Jang (2016) explained, cosmopolitanism "is the ethics we must learn to practice in a shared world where hard-and-fast, age-old identity boundaries are fast disappearing" (p. 40).

Two important principles of cosmopolitanism are *universal concern* and *respect for difference,* which Appiah (2006) clarified via four assumptions aimed at bridging the moral divide between an individual and the rest of humanity. First, we must balance our commitment to human rights with an obligation to preserve our own people. Second, although we must do what we can to advance justice, we are limited by our personal capacities and resources. Third, our actions must be authentic, reflecting our culture of origin. And, fourth, we must be willing to engage with a variety of ethical values and perspectives (pp. 163–164). These assumptions underscore that our moral obligations to humanity have reasonable limitations bounded by our individual abilities and cultural backgrounds.

Similarly, the Dalai Lama (2012) has said that a global ethics distinct from any religion or ideology must be organized around the principle of *compassion,* which seeks to alleviate human suffering and promote justice (p. 59). The Dalai Lama explained that genuine concern for others is far more persuasive than violence; however, depending on the context, compassion does not preclude self-defense. To act with compassion requires a combination of *motivation* and *discernment.* Our moral motivation is grounded in what we believe about the dignity and worth of others. Discernment is intellectual reasoning, which we use to sort out our actions leading to the best outcomes. These processes reinforce each other, enhancing self-awareness and compassion.

From this short description, we see that cosmopolitanism is different from the other ethical theories on which student affairs was based. Cosmopolites think beyond principles or maximizing benefits to a global perspective advancing human dignity and equality. Nash and Jang (2016) asserted that most college students today "are actually cosmopolites because they understand that the United States can no longer exist as an entity independent to other countries" (p. 42). Indeed, increases in social media use and international travel for study and pleasure make it easier to learn about and connect with others, increasing our awareness of how local decisions have global implications.

Attempts to move toward cosmopolitanism have generally been met with resistance, in part because the world is structured around the interests of governments, rather than the needs of individuals. In 1948, the United Nations (2015) enacted the *Universal Declaration of Human Rights,* a list of 30 "inalienable entitlements of all people, at all times, and in all places" (pp. v–vi) that promote "universal respect for and observance of human rights and fundamental freedoms" (p. 2). Although the Declaration is not a cosmopolitan manifesto (it was created by governments on *behalf* of their citizens and is not enforceable), the principles it espouses are a noteworthy effort to codify the duties and rights to which all individuals are ostensibly entitled. Other sources of resistance to cosmopolitanism include nationalist movements that see it as a threat to state sovereignty and others who oppose attempts to substitute moral universalism in place of religious beliefs or dominant political ideologies (Appiah, 2006).

The pluralistic vision of a cosmopolitan ethic and its principles of *respect for difference, universal concern,* and *compassion* broaden the scope of the respect campaign to a global scale. While respect may be happening *here,* on campus, cosmopolitanism reminds us that our local actions have wide-ranging implications for the environment, human rights, and economic security. When we learn to see the world from other perspectives, the biases in our own culture are revealed. Accordingly, organizers can help participants to explore their motivations for respecting others and model a process of discernment that leads to choices that engender respect in our own communities without undermining our responsibility as citizens of the world.

Virtue Ethics

Virtue ethics emphasizes the development of individual moral character within the context of a community that values and reinforces them. As Aristotle (Ackrill,1981) explained, virtues like *loyalty, temperance,* and *honesty* are cultivated over a lifetime focused on achieving what the Greeks called, *arête,* or excellence. Virtues are an ideal, situated between excesses and deficiencies of character to be avoided. *Courage,* for example, is a virtuous ideal that can spiral into foolishness or devolve into cowardice without self-discipline and focus. Nash and Jang (2016) summarized virtues in the contemporary context as "qualities, habits, dispositions, or skills that provide us with the moral impetus for doing what is right and good. A virtue is a core trait of one's moral character" (p. 76).

According to the *ACPA Ethical Principles and Standards* (2006), professionals should demonstrate virtues of *prudence, integrity, respectfulness,* and *benevolence* (p. 7). These and other virtues are acquired through direct instruction and mentoring in the context of professional development, graduate preparation, and lived experience. Even the most virtuous professional can suppress their morals when their reputation or livelihood is at stake. As Fried (1997) observed, "a person can easily know what he or she ought to do, based on principled reasoning, and still be unable or unwilling to do it" (p. 14). Over time, however, our character develops and our response to novel situations is more confident. We focus on becoming the kind of person we should be rather than relying on principles or other external factors to tell us what to do.

Virtues are reflected in student affairs practice as dispositional competencies, the "relatively stable patterns of behavior that are grounded in an educator's values and motives" (ACPA/ NASPA, 2016, pp. 4–5). The *Professional Competencies Rubrics* (ACPA/NASPA, 2016) offers many examples of dispositions for each of the ten professional competences. For example, the *personal and ethical foundations* competency includes dispositions "to seek help, to accept ethical guidance, to support others' development, and to sustain an ethical workplace culture" (p. 26). Similarly, the *advising and supporting* competency lists "dispositions to support others, foster trust, and respect the identities, views, and choices of others" (p. 10). In student affairs, professionals work toward excellence in professional competencies, which includes cultivating the dispositions to put their knowledge and skills into practice.

Critics of virtue ethics regard them as too self-centered, diverting attention from ethical principles, or from pursuing positive outcomes for the least advantaged. Others call them outdated, random, and unteachable (Nash, 1997, p. 15). Opinions about ideal virtues vary across cultures, making it difficult to know what is praiseworthy or reprehensible. Even in the same culture or group, virtues can be valued differently depending on the person and the situation. In education, dispositional competencies have been criticized by some as an ideological *litmus test,* in which educators must publicly avow a set of principles perceived to be politically motivated (i.e., social justice, equity, excellence) or risk public shaming and employer retaliation (Splitter, 2010).

The respect campaign can focus on helping members of the campus community strive for *respectfulness* and other qualities of personal excellence that are aligned with the institution's values and mission. Organizers can facilitate dialogue about why respect is a worthy virtue and explore ways to avoid the vices of contempt or incivility. Existing training programs for student employees and professional development must include content on ethical leadership. The core message is that we do not have to be perfect, but the journey toward personal and professional excellence is commendable (O'Brien, 2016).

Complex Theoretical Frameworks

Thus far, I have discussed five foundational theories relevant to student affairs practice. Now, I turn to ethical frameworks that blend these theories together to demonstrate how to approach moral challenges from multiple perspectives. To guide this discussion, I adapt a framework proposed by Nash and Jang (2016) that describes four, interrelated moral domains. First, is the *private moral space,* a repository of beliefs and values that is the subjective basis of our ethical conduct. Second, *small-community moral spaces* are intimate and formative groups, like family, ethnic groups, and religion that teach us a moral language, validate its meaning, and provide a cultural reference for the choices we make throughout life. Third, the *secular pluralist space of large organizations* is the public arena of formal education, politics, and professional pursuits in which ethical codes and laws clarify our roles and duties, and regulate how we work with others to achieve the greater good. And, fourth, the *cosmopolitan global space,* transcends national borders and competing ideologies in pursuit of an ethical world view that respects pluralism while honoring the moral beliefs of individuals. In this discussion, I combine the *private* and *small-community* spaces into one category, which I call *personal moral space,* and retain the *organizational* and *cosmopolitan* spaces as separate categories. Separating the frameworks helps to clarify their presentation; however, in practice, as I indicate in the descriptions, they frequently overlap.

Personal Moral Space

The personal moral space combines the beliefs and commitments acquired over a lifetime of experiences along with the moral teachings and cultural rituals found in small communities of family, faith, and other intimate networks (see Nash & Jang, 2016). The foundational ethical theories associated with this space are *virtue* and *care.* We develop virtues in small communities like families and significant relationships where we are cared for and learn to care for others. Eventually, we learn to take responsibility for those with whom we have no personal connection. In this space, I locate three ethical frameworks: *moral maturity* (Rest, 1994), *moral identity* (Aquino & Freeman, 2009), and *moral intuition* (Haidt, 2012).

For decades, judgment was considered the basis of moral development (Kohlberg, 1971). A major shift in this position was articulated by James Rest and his colleagues (Rest, Narváez, Bebeau, & Thoma, 1999) who proposed a four-component model of moral maturity situating *judgment* among three additional functions: *sensitivity, motivation,* and *character.* Moral *sensitivity* is the awareness that a social situation has ethical implications that merit our attention. Judgment is the intellectual discernment we use to weigh the principles and consequences involved in the situation. *Motivation* is the intuitive sense, our emotional instincts that balance judgment by assessing our resolve to act and prioritize principles and personal values. Moral *character* is the will to act, based on the accumulation of insights acquired from the previous functions. The inclusion of character in the model emphasizes that the outcome of ethical discernment must be action. Like virtues, aimed at achieving excellence of character, moral maturity entails cultivating the four components over time until we become adept at spotting ethical quandaries around us, making sound decisions that resonate with a sense of what is right, and acting with confidence that our conduct is reasonable (Rest & Narváez, 1991).

Of the four components of moral maturity described by Rest (1994), *motivation* has garnered increased attention among other researchers. The *model of moral identity* (Aquino & Freeman, 2009) posits that the link between moral judgment (what we think) and moral action (what we do) is mediated by the salience or importance we place on our moral identity. *Moral identity* is a conscious process that "motivates choices and actions that demonstrate social responsiveness to the needs of others," while allowing us to meet our "desire for self-consistency" (p. 379). In short, we are motivated to do the right thing based on a yearning to be the moral person we imagine ourselves to be, effectively integrating our self-concept with our conduct (Blasi, 1983). For example, if I have a highly salient moral identity, I am constantly attuned to the ethical cues that surround me and I will want to act in ways that reinforce my character. Of course, for most individuals, moral concerns are not always top of mind. According to Aquino and Freeman (2009), the salience of our moral identity can be influenced by incentives (e.g., money, prestige, peers, mentors) in positive or negative ways. If we harm another unintentionally, we disrupt our moral self-concept (Aquino & Freeman, 2009). To avoid the pain or shame, we may engage in strategies of self-deception, such as or sanitizing our language when we talk about the situation, evading personal responsibility, or reframing our opponents as simplistic or malevolent (see Bandura, 1991).

Moral psychologist Jonathan Haidt (2012) has likewise argued that moral judgment is more dependent on *intuition* (motivation) than previously believed. According to Haidt, ethical reasoning contributes only a small part to how we resolve moral problems; in fact, we neglect the degree to which feelings and passion influence moral action. Based on research conducted with people around the world, Haidt found that we share at least five moral intuitions: *care, fairness, loyalty, authority,* and *sanctity. Care,* which evolved to enhance the bond of parent and child, now heightens our awareness of pain in others and the desire to prevent harm. The evolution of *fairness, loyalty,* and *authority* emerged from the tribal dynamics of early humans to establish standards for reciprocity, allegiance, and status among members. *Sanctity* protected our ancestors from unsanitary conditions and has since evolved into cultural symbols of impurity and sin. As with virtues, the degree to which individuals express these intuitions varies by culture (Haidt & Joseph, 2004). Haidt (2012) has used this theory to explain the underlying motives of conservative and liberal partisans in the U.S. who cling tenaciously to ideological positions on contested issues like gender-neutral bathrooms, universal healthcare, and abortion.

In the respect campaign, these personal space frameworks remind us that framing respect as caring for others and promoting *respectfulness,* as a virtue is merely the beginning. Ethical action is deeply rooted in identity. We have agency, as moral beings, to work toward excellence by avoiding the vices of self-deception. These frameworks account for how moral judgment is influenced by intuitions like *care, authority,* and *purity,* which contribute to profound ideological divides between individuals who observe the same events but respond in opposing ways. Respect campaign participants must be able to articulate their ideal moral selves and explore the motives they have for being respectful, such as a desire for social justice, the pursuit of the greatest good, or the command of a deity. Together, participants can learn to dialogue around shared passions and negotiate moral differences to achieve a respectful campus community.

Organizational Moral Space

In the *organizational moral space,* we engage each other through political, legal, and ethical structures and negotiate our interests using foundational theories like *principlism* and *consequentialism* (Nash & Jang, 2016). Dissimilar as they are, these theories are used interchangeably by student affairs professionals, depending on the context. An assortment of frameworks in the organizational space describe how professionals integrate their ethical identities with institutional culture (Anderson, Harbor, & Davies, 2007), reconcile conflicts among personal and professional ethical codes (Shapiro & Stefkovich, 2016), and understand moral problems of practice (O'Brien, 2017; Reybold, Halx, & Jimenez, 2008).

A four-stage ethical identity framework proposed by Anderson et al. (2007) bridges the *personal* and *organizational* moral spaces. Just as virtues are cultivated in community, professionals develop as ethical leaders by integrating their personal beliefs with organizational values. First, *assimilation* is marked by openness to learning and adopting the ethical values of the institution. Second, *separation* describes a state of detachment from organizational values, either because members hold a contingent status in the group or they regard the values they brought with them to be preferable to those they observe in the new culture. Third, *marginalization* is an ethical apathy or general disinterest in standards and a lack of motivation to accept institutional values. Fourth, *integration* is an ideal balance between a professional's personal values and those of the institution. This framework posits that professionals can move from uncritical acceptance of institutional values to an ethical identity that is balanced between personal values and institutional obligations.

While adaptation to ethical culture is one way for professionals to navigate the organizational moral space, another approach locates students at the center of an *ethic of the profession* (Shapiro & Stefkovich, 2016). Placing students as the *telos* or purpose of ethical conduct clearly establishes that decision-making and leadership must always result in the best possible circumstances for student learning and success. The professional ethic is a dynamic and pragmatic framework, meaning that there is no preferred way to resolve a dilemma; rather, we develop a unique response to ethical challenges by drawing from different theoretical approaches and consulting with colleagues. We act to benefit students by integrating personal conscience with various codes, standards, and stakeholder expectations.

Another pair of frameworks, based on empirical evidence, describes how student affairs professionals make meaning of the moral problems they encounter in practice. In the first, O'Brien (2017) analyzed self-reported incidents of student affairs professionals and proposed a typology of four moral positions: *authority, equity, compliance,* and *strategy*. The *authority* position was characterized by respect for ethical principles and reliance on an internal compass to meet them. An *equity* position favored interpersonal relationships, seeking outcomes that benefitted those who needed the most help. The *compliance* position valued fairness and implemented processes with objectivity, rationality, and efficiency. *Strategy* was the most pragmatic position, in which participants generated multiple options and selected those most likely to be successful. As positions, rather than developmental stages, the types suggested a flexible repertoire that professionals take up depending on the situation.

The second study by Reybold et al. (2008) explored *professional ethicality* or the ways practitioners implemented student affairs principles in their work. Ethicality was manifest across three dimensions: *regulatory, situational,* and *collective*. Participants using the *regulatory dimension* relied on principles, rules, and codes to guide conduct and monitor transgressions. The *situated dimension* was more contextual and relational, relegating codes to one step in the process of resolving a dilemma rather than the basis of a decision. Individuals resolving ethical dilemmas through *collective ethicality* built on *regulatory* and *situated* dimensions and engaged others in making decisions that were "subject to collective critique according to professional codes, principles, and shared values" (p. 118). With coaching and professional maturity, individuals were posited to move from deductive application of principles in the *regulatory* dimension to the inductive approach of *collective ethicality*.

The respect campaign is perhaps most at home in the organizational space, with these frameworks that bring together theories of consequentialism and principlism while recognizing the influence of institutional context on ethical practice. Professionals move from undisputed acceptance of ethical norms to a nuanced integration of institutional values, personal beliefs, and the interests of diverse stakeholders, which are focused on the best interests of students. These frameworks also show how principle-based thinking can be applied to situations with many possible consequences. For example, when *respect* is defined as both a principle and an outcome, campaign participants can work together to find instances that demonstrate respect and highlight these exemplars as they propose new ways to achieve desirable outcomes in other situations where respect is lacking.

Cosmopolitan Moral Space

The cosmopolitan moral space is a global ethic focused on concern for all people because of their individual differences, not despite them. Cosmopolitanism entails setting aside our individual prejudices to take some responsibility for resolving the ethical problems that plague our world (Nash & Jang, 2016). Student affairs in the U.S. has been slow to embrace cosmopolitanism, in part because the nation is geographically separated from most other countries and it has a long history of political and economic isolationism. Fortunately, professional associations and graduate programs in the U.S. have been making progress toward reversing this trend via international exchanges and global partnerships (Dalton, 1999). Few frameworks articulate a cosmopolitan ethic in student affairs; however, the literature on civic engagement and study abroad offers insights for future directions.

Campus-based civic engagement initiatives vary widely, but their general purpose is to build the capacity of students to analyze real problems critically and learn to navigate democratic institutions to improve the human condition (Colby, Ehrlich, Beaumont, & Stephens, 2003). This assumes that social problems have moral implications and that individuals can work together to change society; thus, civic engagement brings together the *person-*

al, organizational, and *cosmopolitan* spaces. Colby et al. identified *understanding, motivation,* and *skill* as the overarching competencies needed for moral and civic engagement. First, *understanding* includes cognitive functions like "interpretation, judgment and knowledge" (p. 19). Second, *motivation* is the "values, interests, emotions such as empathy and hope, sense of efficacy, and moral and civic identity" (p. 19) that prioritize our actions. Third, *skills* are behavioral abilities and practices that put *understanding* and *motivation* into action, such as conducting research, written and verbal communication, and organizing others.

Other opportunities to develop a cosmopolitan ethic occur when we are fully immersed in another culture, such as international study (Starcher, 2013) or gap-year programs (O'Shea, 2010). Living among others, in their native cultures, allows us to observe the priorities they place on moral concerns, like individual expression, collective responsibility, the roles of government and religion in daily life, and the rights of women, minorities, and the poor. We learn that most cultures have a coherent belief system, which allows us to compare and critique our own moral norms. Johnson and Hathcock (2014) explained that students often begin study abroad experiences from a position of naïve cultural relativism, until they encounter local customs that provoke unease or injustice; unable to escape the situation completely, they must reconcile their differences and move closer to understanding moral pluralism.

Starcher (2013) described how students in a three-year, residential study abroad program developed "acceptance, understanding, patience, respect, and compromise" (p. 157) via four processes: *agency, constant comparison, risk-taking,* and *reflection.* Through *agency,* students spontaneously formed peer groups and initiated their own experiential learning activities. When students traveled on their own, they engaged in *constant comparison,* interpreting firsthand what they learned in the classroom. Students engaged in *risk taking* by shedding the security of their home cultures, being open to the unknown, and meeting new friends. Ongoing *reflection* allowed students to process thoughts and feelings about their encounters with different worldviews. While this is a robust model of development in the cosmopolitan moral space, it favors those who are inclined to seek out novel experiences and have the means and ability to travel for extended periods. Despite these limitations, the four processes can be transferred to on-campus and community-based contexts where strangers of good will come into contact.

The cosmopolitan space reminds organizers of the respect campaign that our campuses are not the only location that demands our attention. While not the primary arena for the moral problems we face on our campuses every day, this space situates our experiences in a global context where we have some responsibility to fellow humans, no matter where they live.

Campaign organizers can use the competencies and processes described in this section to help participants distinguish between moral pluralism and the dangers of relativism, a lazy form of ethical reasoning that rationalizes ethical lapses observed in another group as part of their identity that must not be challenged. Seemingly well-intentioned, the danger of this thinking is evident when *their* problems metastasize, threatening bystanders and ourselves with harm. Partnerships with campus-based civic engagement and study abroad programs can help participants to develop skills and to explore and challenge their assumptions.

Conclusion

The *Respect Happens Here* campaign has honorable goals that are in line with a long tradition in the profession of facilitating the moral development of students. The campaign draws attention to the desperate need for campus-wide conversations about how we should treat each other. Further, it emphasizes that we may not always agree, but we share a professional commitment to advance student flourishing at educational institutions where everyone can learn, work, and build the foundation for a good life. In this chapter, I presented ethical foundations and frameworks that integrate theories across *personal, organizational,* and *cosmopolitan* domains. The ethical perspectives we learned in childhood are developed throughout our careers in spaces that define, challenge, and shape them. In the organizational context, we integrate our interpretations of theories, like those presented in this chapter, into a professional ethic reflective of personal character and commitment to institutional values (Ortiz, O'Brien, & Martinez, 2015). This process looks different for everyone. For some, moral action must be weighed against personal needs and professional obligations; wheras for others, action is part of a greater moral obligation to humanity that has few boundaries. Regardless of what we decide, our student's benefit by seeing us grapple with ethical issues and observing how we weigh the moral dimensions before we act. By expanding our knowledge of the theories behind the actions we believe are right, we move that much closer to being better educators and fellow human beings.

REFERENCES

Ackrill, J. L. (1981). Aristotle the philosopher. New York: Oxford University Press.

American College Personnel Association. (2006). *Statement of ethical principles and standards.* Retrieved from http://www.myacpa.org/sites/default/files/Ethical _ Principles_Standards.pdf

American College Personnel Association. (2017, May 24). *Join the respect movement!* Retrieved July 10, 2017, from http://www.myacpa.org/where-respect-happens

American College Personnel Association, & National Association of Student Personnel Administrators. (2016). *ACPA/NASPA Professional Competencies Rubrics.* Washington, DC: Authors.

Anderson, S. K., Harbour, C. P., & Davies, T. G. (2007). Professional ethical identity development and community college leadership. In D. M. Hellmich & G. R. Boggs (Eds.), *Ethical leadership in the community college: Bridging theory and daily practice* (pp. 256–266). San Francisco: Jossey-Bass.

Appiah, K. A. (2006). *Cosmopolitanism: Ethics in a world of strangers.* New York: W.W. Norton.

Aquino, K., & Freeman, D. (2009). Understanding moral functioning. In D. Narváez & D. K. Lapsley (Eds.), *Personality, identity, and character: Explorations in moral psychology* (pp. 375–395). New York: Cambridge University Press.

Bandura, A. (1981). Self-referent thought: A developmental analysis of self-efficacy. In J. H. Flavell & L. Ross (Eds.), *Social cognitive development: Frontiers and possible futures* (pp. 200–239). Cambridge, UK: Cambridge University Press.

Blasi, A. (1983). Moral cognition and moral action: A theoretical perspective. *Developmental Review, 3*(2), 178–210.

Blimling, G. S. (1998). Navigating the changing climate of moral and ethical issues in student affairs. In D. Cooper and J. Lancaster (Eds.), *Beyond law and policy: Reaffirming the role of student affairs* (New Directions for Student Services, no. 82, pp. 65–76). San Francisco: Jossey-Bass.

Brown, R.D. (1985). Creating an ethical community. In H. J. Canon & R. D. Brown (Eds.), *Applied ethics in student services* (New Directions for Student Services, no. 30, pp. 67–79). San Francisco: Jossey-Bass.

Colby, A., Ehrlich, T., Beaumont, E., & Stephens, J. (2003). *Educating citizens: Preparing undergraduates for lives of civic and moral responsibility.* San Francisco: Jossey-Bass.

Council for the Advancement of Standards. (2006). *CAS professional standards for higher education* (6th ed.). Washington, DC: Author.

Dalai Lama. (2012). *Beyond religion: Ethics for a whole world.* New York: Random House.

Dalton, J. C. (1999). The significance of international issues and responsibilities in the contemporary work of student affairs. In J. C. Dalton (Ed.), *Beyond borders: How international developments are changing Student Affairs practice* (New Directions for Student Services, no. 86, pp. 3–11). San Francisco: Jossey-Bass.

Dillon, R. S. (1992). Respect and care: Toward moral integration. *Canadian Journal of Philosophy, 22*(1), 105–131.

Fried, J. (1997). Changing ethical frameworks for a multicultural world. In J. Fried (Ed.), *Ethics for today's campus: New perspectives on education, student development, and institutional management* (New Directions for Student Services, no. 77, pp. 5–22). San Francisco: Jossey-Bass.

Fried, J. (2011). Ethical standards and principles. In J. H. Schuh, S. R. Jones, & S. R. Harper (Eds.), *Student services: A handbook for the profession* (pp. 96–119). New York: John Wiley & Sons.

Gilligan, C. (1977). In a different voice: Women's conceptions of self and of morality. *Harvard Educational Review, 47*(4), 481–517.

Gilligan, C. (1982). *In a different voice.* Cambridge, MA: Harvard University Press.

Goodchild, L. F. (2011). Enhancing individual responsibility in higher education: Embracing ethical theory in professional decision-making frameworks. In T. B. Gallant (Ed.), *Creating the ethical academy: A systems approach to understanding misconduct and empowering change* (pp. 135–152). New York: Routledge.

Haidt, J. (2012). *The righteous mind: Why good people are divided by politics and religion.* New York: Vintage.

Haidt, J., & Joseph, C. (2004). Intuitive ethics: How innately prepared intuitions generate culturally variable virtues. *Daedalus, 133*(4), 55–66.

Hawkes, A. L. R. (1954) Learning more about purpose-formation and self-control. In E. M. Lloyd-Jones & M. R. Smith (Eds.), *Student personnel work as deeper teaching* (pp. 256–266). New York: Harper.

Healy, M. A., Lancaster, J. M., Liddell, D. L., & Stewart, D. L. (2012). The role of the campus professional as a moral mentor. In D. L. Liddell & D. L. Cooper (Eds.), *Facilitating the moral growth of college students* (New Directions for Student Services, no. 139, pp. 83–92). San Francisco: Jossey-Bass.

Janosik, S. M., Creamer, D. G., & Humphrey, E. (2004). An analysis of ethical problems facing student affairs administrators. *NASPA Journal, 41*(2), 356–374.

Johnson, A. B., & Hathcock, D. R. (2014). Study abroad and moral development. *eJournal of Public Affairs, 3*(3) 52–70.

Kant, I. (1785/2002). *Groundwork for the metaphysics of morals.* New York: Oxford University Press.

Khan, H. H. A. (2015, November). *The cosmopolitan ethic in a fragmented world.* Speech presented at Jodidi Lecture in Harvard University, Cambridge, MA. Retrieved July 10, 2017.

Kidder, R. M. (2005). *Moral courage.* New York: Harper.

Kitchener, K. S. (1995). Ethical principles and ethical decisions in student affairs. In H. J. Canon & R. D. Brown (Eds.), *Applied ethics in student services* (New Directions for Student Services, no. 30, pp. 17–30). San Francisco: Jossey-Bass.

Kohlberg, L. (1986). A current statement on some theoretical issues. In S. Modgil & C. Modgil (Eds.), *Lawrence Kohlberg: Consensus and controversy* (pp. 485–546). Philadelphia: Falmer Press.

Kohlberg, L. (1971). Stages of moral development. *Moral Education, 1,* 23–92.

Lampkin, P. M., & Gibson, E. M. (1999). Mountains and passes: Traversing the landscape of ethics and student affairs administration. *NASPA Monograph Series, 22.* Washington, DC: National Association of Student Personnel Administrators.

Lekan, T. (2003). *Making morality: Pragmatist reconstruction in ethical theory.* Nashville, TN: Vanderbilt University Press.

Mill, J. S. (1975). *Three essays: On liberty; Representative government; The subjection of women.* New York: Oxford University Press.

Nash, R. J. & Jang, J. J. J. (2016). *Teaching college students how to solve real-life moral dilemmas: An ethical compass for quarterlifers.* New York: Peter Lang.

Nash, R. J. (1997). Answering the "virtuecrats": A moral conversation on character education. *Advances in Contemporary Educational Thought Series, 21.* New York: Teachers College Press.

Nash, R. J., & Jang, J. J. J. (2016). *Teaching college students how to solve real-life moral dilemmas: An ethical compass for quarterlifers.* New York: Peter Lang.

O'Brien, J. J. (2016). Toward an ethic of becoming. *About Campus, 21*(1), 4–11.

O'Brien, J. J. (2017). An emerging typology of moral positionality for educational leaders. *Journal of College and Character, 18*(4), 1–15.

Ortiz, A. M., O'Brien, J. J., & Martinez, C. R. (2015). Developing a professional ethic. In M. A. Amey & L. M. Ressor (Eds.), *Beginning your journey* (4th ed. pp. 39–60). Washington, DC: National Association of Student Personnel Administrators.

O'Shea, J. (2010). From Florida State to Oxford: Character, the Rhodes scholarship, and the gap year. *Journal of College and Character, 11*(2), doi: 10.2202/1940-1639 .1260

Perry, Jr, W. G. (1999). *Forms of intellectual and ethical development in the college years: A scheme.* San Francisco: Jossey-Bass.

Rawls, J. (2001). *Justice as fairness: A restatement.* Cambridge, MA: Harvard University Press.

Rest, J. R. (Ed.). (1994). *Moral development in the professions: Psychology and applied ethics.* Hillsdale, NJ: Lawrence Earlbaum.

Rest, J. R., & Narváez, D. (1991). College experience and moral development. In W. M. Kurtines & J. L. Gewirtz (Eds.), *Handbook of moral behavior and development, vol. 2: Research* (pp. 229–245). Hillsdale, NJ: Lawrence Erlbaum.

Rest, J., Narváez, D., Bebeau, M., & Thoma, S. (1999). *Postconventional moral thinking: A Neo-Kohlbergian approach.* Mahwah, NJ: Lawrence Erlbaum.

Reybold, L. E., Halx, M. D., & Jimenez, A. L. (2008). Professional integrity in higher education: A study of administrative staff ethics in student affairs. *Journal of College Student Development, 49*(2), 110–124.

Shapiro, J.P., & Stefkovich, J. A. (2016). *Ethical leadership and decision making in education: Applying theoretical perspectives to complex dilemmas.* New York: Routledge.

Splitter, L. J. (2010). Dispositions in education: Non-entities worth talking about. *Educational Theory, 60*(2), 203–230.

Starcher, A. (2013). *Four years on the road to cosmopolitan lives: Student development through the extended international education experience* (Doctoral dissertation, University of Bath).

Tronto, J. (1987). Beyond gender difference to a theory of care. *Signs, 12,* 644–661.

United Nations. (2015). *Universal declaration of human rights.* New York: Author.

Upcraft, M. L., & Poole, T. G. (1991). Ethical issues and administrative policies. In P. L. Moore (Ed.), *Managing the political dimension of student affairs* (New Directions for Student Services, no. 55, pp. 75–92). San Francisco: Jossey-Bass.

Chapter 3

PRACTICAL OVERVIEW OF ETHICAL DECISION-MAKING MODELS

Anne M. Hornak

This chapter will provide an overview of the ethical decision-making models that are often used for making ethical decisions. The models that will be included represent multiple disciplinary perspectives, including but not limited to counseling and psychology, social work, sociology, business, accounting, and education. The chapter concludes with a case study and questions for student affairs educators to use as a tool in professional development.

Ethical decision-making models in higher education and student affairs draw heavily from multiples disciplines. Many of these models focus on a practice-based approach that are grounded in theoretical and philosophical perspectives outside the discipline. This chapter overview models related to both a theoretical and a practice-based perspective, which offers student affairs educators tools for multiple analysis.

Ethical issues within higher education and student affairs often gets lost or overlooked in the legal and privacy concerns that can override the ethical implications of a situation. In 2015, James Keenan explored ethical issues in academia is his book "University Ethics." In the book Keenan argues that we are quick to call the legal counsel, but oftentimes overlook consultation with an ethicist or individuals that specialize in ethics (Keenan, 2015). Failing to recognize and attend to the ethical issues involved can lead to damaging situations for institutions. For example, if an institution is faced with rampant cheating the reaction often is to look at the faculty and how they are teaching, what is being done in the classrooms related to teaching academic integrity. This is important, it is also essential to broaden the discussion to the entire university community and look at the culture and ethos around academic integrity and honesty. Changing the behavior is critical, as well as the

culture that cultivates the behaviors. These situations do not happen overnight, it takes a long time of looking the other way when something does not
seem right, rather than taking the time to investigate what is going on and
addressing the situation. The standards of ethical behavior belong to every
member of a campus community and are created from top to bottom. With
membership in an academic community comes great privilege and responsibility.

In the next few sections I will explore ethical decision-making models.
These models come from various disciplines and represent varying approaches to an outcome. Within student affairs and student development,
the guidance for ethical conduct comes from a variety of professional organizations including, but not limited to, the 2015 ACPA/NASPA Professional
Competency Areas for Student Affairs Educators (ACPA/NASPA, 2015), as
well as the ACPA Statement of Ethical Principles (2006). The ACPA/NASPA
document is designed to offer a common set of competency areas for student affairs professionals. The competencies compliment the Council for the
Advancement of Standards in Higher Education which also offer general
standards for practice and competencies in the field (https://www.cas.edu
/standards). All three documents are used across student affairs and higher
education professional preparation programs, as well as a tool for professionals in the field. The ACPA/NASPA competencies also include rubrics to
use in assessing the level of competency, including foundational, intermediate, and advanced (ACPA/NASPA, 2015).

The Personal and Ethical Foundations Competency states:

> The Personal and Ethical Foundations competency area involves the knowl-
> edge, skills, and dispositions to develop and maintain integrity in one's life
> and work; this includes thoughtful development, critique, and adherence to
> a holistic and comprehensive standard of ethics and commitment to one's
> own wellness and growth. Personal and ethical foundations are aligned
> because integrity has an internal locus informed by a combination of exter-
> nal ethical guidelines, an internal voice of care, and our own lived experi-
> ences. Our personal and ethical foundations grow through a process of
> curiosity, reflection, and self-authorship. (ACPA/NASPA, 2015, p. 16)

Overview of Decision-Making Frameworks

There are many different ways to approach ethical decision making. In
practice, the process is not often formalized with a specific framework; however, it is critical that when a decision is made those in decision-making roles
are able to articulate the process and how a conclusion was reached. This is
demanded most often when the decision is questioned or the outcomes have
consequences that were not anticipated, which is many times the case. When

decisions are ground in a process that offers transparency and rigor, the conclusions may still be questioned; however, the decision-making process offers more credibility and trustworthiness. Another important reason for guiding decisions within a framework is to avoid two things; moral negligence and moral recklessness (Cohen, 2004). Moral negligence is failing to consider the ethical issues within a situation. As stated earlier, Keenan (2015) focuses on this in his book. The biggest problem is that many in the academy are not trained in university ethics but arrive in university administrative positions through other disciplines (e.g., engineering, philosophy, English) and have studied ethics within their discipline, but not higher education ethics. This lack of understanding of the unique ethical issues involved with higher education and student affairs leadership can lead to moral negligence. The other issue to avoid is moral recklessness. Moral recklessness is failing to consider the moral and ethical elements within a situation (Cohen, 2004). This can happen when decisions are made hastily or without careful consideration of the true issues, as well as not particularly taking the time to care about the ethical implications. Individuals and groups can "target the avoidance" (Cohen, 2004, p. 131) of these pitfalls by using ethical frameworks in decision making.

As I begin the discussion about ethical frameworks, I should remind readers that this chapter is not written to advance the theoretical discussion about ethics. These frameworks are structured steps a leader might take in their decision-making process and offer a deliberative process to help avoid moral negligence and moral recklessness. In this section, I will explore three frameworks for student affairs educators and leaders to use as they work through ethical decisions. The frameworks are based across diverse disciplines, not just student affairs/higher education, but can be used within the work done by student affairs educators. The three frameworks that will be overviewed below are first, the Tarvydas Integrative Decision-Making Model of Ethical Behavior (Tarvydas, 2012); second, the Issue-contingent model by Thomas Jones (1991); and finally, the Mary Guy's values, rules, and a decision-making model (1990). The reasons for selecting these three frameworks in this chapter is to offer student affairs educators a diverse perspective on ethical decision making in terms of discipline, as well as focus. The selection of these three frameworks is not an endorsement over other models, more an expansion of frameworks and a compliment to other authors' frameworks in this book.

Tarvydas Integrative Decision-Making Model of Ethical Behavior

The Tarvydas Intergrative Decision-Making Model of Ethical Behavior (Tarvydas, 2012) was selected because the model draws heavily on the work of Rest (1984), Kitchener (1984), and Cottone and Tarvydas (2016). These authors are widely cited and used to guide the work of student affairs educators as they develop programs and co-curricular activities for students. The model stresses the importance of the decision maker's self-awareness, attention to context, and collaboration with all stakeholders, which are important in assessing ethical situations on college and university campuses. The model also heavily stresses the importance of slowing down, remaining calm, and thoroughly assessing all aspects of a situation (Cottone & Tarvydas, 2016). The model has specific steps for analysis and then sub-steps that are embedded. The first major step is to identify the problem and the sub-step is the interpret the situation. This involves considering how the situation impacts those involved and developing an intentional awareness of the facts in the situation. The next step is to identify the potential issues involved, with the minor steps to gather information and review the problem or dilemma. Within these steps the goal is to take an inventory of all those involved and the relevant issues within the multiple environments impacted. This may include, but is not limited to: a residential community, academic spaces, family, administrative structures.

The next major step is to review relevant ethical guidelines, with the sub-steps of consulting legal and ethical guidelines and determining standards that apply to the dilemma. It is critical that all ethical guidelines are consulted. This is important because colleges and universities have multiple and sometimes competing interests. The work of student affairs educators varies across functional areas and the standards of practice may be more prescribed in some units (e.g., licensed mental health providers) and more ambiguous for other units (e.g., student activities, orientation) where the standards of practice are outlined but less specific related to right and wrong behaviors. The next major step is to obtain consultation. This should be done with trusted professionals. These individuals do not need to be on the same campus, but should be professionals who have a contextual understanding of the work. The fifth major step is to consider the possible and probably courses of action. The sub-steps are to generate possible decisions and generate possible and probable courses of action. This stage involves "selecting an action by weighing competing, nonmoral values, personal blind spots, or prejudices" (Cottone & Tarvydas, 2016, p. 73). This stage requires a high degree of reflective processing and practice by the decision maker. This is interwoven throughout the model, but most highlighted during this step.

The next major step is to enumerate consequences of various decisions. The three sub-steps within this step is to examine possible outcomes, consider consequences for each course of action, and consult with supervisor and peers. This requires thinking about reasonable consequences of each decision and the intended consequences as well as the unintended consequences of each decision. The consultation done during this step can be critical in seeing outside of your own decision, which often illuminates your own blind spots.

The next major step is to decide on the best course of action. The substeps are selecting an action by weighing competing values, implementing best choice and evaluating, plan and execute the selected action, modifying practices to avoid future problems, and finally to evaluate course of action. The critical aspect of this final step is to document the course of action and each step within the decision. Student affairs educators make decisions based on the information they have at that time. Professionals who engage in reviewing their decisions and revise based on new information demonstrate a willingness to truly select the best course of action, over being right.

Issue-Contingent Model

The issue-contingent model is a framework that was designed by Thomas Jones (1991) in response to his critique of other frameworks that lacked emphasis on characteristics of the ethical issue, or more simply put the badness of an act. Jones created the model around the construct of moral intensity. Jones argues that moral intensity influences every component of decision making and behavior. The model includes six components. The first component is, magnitude of consequences. "The magnitude of consequences of the moral issue is defined as the sum of the harms (or benefits) done to victims (or beneficiaries) of the moral act in question" (p. 374). An example would be an event on campus that causes 100 people to suffer an injury is of greater magnitude of consequence than an event on campus that causes only five people to suffer the same injury. This would cause outrage in either case; however, when more people are impacted the outrage is intensified. Most moral issues do not rise to the level of widespread outrage because the consequences seem trivial to most, so often times we overlook the magnitude of consequences because they fail to reach a high threshold. The link between how outraged individuals get can be connected to the magnitude and seriousness of the ethical behavior.

The next component of the model is social consensus. "The social consensus of the moral issue is defined as the degree of social agreement that a proposed act is evil (or good)" (Jones, 1991, p. 375). Social consensus involves both a logical and empirical basis for judgement. Logically, it is difficult to act ethically if a person is unfamiliar or ambiguous about defining ethical behavior in a given situation. For example, the social consequences of a college student refusing to live with individuals that identify differently than them. This is an ambitious situation; some could argue that it is the individual's right to select who they do and do not choose to live with. Others may argue that it is our moral responsibility to be inclusive and to learn about others. The degree of ambiguity in the situation leads to a lack of social consensus. Empirically, Laczniak and Inderrieden (1987) offer that more social consensus exists when the situation has a clear legal consequence and not just an ethical consequence. Individuals reject illegal behaviors with far greater frequency than behaviors that are only unethical (but not illegal).

The third component of the Jones model is the probability of effect. "The probability of effect of the moral act in question is a joint function of the probability that the act in question will actually take place and the act in question will actually cause the harm (benefit) predicted" (p. 375). For example, on a college campus, selling alcohol to an underage individual has greater probability of harm than selling alcohol to an individual of legal drinking age. Embedded within the probability of effect is the idea that the expected consequences of a moral act would be the product of the magnitude of consequences, both the probability that the act will take place, and the probability that harm will take place. Oftentimes on college campuses the probability effect is mitigated by the normative nature of behavior. The example of selling to an underage drinker, in most cases, no harm (or benefit) would occur; therefore the behavior does not change and becomes part of the culture. Within this component it may take an unexpected consequence (getting caught) for individuals to address their behavior and change it.

Temporal immediacy is the fourth component of the model. "The temporal immediacy of the moral issue is the length of time between the present and the onset of consequences of the moral act in question (shorter length of time implies greater immediacy)" (Jones, 1991, p. 376). For example, students who are found in violation of a university policy and are not punished for months after the violation will have little reason to change their behavior, thus impacting the moral urgency of the issue. This creates a domino effect on college campuses and for student affairs educators, other students take note of the time gap and it discounts the magnitude of consequences of specific acts, potentially creating spaces where students can behave badly and not face consequences immediately, thus reducing the impact of the consequence.

The fifth component of the model is proximity. "The proximity of the moral issue is the feeling of nearness (social, cultural, psychological, or physical) that the moral agent has for victims (beneficiaries) of the evil (beneficial) act in question" (Jones, 1991, p. 376). Proximity is a critical measure of moral intensity because people care more about people who are close to them. College students tend to get involved with issues related to justice and equity on their own campuses and communities more than issues that are geographically far from their learning spaces. This is why efforts to internationalize college campuses in the U.S. can be a critical learning tool in helping students expand their zones of proximity and feeling of nearness to certain moral issues.

The sixth and final component of the Jones model is the concentration of effect. "The concentration of effect of the moral act is an inverse function of the number of people affected by an act of given magnitude" (Jones, 1991, p. 377). Jones included the concentration of effect in the moral intensity construct because people intuitively are more incensed by acts that have high concentrated effects. For example, cheating scandals that are institution-wide have more effect than individuals who cheat in their own classes. The act of cheating is the same but when entire classes cheat it reflects more on the institution and what is happening to facilitate widespread academic dishonestly. The underlying premise Jones is working to advance in the issue-contingent model of ethical decision-making is that every moral issue or problem can be characterized in terms of moral intensity and the model guides that process of determining moral intensity (Jones, 1991).

Values, Rules, and a Decision-Making Model (Guy, 1990)

This framework was selected because Guy begins the analysis by suggesting that decision makers need to consider "Ten Core Values" (p. 135) prior to jumping into evaluation mode. The ten core values are:

> *Caring*—Treating people as ends in themselves, not as means to ends. This means having compassion, treating people courteously and with dignity, helping those in need, and avoiding harm to others.
> *Honesty*—Being truthful and not deceiving or distorting. One by one, deceptions undermine the capacity for open exchange and erode credibility.
> *Accountability*—Accepting the consequences of one's action and accepting the responsibility for one's decisions and their consequences. This means setting an example for others and avoiding even the appearance of impropriety.
> *Promise-Keeping*—Keeping one's commitments. The obligations to keep promises is among the most important of generally accepted obligations. To be worthy of trust, one must keep one's promises and fulfil one's commitments.
> *Pursuit of Excellence*—Striving to be as good as one can be. It means being diligent, industrious, and committed; and becoming well informed and well prepared. Results are important, but so is the manner and the method of achievement.
> *Loyalty*—Being faithful and loyal to those with whom one has dealings. This involves safeguarding the ability to make independent professional judgements by scrupulously avoiding undue influence and conflicts of interest.

Fairness–Being open-minded, willing to admit error, and not overreaching or taking undue advantage of another's adversities. For example, avoiding arbitrary and capricious favoritism, treating people equally and making decisions based on notions of justice.

Integrity–Using independent judgement and avoiding conflicts of interest, restraining from self-aggrandizement, and resisting economic pressure. Also, being faithful to one's deepest beliefs, acting on one's conviction, and not adopting an end-justifies-the-means philosophy that ignores principle.

Respect for Others–Recognizing each person's right to privacy and self-determination and having respect for human dignity. This involves being courteous, prompt, and decent, and providing others with information that they need to make informed decisions.

Responsibility Citizenship–Having one's actions in accord with societal values. Appropriate standards for the exercise of discretion must be practiced. (Guy, 1990, pp. 135–136)

In addition to the ten-core values Mary Guy suggests five rules which integrate the values and offer guidance in guiding the ethical decision. The five rules are:

Rule 1–Consider the well-being of others, including non-participants. This rule emphasizes caring and respect for others.

Rule 2–Think as a member of the community, not as an isolated individual. This emphasizes loyalty, integrity, respect for others, and responsibility citizenship.

Rule 3–Obey, but do not depend solely on the law. This emphasizes integrity and responsibility citizenship.

Rule 4–Ask: "What sort of person would do such a thing?' This emphasizes all the values by calling each into question.

Rule 5–Respect the customs of others, but not at the expense of your own ethics. This emphasizes accountability, fairness, integrity, and respect for others. (p. 137)

Guys' decision-making model (1990) offers a six-step model for ethical issue analysis. The first step in the model is defining the problem. This involves isolating key factors of the situation and is critical to not solving the wrong problem. Many times, there is more than one problem that needs to be solved, but it is important to isolate each problem and define them separately even though they most likely are created in concert. The second step is, identify the goal to be achieved. You need to know where you are going to actually create a goal to get there. The third step is, list all possible solutions to the problem. This involves listing all possible solutions and alternatives to help achieve the goal set in step two.

The fourth step is to evaluate each alternative to determine which one best meets the requirements of the situation. This step may take time as each solution listed in step three needs to be fully explored measuring, benefits, costs, and risks of each. As well the intended consequences and the unintended consequences need to be identified. As each solution is being analyzed, it is important to remind yourself about the goals identified in step two. The fifth step is to identify the one course of action that is most likely to produce the desired consequences within the constraints of the situation. This involves selecting the solution that most meets the goals identified, maximizes the values of the group or institution, and essentially solves the problem most effectively. The sixth and final step is to make a commitment and implement it. This requires believing you have the best information possible and have explored all solutions to make this decision.

These three frameworks represent diverse disciplinary perspectives of ethical decision making: Tarvydas (2012) Integrative Decision-Making Model of Ethical Behavior is based in the counseling paradigm, Jones (1991) model is grounded in organizational management, and Guy's (1990) model is based from the accounting profession. Each framework offers a different perspective on addressing an ethical dilemma. The underlying point of view of each framework is addressing the issue clearly and then thinking through the possible solutions with solid information. All of these frameworks are theoretically and empirically ground in their disciplinary literature. While this chapter does not explore that grounding, it is important to note. Next, I will present a case study and then offer a brief analysis through the three frameworks discussed in this chapter.

Case Study

Ellen and Kay live together in a residence hall on a large campus. They are both juniors in college and of legal drinking age and have been friends since their first year in college. They are pursuing different academic majors, but are involved in many of the same co-curricular activities. Ellen is on the student government as an officer. Kay is also on student government, but prefers to serve on committees. The two also play floor hockey and intramural soccer together. Additionally, they have been to each other's home towns and have traveled with each other's families. Both have supportive and loving families. Kay often hosts her younger brother for little siblings' weekend.

On one particularly warm October day, Kay returns from class to find Ellen sleeping on the couch with the windows wide open. It was really a nice breeze, but confused Kay because she knew Ellen had class. She attempted to wake her but with no response. She tried again and Ellen said, class had been cancelled. Ellen slept for the next two hours and woke up in time for their evening soccer game. After the game a few of the team members decided to grab a bite at the local bar. Both Ellen and Kay joined and after one beer Kay said, "I need to get back I have a test tomorrow. Ellen are you coming with?" Ellen said, "no I think I will stay for a bit longer." Around 1:30 am as Kay was getting ready for bed she noticed Ellen was still not home and knew she had an 8:00 am class. She texted Ellen and asked where she was. Ellen wrote back, "I am with Ron and Eddie at their house." Kay thought this strange as she has heard Ellen talk about how they drink too much and how they really do not care much about school. Kay caulked it up to Ellen having too much to drink and went to bed.

For the next three to four weeks, Kay noticed Ellen's behavior changing dramatically. She returned to their room daily to find Ellen sleeping in the middle of the day. Some of their other mutual friends started asking about Ellen, stating she was hardly ever in class and she quit her campus job in the training room, which Kay thought was very strange because Ellen worked so hard to get the position. The final straw was when Kay came back to the room one day and found five empty vodka bottles under Ellen's bed. She was shocked, she had never seen Ellen drink anything but beer or wine. When Ellen returned she was extremely flustered and acting strange.

Kay said, "What is wrong?".

Ellen replied, "I was running to the store and when I turned left onto Main Street my car started making a very loud noise. I stopped to see what was going on and noticed that someone hit the front end of my car and the bumper is rubbing against the tire."

Kay replies, "but you are the only one who has been driving it. I saw how you were parked and the fence would have protected the front end. Could you have hit something?"

Ellen gets very angry starts yelling at Kay, "I did not hit anything, how could you think I hit something? I am a great driver!"

Kay: "I am not accusing you of anything just asking for any insights. Is everything all right? I am worried about you and found all [vodka bottles] these under your bed?"

Ellen: "Why are you in my room? Why are you spying on me? What is your problem? Are you accusing me of something?"

Kay: "I am very worried about you and think you might have a drinking problem?"

Ellen: "Well it is none of your business." And she storms out of the room.

Analysis

It has become apparent to Kay that Ellen has a drinking problem and she is not ready to admit or acknowledge it. Kay is under no legal obligation to report this situation; however, as an ethical friend and roommate, it might save Ellen's life and college career. What should Kay do?

As you think through the steps in helping Kay, the analysis should first be guided by the selection of an ethical decision-making framework. Three diverse models were presented earlier in this chapter. Each model has a different focus of importance in how the ethical issue is addressed and then resolved. In analyzing ethical issues, student affairs educators should remember that the first choice in ethical decision making is to do nothing. However, it should be cautioned that doing nothing has consequences and sometimes those can be very serious. As history shows a lack of interest in isolating and focusing on unethical behavior can have serious and damaging effects on colleges and universities (Keenan, 2015).

As you work through the case study and select a model for analysis, here are some ideas to guide your considerations. If you select the Tarvydas Model (2012), the focus should be to take the time needed to analyze Ellen's behavior from all impacted stakeholders possible. You might consider questions like; do I start by including campus resources or go directly to her parents for support? How will reporting the suspected drinking problem impact her standing on campus in her leadership roles and course work? It is important to also remember that being reflective is embedded throughout the Tarvydas model.

If you select the Jones model, the focus will be on the moral intensity of the situation. As Kay works through each component of the model, the focus is on measuring the moral intensity of Ellen's behavior. This could be encouraging as a frame as there is evidence that Kay cares about Ellen and part of this framework is that people often act more ethically when the issue is of substantive importance to them. The final framework discussed in this chapter was Guy's decision-making model which is more of a step-by-step analysis of ethical issues. This model would require that you have a clear goal for Kay as she navigates how to help Ellen. You would ask questions like, what are my goals in helping Ellen realize the impact alcohol is having on our relationship and across campus? What does Kay hope to have as the outcome of reporting Ellen's behavior to campus officials or even her family? Each model offers student affairs educators and Kay the opportunity to identify the issues involved with addressing Ellen's behaviors and then working through to a solution. In the end, one might arrive at the same result by differing paths. The path is only important as it helps guide and offer rigor to the results.

The challenge for student affairs educators is that they are bound by ethical codes and standards (ACPA, 2006; ACPA/NASPA, 2016; CAS, 2006) but are not bound by licensure or certification like other professions. For example, licensed mental health counselors are usually bound by their state licensure board, as well as a national licensure board, which makes reporting unethical behavior clear. The responsibility for investigating the behavior and determining the outcome falls to the designated ethics board. For student affairs educators, both ACPA and NASPA have ethics committees that consult and offer consultation services to members. However, the authority of each of these boards is limited in scope as they do not have authority to discipline on the individual's campus. In addition, these ethics committees do not govern the behavior of students. The responsibility of student affairs educators on college and university campuses is to create the climate for responsible and ethical behavior for all students. There are particular aspects of higher education and the work of student affairs educators that lack clear guidance related to ethic and ethical decision making. It is critical that campuses offer clear and visible guidelines related to ethical conduct.

REFERENCES

American College Personnel Association. (2006). *Statement of ethical principles and standards.* Retrieved from http://www.myacpa.org/sites/default/files/Ethical _ Principles_Standards.pdf

American College Personnel Association & National Association of Student Personnel Administrators. (2016). *ACPA/NASPA Professional Competencies Rubrics.* Washington, DC: Authors.

Council for the Advancement of Standards. (2006). *CAS professional standards for higher education* (6th ed.). Washington, DC: Author.

Cohen, S. (2004). *The nature of moral reasoning: The frameworks and activities of ethical deliberation, argument, and decision-making.* Victoria, AU: Oxford University Press.

Cottone, R. R., & Tarvydas, V. (2016). *Ethics and decision making in counseling and psychotherapy.* New York: Springer.

Guy, M. (1990). Ethical decision making in everyday work situations. New York: Quorum Books.

Jones, T. M. (1991). Ethical decision making by individuals in organizations: An issue-contingent model. *The Academy of Management Review, Vol. 16, No. 2,* pp. 366–395.

Kitchener, K. S. (1984). Intuition, critical evaluation, and ethical principles: The foundation for ethical decisions in counseling psychology. *The Counseling Psychologist, 12,* pp. 43–55.

Laczniak, G. R., & Inderrieden, E. J. (1987). The influence of stated organizational concern upon ethical decision making. *Journal of Business Ethics, 6:* pp. 297–307.

Rest. J. R. (1984). Research on moral development: Implications for training counseling psychologists. *Counseling Psychologists, 12,* pp. 19–29.

Tarvydas, V. M. (2012). Ethics and ethical decision-making. In D. R. Maki & V. M. Tarvydas (Eds.), *The professional practice of rehabilitation counseling* (pp. 339–370). New York: Springer.

Chapter 4

CREATING A CAMPUS CONVERSATION ABOUT ETHICS

V. Barbara Bush and Daniel Chen

Many researchers and educators have stated the need for ethics curriculum in undergraduate, graduate, and professional education (DuBois & Burkemper, 2002; Lowry, 2003; McNeel, 1994). However, most of the discussion tends to focus on training for students and not on the need for a campus-wide conversation of ethics among all members of the institution. Indeed, though most people recognize the importance of ethical culture, in practice most people assume ethics as an individual responsibility. For this chapter, we as the authors would like to stress the importance of ethics as an organizational responsibility and that an ethical culture is crucial for individuals within the organization to make the right decisions. We also believe that ethics must be explicitly discussed and ethical behaviors should be recognized in order to create an ethical culture. Therefore, it is extremely important for institutional leaders to create conversations on ethics among all members of the organization. In this chapter, we will first provide a theoretical framework on why a campus conversation on ethics is needed. We will then use our institution's journey and goal of creating a campus culture of ethics and a shared language and vision for ethics among administrators, faculty, staff, and students as a replicable case study for others.

WHY DO WE NEED A CAMPUS CONVERSATION ABOUT ETHICS?

In the previous chapters, authors have discussed the theoretical framework for ethical decision making and practical models for ethical decision making. Ethical theories and models of decision making in disciplines such as counseling and psychology, social work, sociology, and education are also discussed in the previous chapters. For this chapter, we adopted Lickona's three-component definition of effective character education (Lickona, 1991, 1993, 1998; Lickona, Schaps, & Lewis, 2002) as the theoretical framework. Lickona is a developmental psychologist and educational scholar whose academic works focus on character development and moral education for young people. Even though Lickona's theory was not designed specifically for higher education, we believe it is applicable as a theoretical framework for our discussion.

THEORETICAL FRAMEWORK

Many articles have been written about character development and moral education (Durkheim, 1961; Noddings, 2002; Power, Higgins, & Kohlberg, 1989). What separates Lickona's work from other scholars' work is his advocacy for a comprehensive definition of effective character that includes cognitive, emotional, and behavioral aspects of ethical life (Lickona, Schaps, & Lewis, 2002). Lickona and his coauthors stated the outcome of ethical behavior is built on the foundation of a good understanding of values and ethical principles and an internal motivation to act on the ethical principles. Chen, Dalton, and Crosby (2006) conducted a study using Lickona's definition of effective character education to investigate how colleges and universities promote moral and ethical development on campus. They concluded that most American colleges and universities focus their character education efforts on cognitive and behavioral aspects of ethical life because the outcomes of these two aspects are easier to measure than the emotional aspect of ethical life. Indeed, most writings on ethical education tend to aim at the cognitive aspect, such as moral reasoning, or behavioral aspect, such as honesty and respect. The result of this emphasis on measurable outcomes is that most higher education institutions use benchmarks such as the number of students taking ethical courses and the number of hours students spend on community service work as evidence of institutional efforts to promote moral and ethical development. However, real life evidence has shown that the lack of emotional aspect in ethical training may lead to a total failure in moral and ethical development.

The prevalence of white-collar crime in American business and corporations has prompted many business scholars to study the reasons people chose to commit unethical and/or criminal behaviors in the corporate environment. Despite long-term governmental and public efforts to curtail white-collar crimes, ethical scandals and crimes such as unlawful accounting practices (Millman, 2002), predatory business practices targeting vulnerable populations (Santoro & Strauss, 2013), discriminatory practices in business operations (Bobbitt-Zeher, 2011; Offermann, Basford, Graebner, Jaffer, De Graaf, & Kaminsky, 2014), and sexual harassment (McDonald, 2011) continue to be prevalent in society. As pointed out by Heath (2008), in business there is usually no real dispute about the content of ethical decisions, the question is rather how to motivate people to act in an ethical way. In other words, people who commit unethical behaviors usually know what they do is wrong, but they still consciously choose the unethical path. Researchers in ethical decision making pointed out that personality (Singhapakdi & Vitell, 1990), beliefs (Zahra, 1989), values (Hegarty & Sims, 1978, 1979), and situational factors such as peer group influence (Izraeli, 1988; Zey-Ferrell, Weaver, & Ferrell, 1979) and risk and reward (Tang, Chen, & Sutarso, 2008; Tang & Sutarso, 2013) all affect an individual's likelihood to knowingly commit unethical acts. Simply put, being an ethical person takes more than knowing what is right and wrong. We believe higher education institutions have the responsibility to promote the whole spectrum development of ethical life from knowing what is right, motivating to do what is right, and eventually cultivating moral and ethical behaviors in everyday decision making.

THE GUIDING QUESTIONS

Based on this framework, we recommend that campus conversations about ethics focus on the following guiding questions. First is the "why" question. Why is it important to be ethical for the individual and for the organization? The why question addresses the emotional aspect of ethics and it requires soul searching. We believe that every individual and organization must anchor their moral compass on convictions. The trickiness of convictions is that every individual must take on and internalize them for himself/herself. No one can force others to believe in a conviction. As a leader of an organization, you can require members of your organization to sign an ethical statement, but signing an ethical statement does not equal to believe in the statement. Before encouraging members of the organization to behave ethically, leaders of the organization should first ask members to think why they should behave ethically. An ethical culture will not last if members of the organization are not internally motivated to think and behave ethically. Some people build their moral compass on religious beliefs while others anchor their moral compass on shared social norms such as justice and care (Kohlberg & Ryncarz, 1990; Noddings, 2002). Similarly, some organizations establish their ethical guidelines on religious doctrines while others develop their ethical guidelines on shared social norms. No matter what individuals and organizations believe, they must develop a deep conviction on morality and ethics in order to form the foundation of ethical thinking and ethical behaviors. A campus conversation on the "why" question will not immediately create an ethical conviction for members of the organization, but these kinds of conversations will encourage people to reflect and affirm their own ethical conviction.

The second guiding question is the "what" question: What ethical principles or guiding system should the individual or organization use to guide their ethical decision making? This question addresses the cognitive aspect of ethics. The difficulty of ethical decision making is the fact that each ethical situation is unique. A campus conversation about ethics should create opportunities for members of the institution to discuss principles and difficulties in making day-to-day ethical decisions. The conversation should also address the potential conflicts between an individual's ethical conviction and the organizational ethical guidelines.

The third guiding question is the "how" question: How do individuals find supports when facing difficult ethical situations? An ethical organization should provide supports when members of the organization face difficult ethical dilemmas. Is there someone within or outside the organization with whom individuals can feel comfortable discussing the ethical issues in workplace? When an individual observes unethical behaviors or incidents in the organization, is there a system for reporting the behaviors or incidents without retribution to the whistleblower? These questions belong to the behavioral aspect of ethics and they are equally important as the emotional and cognitive aspects of ethics for individuals and organizations.

WHAT CAN CAMPUS LEADERS DO TO CREATE A CONVERSATION: AFFIRMING AN ETHICAL STANCE

Following Lickona's framework, there are steps campus leaders can follow to create a culture of ethics. First, institutional leaders must affirm a broad ethical stance in order for students and other members of the campus community to obtain guidance in ethical decision making. Many educational institutions have published their guiding ethical principles, either as stand-alones or as part of their mission and/or vision statements. Institutions that do not have such guiding ethical principles should consider adapting. For example, Harvard University's Office of the President published a Statement of Values in 2012 as guiding principles for all policy and practice throughout the university. The statement is short but self-explanatory:

- Respect for the rights, differences, and dignity of others
- Honesty and integrity in all dealings
- Conscientious pursuit of excellence in one's work

- Accountability for actions and conduct in the workplace (Harvard, 2002, "Statement of Values," para. 6)

When institutional leaders are clear on their ethical stance, it is easier for campus communities including faculty, students, administrators, and staff members to follow through in everyday practice. It also makes it possible for campus communities to adapt the ethical principles and create their own guidelines that suit better with their specific circumstances. For example, Harvard Business School posts their own community values based on the university's statement of values:

At Harvard Business School we believe that leadership and values are inseparable. The teaching of ethics here is explicit, not implicit, and our Community Values of mutual respect, honesty and integrity, and personal accountability support the HBS learning environment and are at the heart of a School-wide aspiration: to make HBS a model of the highest standards essential to responsible leadership in the modern business world. Our values are a set of guiding principles for all that we do wherever we are and with everyone we meet. (Harvard Business School, n.d., "Community Values," para.5)

Imperial Valley College, a public community college in California, passed a resolution in 2007 to create a college-wide institutional code of ethics statement:

All employees of Imperial Valley College embrace a code of conduct in which we recognize the value and dignity of each individual within the framework of the campus community. We strive to:

- Respect the opinions, values, and traditions of others.
- Be responsible for our own behavior.
- Be honest, open, and trustworthy.
- Be fair and equitable in our treatment of others.
- Promote democratic principles, good citizenship, and the standards of academic freedom.
- Perform our duties and responsibilities with integrity and professionalism.
- As appropriate, use effective teaching practices and teach our students with rigor and compassion.
- As appropriate, maintain confidentiality, objectivity, and impartiality in all evaluative activities involving students and colleagues. (Imperial Valley College, n.d., "Ethics Statement," para. 5)

It is clear when comparing the statements between Harvard University and Imperial Valley College that there are some shared values and some distinctive values between these very different institutions. For example, both institutions list respecting others as the number one value statement. Honesty and integrity are also shared between the two institutions. On the other hand, Harvard University has "conscientious pursuit of excellence" as one of their core ethical values whereas Imperial Valley College stressed the importance of promoting democratic principles, good citizenship, and the standards of academic freedom. The lesson here is that each institution must create its own core ethical stance through campus conversation and dialogues. These statements from colleges and universities that show their values can be a good starting point of the "what" questions. Individuals must know the ethical standards to which they are subscribing before they can make an emotional affirmation.

CREATING CONVERSATIONS ON ETHICS

Creating an ethics statement is the first step in developing a campus culture of ethics. The second step, and usually the most difficult step, is to work on the heart: Why is it important to be an ethical person or ethical campus? On a fundamental level, this is a question every individual has to answer for themselves. However, campus leaders can create opportunities for individuals to reflect on ethical decision making in order for each individual to reach an answer for the "why" question. One way to achieve this is to create campus-wide ethical case study competitions. Case study competitions are regularly held in student affairs professional conferences and many student affairs practitioners are familiar with the format. It is up to the campus leaders and student affairs professionals to create compelling ethical cases and marketing the event to attract wide participation from all campus communities.

There are other ways to encourage campus conversations on ethics; and one of them is to include ethics case studies in curriculum. To achieve this, campus leaders must utilize academic resources to support faculty members and create ethical components tailored toward different disciplines and subjects. Ethical decisions happen in all disciplines and areas of life, but different professions tend to encounter different types of ethical dilemmas. The following scenario is a case study example for students in higher education and university employees who interact with students on a regular basis.

Case Study: The Scenario

Janice is a resident director at a university residence hall. She has been in that position for one year. Janice graduated from a student affairs master's program, so she has had exposure to all of the theories related to working with students. However, the vast majority of the residential life experiences Janice has had are from her postgraduate living arrangements as a student. Currently, she is in a position in which she is very close in age to the residents in her hall. As a graduate student, she was highly sociable and liked by her residence hall learning community.

On Friday afternoon, Janice was invited to a party to be held in one of the student suites in a hall other than her own. The party planners had obtained permission for hosting the party from the residence director, Janice's supervisor. The only stipulations given were that there should be no alcohol served to minor students. The planners were asked to set up a means of identifying underage participants.

Because she was had considerable interaction with the party planners, Janice decided to attend the party. When she arrived, she was aware of some scrambling at the back of the suite lounge. There was no one at the door checking for IDs, so she walked in to find several freshman students holding telltale red cups and the distinguishing smell of beer. The scuffling in the rear of the lounge seemed to be the result of an attempt to hide a keg. Upon seeing Janice, two male residents of the lounge appeared from the back door and apologized for the beer and the first-year students saying they did not know they were coming and they were asking them to leave. They asked that Janice please give them a chance to "make things right."

Janice is perplexed. It is her duty to report what she has seen, but in doing so, she will have lost the confidence of the residents sponsoring the party. How should she decide her next actions?

An Ethical Decision-Making Model

For purposes of this case and the explanation of the process, we use Ethical Decision-Making Model developed by Forester-Miller and Davis (2016) as the guiding framework. This model involves the following processes: (a) identifying the problem, (b) apply an existing code of ethics, (c) determining the nature and dimensions of the dilemma, (d) generating potential courses of action, (e) considering the potential consequences of all options and determining a course of action, (f) evaluating the selected course of action, and (g) implementing the course of action (p. 5).

Case Study Analysis. Using the Ethical Decision-Making Model (Forester-Miller & Davis, 2016), we can analyze the case and make recommendations and steps for Janice to take:

1. **Identifying the problem** of involved in her role as a resident assistant and her relationship with the students. Janice must consider the

rules that may have been violated with the consequence involved in a legal situation. Also, she should consider what actions are involved in her relationship with the students. Do they understand the position in which they are placing her? Does their relationship depend on acquiescence?

2. **In applying the university code of ethics and conduct**, asking what is expected of each member of the university community? Is honor based on following rules and regulations and respect for the roles of others? Also, what is the professional code that Janice must follow? Is there a conflict in applying the code to the behavior of both she and the students?

3. Determining the **nature of the dilemma. The dimensions of the dilemma** are many. Any one decision could affect the future of the students involved and Janice's employment. Where legal issues are involved, this could be even more serious.

4. Determining possible **courses of action**? The **courses of action** for Janice include (a) reporting the incident to the appropriate residence director, (b) ignoring what she saw and leaving the party, (c) telling the students her responsibility and outlining their next action, and (d) staying at the party as if nothing happened.

5. **Asking what could be the consequences of each action.** Reporting the incident could mean that the students were sent forward for judicial action with the possibility of Janice's relationship with these students in jeopardy. Ignoring what she saw would call into question her professional integrity possibly resulting in the loss of both her job and the respect of students. Confronting the students and advising them as to her next action and its consequences could be recognition of her duties as both an "enforcer" and an advisor. Staying at the party and ignoring the events could result in the same consequences, as would ignoring events and leaving. Staying, however, may be condoning the activity.

6. Evaluating each option. In selecting the course of action, Janice must **evaluate each option.** There is nothing here that is clear-cut, so many of the consequences may overlap. She needs to give value, from her own perspective as to the possible outcomes of each action and how it fits within her own ethical foundation.

7. **Taking action. This can be** the most difficult, but also the most rewarding part of this scenario.

HOW CAN THE ETHICAL DECISION-MAKING PROCESS BE USED CAMPUSWIDE?

Bowen, Bessette, and Chan (2006) argued that graduate programs should teach the process of deconstructing ethical issues by "analyzing and understanding behaviors and teaching respect for the perception of others" (p.5). As a result, practicing reflective, insightful, and self-critical examination is necessary. While it may seem practical to go through this process in a classroom or an ethics workshop, addressing ethical decision-making becomes more complicated on a campus-wide basis. Who controls the moral and ethical agency of a campus? What are the institutional rules, and how do they affect the process? These are the questions that institutional leaders must grapple and address through campus-wide conversations if they want to create a culture of ethics for the whole campus community.

PROVIDING SUPPORTS FOR AN ETHICAL CAMPUS CULTURE

Ironically, it appears that much of the support for ethical decision-making among students comes for those who have violated some code of the institution. Students who violate student conduct codes are usually required to attend workshops that include ethical decision making as a part of the remedial exercises. However, there are institutions that realize the need to address ethics outside this setting. Some institutions offer ethics classes as an elective or an optional part of the curriculum for a specific certificate, licensure, and degree programs. A requirement for campus wide conversation on ethics is intentional inclusion in a variety of places within campus life.

A university campus in Texas is addressing the concept of ethical decision making in its conduct workshops. Their workshop model was designed by the Dean of Students office, and is used for student conduct violations as disciplinary sanctions. Students are required to complete what are called Ethical Decision-Making Workshops when engaging in any activities that prove to disrupt the learning environment. Sanctions would be used in cases of theft, vandalism, residence hall-related violations, and other violations of the student code of conduct. All violations of the student conduct code are addressed as flawed ethical decision making. Students are required to enroll in the workshop after a violation is determined through a conduct hearing. Their participation in the two-week workshop is evaluated by the responsible conduct official in the Dean of Students office. A negative evaluation shows that a student did not make satisfactory completion of the workshop; and the student may be asked to repeat part or all of the process. The data reported from the workshops show the scores students achieved for each section of the workshop.

Another supporting system needed for an ethical campus is a safe route to report unethical behaviors. No matter how much we want our campus to be an ethical campus, unethical behaviors will happen. Institutional leaders must find a way to provide a safe environment for those who report incidents. Some campuses provide support services through the Dan of Students Office, Campus Police, offices of diversity and inclusion, counseling centers, and academic advisors. Students involved in code violations and those who are struggling with ethical decision making can normally contact any of these offices for advice. With these supports in place, the campus acts on promoting a campus wide conversation about ethics.

CONCLUSION

Campus wide discussion of ethics does not have to address a campus wide problem. It can be an inclusionary discussion of how the campus community can address everyday dilemmas and problems such as the one faced by Janice in our case study scenario. To be consistent in the approach, the problem solvers, be they students, faculty, staff, or administrators, must know, understand, and subscribe to a campus code. This code can be addressed at the orientation of all campus constituents in such a way that they understand the centrality of the code.

To summarize, we recommend these actions to be taken to create a campus culture of ethics:

1. Make a clear statement as to why ethical decision making is important to the future of higher education as well as the campus. When institutions create their strategic goals and state their values, they need to make certain those goals and values are known and understood campus wide. This means that all constituents should be involved, in some way, in campus strategic planning. It would be interesting to know how many goal and values statements are created by the administration alone.
2. Instill all of the principles of the ethics and values statements in the operations of all aspects of the institution. Does the Faculty Senate have these values as part of their charter and bylaws? Do student organizations base their activities on the ethical values and codes established by the university? Does the administration incorporate ethical principles in its policies and procedures? Are all policies and procedures followed using the values of the institution, i.e., respect for each individual.

3. Provide frequent reminders and examples of ethical decision making within the context of daily activities. This recommendation goes beyond campus workshops provided for students who violate campus policy. It extends to decisions that are disseminated through the public voice of the institution, be it the president, chancellor, or designated public relations entity. This shows that practice is consistent with concept.

4. Reward ethical behavior consistent with the institution's values. Awards are given annually for students, staff, faculty, and administrators. Is ethical behavior a consideration in these awards and recognition?

5. If not already present, create an ethics portion to all degree programs, if not all curricula. It may not be enough to provide a singular ethics class, when ethics can be a topic in all classes.

6. Create official campus supports for ethical decision making. This goes beyond sanctions for student violation of code. It includes such entities as ethics centers and career centers as long as the purpose and location is clear to the entire campus community.

Although some of these recommendations require funding for the establishment of centers and personnel to staff those centers, most can be accomplished by a change of focus. Leadership for this kind of effort must come from the top, but the ideas of how to implement the efforts is the responsibility of the entire campus community. It is our hope that creating an ethical culture on college campus is not seen as a special effort but a common requirement for all higher education institutions.

REFERENCES

Bobbitt-Zeher, D. (2011). Gender discrimination at work: Connecting gender stereotypes, institutional policies, and gender composition of workplace. *Gender & Society, 25*(6), 764-786.

Bowen, C., Bessette, H., & Cham, T. C. (2006). Including ethics in the study of educational leadership. *Journal of College & Character, 7*(7), 1–7.

Chen, P. D., Dalton, J. C., & Crosby, P. C. (2006). How colleges differ in their efforts to promote moral and ethical development in college. *Religion & Education, 33*(2), 47–63.

Forester-Miller, H., & Davis, T. E. (2016). Practitioner's guide to ethical decision making. The Center for Counseling Practice, Policy, and Research. *American Counseling Association*. Retrieved from https://www.counseling.org/docs/default-source/ethics/practioner-39-s-guide-to-ethical-decision-making.pdf?sfvrsn=f9e5482c_10

Harvard University. (2002). Retrieved from https://www.harvard.edu/president/speeches/summers_2002/values.php

Harvard Business School. (n.d). Retrieved from https://www.hbs.edu/about/campus-and-culture/Pages/community-values.aspxlife/Pages/community-values.aspx

Heath, J. (2008). Business ethics and moral motivation: A criminological perspective. *Journal of Business Ethics, 83,* 595–614.

Hegarty, W. H., & Sims, H. P., Jr. (1978). Some determinants of unethical decision behavior: An experiment. *Journal of Applied Psychology, 63*(4), 451–457.

Hegarty, W. H., & Sims, H. P., Jr. (1979). Organizational philosophy, policies and objectives related to unethical decision behavior: A laboratory experiment. *Journal of Applied Psychology, 64*(3), 331–338.

Imperial Valley College. (n.d.). Retrieved from https://www.imperial.edu/about/mission-vision-and-core-values/ethics-statement/

Izraeli, D. (1988). Ethical beliefs and behavior among managers: A cross-cultural perspective. *Journal of Business Ethics, 7,* 263–271.

Lickona, T. (1991). *Educating for character: How our schools can teach respect and responsibility.* New York: Bantam Book.

Lickona, T. (1993). The return of character education. *Educational Leadership, 51*(3), 6–11. Retrieved from http://www.ascd.org/publications/ed_lead/199311/Lickona.html

Lickona, T. (1998). Character education: Seven crucial issues. *Action in Teacher Education, 19*(4), 77–84.

Lickona, T., Schaps, E., & Lewis, C. (2007). *CEP's eleven principles of effective character education.* Washington, DC: Character Education Partnership. Retrieved from https://files.eric.ed.gov/fulltext/ED505086.pdf

McDonald, P. (2011). Workplace sexual harassment 30 years on: A review of the literature. *International Journal of Management Review, 14*(1), 1–17.

Millman, G. J. (2002). New scandals, old lessons financial ethics after Enron. *Financial Executive, 18*(5), 16–19.

Offermann, L. R., Basford, T. E., Graebner, R., Jaffer, S., De Graaf, S. B., & Kaminsky, S. E. (2014). See no evil: Color blindness and perceptions of subtle racial discrimination in the workplace. *Cultural Diversity and Ethnic Minority Psychology, 20*(4), 499–507.

Santoro, M. A., & Strauss, R. J. (2013). *Wall Street values: Business ethics and the global financial crisis.* New York: Cambridge University Press.

Singhapakdi, A., & Vitell, S. J. (1990). Marketing ethics: Factors influencing perceptions of ethical problems and alternatives. *Journal of Macromarketing, 10,* 4–18.

Tang, T. L., Chen, Y., & Sutarso, T. (2008). Bad apples in bad (business) barrels: The love of money, Machiavellianism, risk tolerance, and unethical behavior. *Management Decision, 46*(2), 243–263.

Tang, T. L., & Sutarso, T. (2013). Falling or not falling into temptation? Multiple faces of temptation, monetary intelligence, and unethical intentions across gender. *Journal of Business Ethics, 116*(3), 529–552.

Zahra, S. A. (1989). Executive values and the ethics of company politics: Some preliminary findings. *Journal of Business Ethics, 8,* 15–29.

Zey-Ferrell, M. K., Weaver, M., & Ferrell, O. C. (1979). Predicting unethical behavior among marketing practitioners. *Human Relations, 32*(7), 557–569.

Chapter 5

ETHICAL DECISION MAKING IN PRACTICE

Regina Garza Mitchell, Ramona Meraz Lewis, and Brian Deitz

Professionals working in student affairs and higher education make countless decisions on a daily basis. Each of those decisions impacts human lives, whether students, faculty, or staff, which requires a focus on ethics in addition to rules and policies. Being aware of the ethical nature of problems, the ethical approaches you prefer, and the codes to which you adhere can lead to more effective decision making.

The nature of working with college students "has ethical issues and ethical choices at its very core" (Kitchener, 1985, p. 17) because each decision impacts someone's life and wellbeing. Although the student affairs profession is built on values that encourage ethical behavior and decision making, often-ethical decisions are difficult to make because there are many choices and interpretations involved in the process. Ethical decisions often also involve emotion and require interpretation of what is right or wrong in a given situation, which can further complicate the situation. Thus, it is imperative that professionals are aware of the values and ethics that undergird their own decision-making processes. It is to this end that we focus on ethical decision making as a professional skill that can be practiced and applied in our day-to-day practice.

ETHICS AND VALUES

The terms ethics and values are often used interchangeably, but they are different. Ethics and values are interconnected and drive each other, which may account for some of the confusion. Ethics tend to be thought of in terms of what is right and wrong (Dalton, 2016), whereas values refer to what a person believes is important (Saunders & Wilson, 2016). Merriam-Webster (n.d.) defines ethics as a set of moral principles, a guiding philosophy, and the principles of conduct that govern an individual or group. These definitions can be applied to further delineate the different types of ethics that guide the behavior of professionals in practice.

PROFESSIONAL AND PERSONAL ETHICS

Professional ethics refer to the shared ethics of a profession. These ethics are often comprised of principles of conduct that govern a particular group, so they may be looked at as rules or guiding principles that help determine an ethical course of action. These ethical principles are often shared through professional groups, such as Student Affairs Professionals in Higher Education (NASPA), American College Personnel Association (ACPA), American Association of Collegiate Registrars, Admissions Offices (AACRAO), and more. Each of these groups has either a stated ethical code or a statement of ethical principles that members are prompted to follow. When joining these groups, members agree to uphold these ethical principles and standards of conduct (Dalton, 2016). Professional codes of ethics guide the specific and broader work that is conducted by professionals at all levels, including those new to the profession. Given that there are numerous professional associations, the Council for the Advancement of Standards in Higher Education (CAS); 2006, 2017) formed an alliance representing a variety of functional area professional organizations within higher education. In an effort to promote and articulate shared ethical principles, CAS (2006, 2017) reviewed the ethical codes and statements of numerous professional member associations and found seven common principles among them: autonomy, nonmalfeasance, beneficence, justice, fidelity, veracity, and affiliation. The ethical statement provided by CAS builds on Kitchener's (1985) work that is discussed below; furthermore, it complements the ethical statements of various member professional organizations (Barr, McClellan, & Sandeen, 2014). This statement provides a shared language among higher education and student affairs professionals, so that "ultimately students are better served" (CAS, 2006, p. 2).

Kitchener (1985) differentiated between ethical rules and principles. In her view, ethical codes comprise the ethical rules that ideally govern decision making. Kitchener described professional rules and ethical codes as the basis for and most specific level of ethical decision making. Kitchener viewed ethical principles as more abstract and general and noted that they provide the justification for ethical codes.

Each of us has a personal code of ethics that governs the way that we behave and the choices we make, although this code may not have ever been explicitly or intentionally articulated. Personal ethics guide our perspectives of what is right and what is wrong (Liddell, Hornak, & Ignelzi, 2016). They guide everything we do as individuals, and they stem from the values we hold dear. Personal ethics may be viewed as a moral compass suggesting that knowledge, process, and skills are integral components of navigating the complex work in which we engage each day (Dalton, Crosby, Velente, & Eberhardt, 2016). These ethics are developed throughout our lives and continue to evolve as we grow and learn; they can be thought of as the foundation of an individual's ethics and are undergirded by the values that guide our thinking.

Each of us has our own personal interpretation and brings our own perspectives to every decision that we make. Our backgrounds, cultural context, level of exposure to various issues, knowledge and understanding of the community and laws, professional maturity, perspective from within the organization, and many other things play a part in how we analyze and interpret the various situations that we encounter. Several codes, statement of principles, and models of ethical decision making discuss the intersection of personal and professional values (e.g., ACPA, 2006). Dalton et al. (2016) suggests that at times situations may require personal conscience to "trump moral considerations" (p. 207). If professionals feel that making a particular decision or moving forward on an action would violate personal values, then they have to decide whether to follow personal conscience or other action. Of course, there may be practical risks and/or consequences associated with doing what an individual view's as "right" from their own perspective, particularly if it clashes with institutional norms or agreed upon rules. It is important to be aware of how personal and professional codes of ethics may be at odds with each other to avoid potential conflicts; yet, knowing when and how to navigate the personal and the professional is difficult. The process of doing so often requires deep personal reflection as suggested below.

Fried (2003) suggested using Rion's (1996) six questions as a way to guide the inner dialogue when approaching an ethical dilemma.

> 1) Why is this bothering me? 2) Who else matters? Are there stakeholders in this situation? 3) Is it my problem? Have I caused the problem and am I responsible for resolving it? 4) What is the ethical concern? What principles, virtues, laws, and cultural, temporal or phenomenological considerations should I take into account? 5) What do others think? Would discussing this with a person who might disagree with me help me to think more clearly? 6) Am I being true to myself? What are my personal beliefs in this issue, beyond consideration for the relevant ethical codes and guidelines? (pp. 13–14)

These questions may provide a helpful guide in reflecting upon situations where personal and professional ethics may seem to clash or when several belief systems may be in play (Reybold, Halax, & Jimenez, 2008).

Values

Values influence ethics, but they are different. Saunders and Wilson (2016) denoted the distinction by stating, "Values describe what a person believes is important in life, whereas ethical principles and standards prescribe what is considered good or bad and right or wrong behavior" (p. 90). Values not only influence ethics, but also the way a person views the world (Harris, 1994). This, in turn, has an effect on how an individual makes decisions, which ethics take priority, and which are most important in determining the best course of action. Values inherently drive the way that we make decisions and how we interpret and enact ethical rules and principles. For example, someone who holds social justice as a core value may first examine existing rules or policies to determine whether they advantage certain groups of students over other groups before determining whether the rule or policy should be followed and/or changed.

Ethical Decision-Making Frameworks

Many ethical decision-making models and frameworks are available that are grounded in theory and practice. In this chapter, we use these terms interchangeably to refer to constructs that provide steps or processes for making decisions. These frameworks are not intended to be absolute or to have everyone come up with the same response but are intended to offer options for considering situations that lead to ethically sound judgments (Kitchener, 1985).

Kitchener (1985) developed a model of ethical justification for decision making that has its roots in psychology. In Kitchener's model, ethical decision-making is situational, and the ethical rules, principles, and theories used for making that decision are dependent upon the context of the situation. These three elements comprise a hierarchy of ethical thinking that moves from the general to the abstract.

RULES, PRINCIPLES, AND THEORIES TO GUIDE DECISION MAKING

In Kitchener's (1985) model, the ethical rules, principles, and theories that are used depend on the facts of the situation. This hierarchy can help provide justification for ethical decisions that are made. In applying this model, the first approach to deciding would be to consult professional rules and codes of ethics. The next level in the model involves ethical principles, which provide a framework for identifying critical issues and selecting, which one is applicable. Ethical theories are the highest level of the model and provide rationale for when ethical principles are in conflict.

Saunders and Wilson (2016) proposed an approach to ethical decision making that is grounded in Kitchener's (1985) model and provides a stepped process for making ethical decisions. The first step in this model is to recognize that there is an ethical decision to be made. This requires determining both the facts and assumptions in the situation. Second, they recommend seeking assistance in the form of policies or legal guidance. Third, consider the context of the situation including campus, professional, and external elements. Next, consider the options and consequences in relation to ethical principles, such as the CAS Statement of Ethical Principles (2012). Saunders and Wilson (2016) also recommend obtaining feedback from colleagues to expand perspective on the issue. This step is key because it is not always easy to see beyond the scope of our personal ethics and values. Consultation with colleagues helps to highlight potential blind spots or omissions that may have critical bearing on the decision. Going through the steps and considering multiple aspects of the case should provide enough information to make the best decision.

ETHICAL LENSES FOR DECISION MAKING

Another approach to ethical decision making involves the application of various ethical lenses or paradigms to make decisions. Dalton, Crosby, Velente, and Eberhardt (2016) present a conceptual framework for examining ethical issues and making moral decisions (p. 201). The authors offer what they call a "multi-lens perspective" presenting a visual model with five domains of ethical responsibility (p. 213). Four of the domains—the student, the profession, the community, the institution—are encircled by the fifth domain, individual conscience. Each of the domains signifies essential professional obligations and responsibilities; yet, there is a recognition that given the multifaceted nature of situations and ethical decision making these domains may conflict with one another. Each of the domains is described in the section below.

Student Welfare. This domain recognizes that students and their welfare are the center and focus of the work of a student affairs educator. This emphasis on the welfare of the student is consistent with other professional codes of ethics such as ACPA's (2006) Ethical Principles and Standards. From this view, ethical decision making requires that we consider the personal wellbeing of not only the individual student, but also the impacts on other students.

Institution. This domain recognizes the context of the work. As employees, professionals are responsible to uphold the mission and values of their institutions. Thus, it is crucial that professionals strive to understand the culture and context of our places of work.

The Profession. This domain highlights responsibility to the larger profession including association standards, principles, and ethical codes. As professionals, whether one is a member of a particular organization or not, there is a responsibility to be familiar with and observe professional practices and values.

The Community. In this domain the broader context of the larger community is emphasized. This community may take into consideration laws, stakeholders, and community members. In essence, the values of the communities in which we serve and abide must be considered in our decision-making.

Personal or Individual Conscience. These four domains are viewed through the lens of personal or individual conscience. Individual conscience is the "domain of one's deeply held personal beliefs" formed from experience (Dalton, Crosby, Valente, & Eberhardt, 2016, p.206). These beliefs provide the personal contexts or schema for interpreting an ethical dilemma (Harris, 1994). In facing an ethical decision, individual conscience is reflected in questions such as: Is this decision something I can stand behind? Do I feel right about this decision?

In summary, this framework highlighting the "multi-lens perspective" calls for professionals to consider both the individual distinctions of the particular situation as well as apply broad normative principles. Thus, this model is also situational, indicating that ethical decisions cannot be made using "fixed moral principles," but rather individuals must consider the unique circumstances as well as those principles (Dalton, Crosby, Valente, & Eberhardt, 2016, p. 214).

Another approach to applying different lenses when making ethical decisions involves the consideration of four multiple ethical paradigms in decision making: ethics of justice, critique, care, and the profession (Shapiro & Stefkovich, 2005, 2016). These four paradigms are presented as broad lenses that are essential to apply when making ethical decisions. These paradigms are related, sometimes overlapping, and provide ways of thinking to help individuals consider decision making from multiple perspectives, including those that may be outside of a person's typical way of thinking (Wood & Hilton, 2012).

The ethic of justice stems from a traditional, rational approach to decision making and focuses on rules, laws, and policies that are relevant to the situation. It is often considered to be a morally objective approach to decision making (Beckner, 2004; Wood & Hilton, 2012). "Viewing ethical dilemmas from this vantage point, one may ask questions related to the rule of law and the more abstract concepts of fairness, equity, and justice" (Shapiro & Stefkovich, 2016, p. 28).

The ethic of critique provides a post positivist perspective that stems from critical theory and critical pedagogy (Shapiro & Stefkovich, 2016). This perspective aligns with a focus on multiculturalism and diversity, to ensure equity despite class, race, gender, sexuality, or other categories that have been used to minoritize groups of people. It provides a lens for critiquing the rules, laws, and policies that may not be fair to all individuals. The ethic of critique ensures a focus on social justice, which can be understood as institutional and structural elements "that provide access, opportunity, and inclusion of historically marginalized or otherwise oppressed individuals or groups of people" (Aragon & Brantmeier, 2009, p. 39). The ethic of critique is employed to ensure that the rules, laws, and policies employed in decision making are fair and just and that they are equitable to all groups.

The ethic of care is prevalent in student affairs, placing students and student development as primary concerns in decision making. This ethic is rooted in feminist approaches that challenge what is viewed as a "patriarchal, ethic of justice in our society by turning to the ethic of care for moral decision making" (Shapiro & Stefkovich, 2016, p. 32). This ethic emphasizes relationships rather than the individual, focusing on empathy, response, reciprocity, and receptivity (Noddings, 2012).

The ethic of the profession includes professional ethics and values that may fall under the ethic of justice, but it also encompasses the development of an individual's personal and professional codes of ethics (Shapiro & Stefkovich, 2016). Rather than broadly applying existing professional codes, Shapiro and Stefkovich recommend that individuals create their own codes based on their professional experiences and expectations combined with their own personal codes. This is a paradigm that will take time and effort to develop, and it will evolve over time as learning occurs and experiences help to redefine issues and concepts.

Wood and Hilton (2012) considered the community college mission of serving their local communities and expanded the framework to include the ethic of local community as a consideration. "The ethic of local community is grounded in the notion that community colleges must serve the needs, interests, and public good of the local community, defined as the service region of the institution" (p. 206). The emphasis here is on local, rather than state- or national-level interests. When considering ethical decisions, the interests and needs of the local community must be considered for those who work at community colleges. Wood and Hilton (2012) point out that other institutional types also serve local communities, but the notion of serving the community is a distinct part of the design and philosophical underpinnings of the community college sector, so it is essential to consider that when making decisions.

Most people tend to lean toward one or two of these paradigms, but ideally leaders will consider a variety of perspectives when making decisions. Starratt (1994) viewed the ethics of justice, care, and critique as a tapestry where the threads of each are woven together. Through examining different paradigms and perspectives, students and new professionals gain a better understanding of their preferred perspectives and will lessen the chance of making decisions based on personal bias (Shapiro & Stefkovich, 2016). Viewing situations through multiple paradigms also helps develop an understanding of how others may perceive similar situations differently, so that they can learn to better understand and work through conflicting views.

A Kaleidoscopic Approach. Ethical decision-making models tend to incorporate four major steps: problem identification, gathering data, conceptualization and evaluation of alternative courses of action, and implementing the decision (Nevarez & Wood, 2010). The critical part of the process for ethical decision making lies in evaluating alternative courses of action (Wood & Hilton, 2012) prior to making the final decision. Often, these courses of action are driven by ethical lenses or paradigms, as demonstrated by Dalton, Crosby, Velente, and Eberhardt's (2016) framework. Similarly, Shapiro and Stefkovich (2016) advocate the use of multiple ethical paradigms in decision making: the ethics of justice, critique, care, and the profession. Starratt (1994) viewed the ethics of justice, care, and critique as a tapestry where the threads of each are woven together. Through examining different paradigms and perspectives, students and professionals gain a better understanding of their preferred perspectives (Shapiro & Stefkovich, 2016), and they will also gain an understanding of how others may perceive similar situations differently, so that they can learn to work through and understand conflicting views. It is rare that ethical decisions are clear cut and agreed upon by all.

Although some frameworks position ethical decision making as a hierarchy (Kitchener, 1985; Shapiro & Stefkovich, 2016), we view ethical decision making as looking through a kaleidoscope. Each situation presents unique challenges, opportunities, and outcomes; each element in the problem creates a different picture; and each person will solve the problem differently in ways that align with their personal and professional codes of ethics. The kaleidoscope metaphor allows for the application of different lenses when considering a problem. If we look only through our own personal lens, then we may be missing key information and may not make the most appropriate decision (Saunders & Wilson, 2016; Wood & Hilton, 2012). This metaphor also represents that people should practice changing the elements of the situation before making the decision, such as considering how placing different weights on ethical perspectives may result in different outcomes or how different decisions result in different outcomes. This metaphor serves as a reminder that many elements comprise the situation as well as how we view it, and each interacts differently given the context. If we do not consider how those different elements create different patterns, the best decision may not be made.

Making Ethical Decisions in Practice

It is often difficult to make decisions as a new practitioner. We want to be sure that we are making the "right" decision. While there are ethical codes and principles as well as many decision-making frameworks that exist there is no one exact or perfect route to making an ethical decision. In fact, some consider navigating the complex nature of decision making to be an art more than a science (Dalton, Crosby, Valente, & Eberhardt, 2016).

In regard to ethics, however, there are usually multiple decisions that may be considered "right" or "correct." The goal, then, is to recognize that the decision you make must be right for you, the students, and the institution, and it should fit within your own personal and professional ethical codes. Although not everyone may agree with the decision that is made, it is important to be able to justify why the decision you made is appropriate and to share the thinking behind the decision in order to gain shared understanding. In the next section, we provide a sample case problem and describe how two people walk through the process of making an ethical decision, what their decisions are, and why each is an appropriate decision.

In an increasingly complex world, our personal and professional lives are full of decision-making opportunities and many times these involve ethical issues requiring us to think through options and responses. Our ability to effectively address ethical issues can be enhanced through personal reflection about our own values, willingness to discuss and hear others' viewpoints and interpretations about situations, and through practice. The case problems provided in this chapter can be used for that very purpose. These cases offer an opportunity for us, as authors, to reflect on our own values, to discuss with one another our approaches to resolving ethical dilemmas, and offer the opportunity for us to practice making decisions about various situations. We encourage our readers to use these cases as an opportunity for reflection, dialogue, and practice as well.

Case Problem

First, we present the case problem, next we demonstrate how each person thought through the steps to making an ethical decision, we briefly highlight our responses, and finally we summarize how we approached our decisions.

CASE PROBLEM: TRANQUIL U

Tranquil University is a small, private college. Its quaint campus is located just outside a major metropolitan setting. The institution draws heavily from the nearby city, and also has a good number of students from the region and state with a small number of students from across the country. There is also a growing international student population, which currently comprises about 15% of the student body, an amount that has tripled in the past 10 years due to intentional recruitment aimed to diversify the student body.

A hallmark of the institution is its rich history in freedom of speech and open exchange of controversial ideas. The faculty, in general, sees this as a hallmark of higher education and views it as essential to the work and learning on campus. Additionally, the student government association funding committee (SGAFC), which funds student organization events and speakers, has within its foundational principles that the exchange of ideas and the freedom to disagree, are essential to their work on campus.

Recently, a student organization, which is known for bringing controversial speakers and divisive debates to campus, was denied funding by the SGAFC for a proposed event. During the funding proposal hearing, concern was voiced by several people on the SGAFC who felt that the speaker would both offend many students on campus and make them feel unwelcome because the speaker advocates for closing international admissions to U.S. colleges and limiting enrollment to U.S. citizens only. They also felt that the speaker went against the college's values. Many questions were asked during the proposal hearing to gain further information, but ultimately the student organization was denied funding to host the speaker on campus. Now the student organization is upset because they do not have the funding to bring the speaker to campus, and they approach you, as the student government advisor, to overturn the decision.

You speak with the SGAFC and find out that although the student organization met the requirements for funding, the SGAFC decided not to fund the event because they did not want Tranquil U students to feel unsupported or unwelcome by the speaker's viewpoints. When you ask the SGAFC about their commitment to the exchange of ideas and freedom of speech, they indicate student safety is more important in their view than the student organizations ability to host the speaker and the speaker's ideas. However, your supervisor encourages you to overturn the decision or use department funding to bring the speaker to campus because the supervisor feels that Tranquil U students must learn to engage with ideas they do not like or support. "We cannot claim to support free speech and then deny it because some students might get offended," is your supervisor's position. As advisor to the student government association, how do you approach the ethical decision?

Authors' Perspectives on the Case Problems

In this section, we walk through the process of making an ethical decision from the perspective of two of the chapter authors.

First, we identified the practical and ethical dilemmas associated with the issue.

Step 1: Identify the practical and ethical dilemma

The practical issue is whether or not to overturn the decision made by the student government association funding committee (SGAFC) to not fund the student organizations request for a speaker.

The practical dilemma is whether or not to recommend an overturn of the decision not to fund a controversial speaker or fund the speaker from another source.

The ethical issues in this case seem to be about: promoting justice and respecting autonomy, which may seem at odds depending on the lenses through which the dilemma is viewed.

The ethical issue in the case involves weighing two values: allowing all voices to be heard in order to encourage healthy discussions and debates, a long-standing value of the college, and creating an environment where all students feel welcome and safe. There is also an issue of respecting the decision made by the SGA Funding Committee.

Justice: Is it just to allow a speaker whose views whose very philosophy attacks the principles of justice that we promote and hold as fundamental to our university?

Autonomy: How do we respect the autonomy of our student government to make decisions about what to fund? Are we infringing upon the student organizations autonomy to host a speaker of their choosing?

Author 1. Using the kaleidoscope lens and viewing both the practical and ethical dilemma from various points of view, there may be a number of competing dilemmas in this situation. I utilized the Dalton et al. (2016) framework to guide my thought process keeping in mind students, the institution, the community, and the profession with recognition that my own personal background and individual conscience and biases do influence how I see the situation. However, the primary practical issue seems to be whether or not to overturn the decision made by the SGAFC. As a former practitioner and now faculty member who works with master's students from a variety of functional areas in higher education I tend to lean towards the CAS Statement of Shared Ethical Principles (2006) and the ACPA Standard of Ethical Principles (2006) which both include justice and autonomy as key aspects.

Author 2. Identifying the practical dilemma was fairly straightforward. The practical dilemma is whether or not to overturn a decision that was made by the SGAFC. Identifying the ethical dilemma was a bit more difficult. I primarily referred to the CAS Statement of Shared Ethical Principles (2006) in determining the ethical dilemmas.

First, overturning a decision made by another group violates the principle of autonomy, which empowers people to make decisions. What message is sent if I overturn that decision? The principle of autonomy must also be considered in that it encourages all voices to be heard. However, the principles of nonmalfeasance and beneficence call for the supportive environments that promote student growth and consider others' thoughts and feelings. Would allowing a speaker of this type violate those principles?

Step 2: Gather Information

The gathering information stage consists of reviewing procedures, documents, and discussing the situation with those involved as well as other constituencies.

Documents and procedures
- Review my institution's mission, standards of practice, as well as codes of conduct as it relates to issues of speech, and promoting justice.
- Reviewing the SGAFC procedures and how other funding requests like this have been handled.
- Gather more information about the specific event, the speaker and how events on other campuses inviting this speaker have been handled. In particular, concern around issues of safety.

Information needs to be gathered in regard to both the speaker and past practice on campus.

- About the Speaker: Have there been negative or harmful outcomes from previous engagements by the speaker? Does the speaker advocate harm?
- About campus: What has past practice been in regard to controversial speakers? If the college has not barred speakers in the past, why is this one considered too controversial?
- Seek information from other colleges that may have hosted the speaker: How did they plan for the event? What were the outcomes? Would they do it again? Do they have recommendations?
- Seek the opinion of other professionals in the college including

- What do professional association documents have to say about handling issues like these? What has been discussed lately by professional organizations?

Gain perspectives and points of view:
- Talk to the SGAFC.
- Talk to the student organization
- Speak with the on-campus. international student organization.
- Speak with the office of international students.
- Consult with any faculty experts (faculty senate-faculty experts on issues of multiculturalism, speech).

both faculty and staff members. This deserves a larger conversation among student affairs professionals also because we may be setting a precedent for future events.
- Yet another consideration is the local community. Will the event disrupt or divide the community? What if community members agree with the speaker—will this create unsafe situations for students when they go off campus?

Author 1. I used the various lenses to consider what information needed to be gathered from the students, the institution, the community, and the profession. It seems that simultaneously information must be gathered along with considering context. In considering context, some of my most urgent concerns included the following questions. How much time do we have? How quickly is a decision required? I also wanted to consider the larger social and community context. What is the current national, community, and campus climate around the issues at hand such as international students and speech?

Author 2. In the midst of gathering information, context must also be considered. The college has a documented history of valuing and encouraging free speech and the open exchange of controversial ideas, so why would that change in regard to this speaker? The logical reason is that the college population has changed, and there is a growing population of international students, the very population that this speaker claims should not be allowed to be students at the college. Rather than an academic debate that could be viewed as harmless when students are not the topic of the debate, it now impacts a considerable population of students. These students may feel that other students, faculty, and staff members share the speaker's views, which may in turn make them feel unsafe. If they attend the talk, students may be impacted by the speaker's comments emotionally, reducing the ability to have civil discourse around the issue and increasing discomfort among students. It is also worth considering the current external climate of "nationalism distorted into nativism" (Bush, 2017, p. 45). Permitting a speaker who claims international students should not be allowed on campus could be viewed as hate speech or bigotry, which is not what I, as a professional educator and former administrator, want to promote.

Step 3: View through the Multiple Perspectives (Kaleidoscope)

Using the kaleidoscope perspective, in each stage of the process I wanted to take into consideration the various points of view: the student, institution, profession, and community.

Student: How does this situation look from various student perspectives? The student government association, the student organization requesting the funding, the overall student body, and students on campus who may feel particularly marginalized or harmed by the viewpoints of the speaker—in this case international students came to the forefront of my thoughts. How do I balance the needs of one group with the needs of another?

Institutional: Consider the institutions mission and history on decisions such as this. Consider that the decision I make does impact the institution and its reputation. What are the institutions guidelines and procedures? Who are the institutional stakeholders in a decision like this? Consider how the outcome may impact international admissions.

Community: What is the community context particularly around issues concerning international populations?

Professional: Consult various professional organizational documents. The principles of do no harm and non-malfeasance (ACPA, 2006; CAS, 2006)

The personal values that undergird my ethical views include lifelong learning, social justice, and fairness and equity.

Professional: CAS principles of autonomy, justice. beneficence, non-malfeasance. Other professional ethics include placing high value on lifelong learning. Does bringing the speaker to campus promote student learning? By not bringing the speaker to campus, can we promote learning in another way through dialogue about why the decision was made?

Justice and Critique: What do policies and laws say in regard to the issue? Are those policies and laws just, fair, and equitable? Does the promotion of free speech promote ideas that highlight discourse of a dominant group and disadvantage an oppressed group?

Care: What is best for students? In this case, students are viewed as a group rather than individuals. How will the decision impact the relation between students and college personnel? How will it impact relationships between domestic and international students? Students and college personnel?

are at the forefront of my mind. Several resources exist beyond statements of ethical standards. Consult the *Bias Incidents Prevention and Response Policy and Protocol* (ACPA, 2014) as a source for ideas.

Author 1. The concepts of do no harm or malfeasance are fundamental to any decision made; thus, I tried to consider harm from each of the perspectives. I asked myself: who is harmed, what might harm look like, and how can harm be minimized? Each of the perspectives mentioned above is encircled by my own personal conscience. Given the current dialogue across the nation about issues of speech as well as the current climate around international populations my individual sensitivities were heightened in analyzing this situation. I think it is important that as professionals we acknowledge our sensitivities and biases. Generally, my personal conscience and leadership style lends me to seeking multiple perspectives before coming to a final decision. Seeking multiple perspectives often takes time and in many situations, time is of the essence. I often do not personally feel right about a decision when I have not sought input from those who may be impacted by a decision. While consulting professional resources, I found the *ACPA Bias Incidents Prevention and Response Policy and Protocol* (2014) helpful in that it provided me insights about specific issues to consider in a situation like this and specific courses of action to take which are explained further in the next section.

Author 2. I viewed the issue through four paradigms: Professional, Justice, Critique, and Care. I see the free speech/healthy debate aspect as aligning with the CAS (2006) Ethical Principle of autonomy, which encourages learning and freedom of discussion and justice, which respects the rights of individuals and groups to express their opinions. The safe environment value aligns with the principles of beneficence and nonmalfeasance, which advocate the consideration of others' feelings and creation of a supportive environment. A personal value that guides my professional ethics is a focus on lifelong learning. Therefore, a key consideration is my decision's potential for and impact on student learning.

The ethic of critique places a focus on social justice, fairness, and equity. Freedom of speech is valued at the college, and stems from the U.S. Constitution. The law says that individuals have the right to free speech, and the college agrees with that. However, what if that speech intentionally invokes harm upon certain groups of people? Does allowing a person of privilege—in this case, a U.S. citizen speaking out against those from other countries—to speak out against a subordinate group support existing systems of oppression? Does this type of event work against notions of equity? In this situation, it is important to consider "whether decision making promotes status quo perpetuation or positive social change" (Aragon & Brantmeier, 2009, p. 49).

The ethic of care places students' well-being as the most important aspect of a decision. Considerations from the Professional paradigm overlap with the ethic of care. Will the speaker's presentation be more helpful or harmful for students? What message is sent by allowing a speaker WHO openly decries 15% of the student population? It is possible that students may think that the college agrees with the speaker, which may cause students to feel unsafe and unwelcome, ultimately impacting their ability to gain a quality education. This conflicts with the CAS (2006) principle of non-malfeasance.

Step 4: Generate Options/Alternative Courses of Action

- Veto the student government ruling and fund the requested amount to the student organization
- Uphold the student government ruling.
- Postpone the event until the future?

Additional considerations for action. Regardless of the final decision made the following action steps should be considered.

- A facilitated conversation between involved parties. Both sides need to be able to clearly express and articulate their points of view both before and after the decision is made.
- Be prepared to hold "restorative circles" (ACPA, 2014).
- Educational programming (active and passive) around the purposes of speech and the university policy.
- A clear and public statement on

- Support the request to either overturn the decision or fund the speaker.
- Support the SGAFC's decision
- Find a solution that both respects the value of free speech and debate and provides support for students.
- Regardless of the decision, more discussion must occur between students, faculty, and staff so that this does not remain a hidden decision that is not shared or discussed by the broader campus population.

what the decision is and why it
was made must be made readily
available.
• A review of policies and procedures.

Author 1. Even in my first read of the situation, I knew that nothing about this case would be simple. The profession and our campus value diversity, inclusion as well as promoting diverse perspectives, and we have a commitment to the safety and inclusion of our students and in this particular case our international students. Given that currently sensitivities are heightened around issues of free speech, it made the decision that much more complex.

I empathize with both the student organization and the SGAFC points of view and I want to balance the values of autonomy and justice. In discussing the situation with the students, consulting professional and institutional documents, I found my answer by checking in with institutional and professional colleagues who often hold different opinions than I do. I found that by listening to the voices of diverse others, I was better able to view the consequences of any decision I might make and ultimately helped me feel more confident. Ultimately, as with most ethical decisions, I was not convinced that in this situation there was a right or wrong decision, but rather a best decision given the circumstances. After evaluating the alternative courses of action, the next best step is to prepare for the post decision with some of the options explored in the table above.

Author 2. At first glance, the options in this case seemed straightforward: either I will support the request to bring in the speaker, by requesting a revised ruling or providing funding to bring in the speaker, or I will support the decision that was already made. Prior to working through the steps and considering the different values and ethics involved, I thought it would be an easy decision, but in working through the options, I found information that ethically supports several different options. Ultimately, the determining factor will be the personal and professional values that comprise my professional paradigm (Shapiro & Stefkovich, 2016).

In addition to merely supporting the request for funding or not supporting it, there are other options. If the speaker is allowed to present on campus, then the campus can provide additional programming to supplement the event. There can be pre- and post-events that focus on how to discuss sensitive topics respectfully, how to disagree with others in ways that promote fruitful conversation, and how to deal with the emotions that may arise. A key consideration, however, would be in ensuring that students actually attend the other events. An alternate option would be to explain to the student organization that I cannot support their request for funding and explain why. If this is the decision, however, there must be discussions with larger groups of students to discuss the reasons why I feel this way, and there should also be broader discussions between members of the SGAFC and the student organization to gain better understanding of the issues from multiple perspectives. It is an opportunity for learning and for students to see the potential broader impact that their decisions may have beyond what they may have envisioned.

In determining which option, I pick, there are several important considerations. One is that the decision should have the potential to result in the least amount of harm to students' well-being, including their growth and development. The decision also has to weigh heavily in favor of doing the right thing from a social justice perspective. Considering the broader current social context, bringing in a nationalist perspective may not be appropriate.

Conclusion

We have explored the literature on ethical decision making and walked through how two of the authors approached a specific ethical dilemma. Finding opportunities to reflect upon our values, dialogue and hear the perspectives of others, and practicing approaching dilemmas through case studies are all ways new professionals and even seasoned practitioners can enhance skills in decision making. Making decisions that impact the lives of students and others is not easy, but the more we can engage in these kinds of reflective activities the more confident we can fee when approaching day-to-day decisions and ethical dilemmas in our professional lives.

Practice Case Problem

To conclude our chapter, we offer another case problem. We encourage you to use this case example as an opportunity explore your own values, ethical principles, and frameworks that fit for you; also you may find it helpful to discuss this and other cases with a colleague, classmates, or you may want to bring a case to a staff meeting as a professional development opportunity. At the end of the case we present questions for consideration.

Case Problem

You are the director of a newly renovated student center on campus. The renovation was a long-time coming and it has greatly boosted student satisfaction on campus; the building has also become a shining star for admissions tours and recruitment videos for the institution over the past year. A generous donor with deep pockets and a strong affinity for the institution funded the renovation. This same donor is interested in helping with another need for the campus by making a gift which would fund two endowed faculty positions in the cultural studies department, a new full-time mental health counselor, and 20 full scholarships for low income students who demonstrate great leadership and academic potential.

You know from experience and data that the counseling center is in desperate need of additional staff to support the growing array of students' mental health needs. You have also been told there is no hope for any new staff positions for the next three to five fiscal years. You also know students have been advocating for more academic ties and institutional research, which focuses on cultural competence. The donor is a good friend to the college and truly wants to help; in fact, the structure of this intended gift was crafted from listening to needs identified by the vice president of student affairs.

Though students love the new renovated student center, they have recently circulated a petition to remodel the restrooms to be designated as all-gender restrooms. Students want these restrooms to help ensure the student center is a safe and welcoming place for all students; they also believe such restrooms are in line with the institutional values of nondiscrimination and desire to have a diverse student body. The donor, whose name is on the building, indicates she does not want to see this restroom change. Although the donor knows that she cannot dictate the decision, she indicates if the restroom change is made, the proposed financial gift may be withdrawn. The donor has no problem with all-gender restrooms on campus; she just does not want them in the new student center, which bears her name. Your vice president asks you not to make the restroom change, but says the decision is up to you. What do you do?

QUESTIONS FOR CONSIDERATION

1. Before solving the problem, take a few minutes and consider your own personal and professional ethical codes. What values are most important? How do those values drive decision-making? Which values overlap between the personal and professional? How does this impact your ethical code?
2. What does a kaleidoscope approach look like to you?
3. What steps would you take to work through the ethical dilemma? What professional resources would you consult?
4. Which lenses/perspectives did you think of first? Why are those most important to you? How do they influence the decisions that you make?
5. View the problem using a lens that you are not comfortable with or do not rely on frequently. How does that lens impact the way that you thought about the problem?

6. Consider how you might approach the case from various positions within the university (as an entry level program coordinator level, as the director of a department, as dean of students). What is similar or different to your current approach?

7. Consider how the case might be approached from someone on the academic affairs side (faculty, college dean). How does that impact the decision?

8. Consider how approaches may vary at different institutional types (community college, private, public, faith-based, special focus or minority serving institution). How do different contexts influence ethical decision making?

9. Compare and contrast your responses with a partner. What was similar? What was different? How might those differences need to be navigated in a professional setting?

REFERENCES

Almutaz Bur News Network. (2017, Oct. 19). *President George W. Bush speaks on divisive state of American politics* [video file]. Retrieved from: https://www.youtube.com/watch?v=_9XfeAqIuf4

American College Personnel Association. (2006). *Statement of ethical principles and standards.* Washington, DC: Author. Retrieved from: http://www.myacpa.org/files/ethicalprinciplesstandardslargepdf

American College Personnel Association. (2014). Bias incidents prevention and response policy and protocol. Washington, DC: Author. Retrieved from: http://www.myacpa.org/docs/bias-incident-prevention-and-response-protocol-final-approved-2-14-14pdf

Aragon, A., & Brantmeier, E. J. (2009). Diversity-affirming ethics and critical epistemology: Institution decision making in community colleges. In P. L. Farrell & C. P. Harbour (Eds.), *Contemporary Issues in Institutional Ethics, New Directions for Community Colleges, 148* (pp. 39–51). San Francisco: Jossey-Bass.

Barr, M. J., McClellan, G. S., & Sandeen, A. (2014). *Making change happen in student affairs.* New York: Wiley.

Beckner, W. (2004). *Ethics for educational leaders.* Boston: Pearson.

Council for the Advancement of Standards (2017). About CAS. Retrieved from: http://www.cas.edu/

Council for the Advancement of Standards (2006). CAS statement of shared ethical principles. In Council for the Advancement of Higher Education (Ed.), *CAS professional standards for higher education* (6th ed.). Washington, DC: Author.

Dalton, J. C., Crosby, P. C., Valente, A., & Eberhardt, D. (2016). Maintaining and modeling everday ethics in student affairs. In G. S. McLellan, J. Stringer, & Associates (Eds.), *The Handbook of Student Affairs Administration* (4th ed.; pp. 199–223). San Francisco: Jossey-Bass.

Ethic. (n.d.). *Merriam-Webster's Collegiate Dictionary* (11th ed.). Retrieved from: https://www.merriam-webster.com/dictionary/ethics

Fried, J. (2003). Ethical standards and principles. In J. H. Schuh, S. R. Jones, & S. R. Harper, and Associates (Eds.), *Student services: A handbook for the profession* (5th ed.; pp. 107–127). San Francisco: Jossey-Bass.

Harris, S. G. (1994). Organizational culture and individual sensemaking: A schema-based perspective. *Organization Science, 5*(3), 309–321. doi: https://doi.org/10.1287/orsc.5.3.309

Kitchener, K. S. (1985). Ethical principles and ethical decisions in student affairs. In H. J. Canon & R. D. Brown (Eds.), *Applied ethics in student services, New directions for student services, 30* (pp. 17–29). San Francisco: Jossey-Bass.

Nevarez, C., & Wood, J. L. (2010). *Community college leadership and administration: Theory, practice, & change.* New York: Peter Lang.

Nevarez, C., & Wood, J. L. (2014). *Ethical leadership and the community college: Paradigms, decision making, and praxis.* Charlotte, NC: Information Age.

Noddings, N. (2012). The language of care ethics. *Knowledge Quest, 40*(5), 52–56.

Noddings, N. (1984). *Caring: A feminine approach to ethics and moral education.* Berkeley, CA: University of California Press.

Reybold, L. E., Halx, M. D., & Jimenez, A. L. (2008). Professional integrity in higher education: A study of administrative staff ethics in student affairs. *Journal of College Student Development, 49*(2), 110–124.

Rion, M. (1996). *The responsible manager.* Amherst, MA: Human Resources Press.

Saunders, S. A., & Wilson, C. M. (2016). What is ethical professional practice? In J. H. Schuh, S. R. Jones, & V. Torres (Eds.), *Student services: A handbook for the profession* (6th ed.; pp. 89–106). San Francisco: Jossey-Bass.

Shapiro, J. P., & Stefkovich, J. A. (2005). *Ethical leadership and decision making in education: Applying theoretical perspectives to complex dilemmas* (3rd ed.). New York: Routledge.

Shapiro, J. P., & Stefkovich, J. A. (2016). *Ethical leadership and decision making in education: Applying theoretical perspectives to complex dilemmas* (4th ed.). New York: Routledge.

Reybold, L. E., Halx, M. D., & Jimenez, A. L. (2008). Professional integrity in higher education: A study of administrative staff ethics in student affairs. *Journal of College Student Development 49*(2), 110–124.

Shapiro, J. P., & Stefkovich, J. A. (2005). *Ethical leadership and decision making in education: Applying theoretical perspectives to complex dilemmas* (2nd ed.). Mahwah, NJ: Lawrence Erlbaum.

St. Olaf College. (n.d.). Personal ethics. In *A guide to ethics.* Retrieved from: https://pages.stolaf.edu/ein/disciplines/personal-ethics/

Wood, J. L., & Hilton, A. A. (2012). Five ethical paradigms for community college leaders: Toward constructing and considering alternative courses of action in ethical decision making. *Community College Review, 40*(3), 196–214. DOI: 10.1177/0091552112448818

Chapter 6

CURRENT LEGAL ISSUES
IN STUDENT AFFAIRS

Natalie Jackson and Janelle Schaller

The relationship between a higher education institution and its students is a complex one that requires student affairs professionals to understand the legal rights of students and an appreciation of the legal responsibilities of the institution. A critical competency for student affairs professionals is the ability to identify legal issues arising within daily practice. Many of the rights afforded to students in the higher education context are based in federal law and regulation related to student civil rights, free speech, discipline, campus safety, and privacy. This chapter will cover each of these topics along with discussion of practical ways to address institutional risk related to these issues.

I. Civil Rights

A panoply of federal (and state) laws require institutions to prohibit discrimination or harassment[1] based on a variety of classifications. As a result, the vast majority of institutions—as recipients of federal funding, as employers, as places of public accommodation, or as other legally defined entities—prohibit discrimination on the basis of sex,[2] race, color, national origin,[3] disability,[4] and age.[5] Many institutions also prohibit discrimination on other bases, which are either required by case law, state law, or local law, or by institutional choice.

---

1. For purposes of this article, "discrimination" and "harassment" are collectively referred to as "discrimination."
2. Title IX of the Education Amendments of 1972, 20 U.S.C. Sec. 1681 *et seq.*
3. Title VI of the Civil Rights Act of 1964, 42 U.S.C. Sec. 2000d *et seq.*
4. Rehabilitation Act of 1973, 29 U.S.C. Sec. 701 et seq.; Americans with Disabilities Act of 1990, 42 U.S.C. Sec. 12101 *et seq.*
5. Age Discrimination Act of 1975, 42 U.S.C. Sec. 6101 *et seq.*

Practically speaking, the prohibition on discrimination means that institutions and those acting on its behalf must not deny participation, benefits, or services to an individual because of the listed bases. Put differently, institutions may not discriminate against a student on the basis of the student's protected classification.

Institutions are also obligated to ensure that a student is not subjected to a hostile environment on the basis of any protected classifications. Typically, a hostile environment is found when harassment is so severe, persistent, or pervasive that it impacts the student's ability to receive the benefits offered by the institution. Sexual harassment additionally can occur as a request for sexual favors in exchange for a benefit—known as *quid pro quo.*

The Rehabilitation Act of 1973, Section 504 and the Americans with Disabilities Act,[6] in addition to forbidding discrimination on the basis of disability, impose additional affirmative obligations on institutions. In addition to complying with certain physical accessibility standards, institutions must provide auxiliary aids, academic adjustments, or reasonable accommodations (collectively referred to in this text as "accommodations") upon request to students with disabilities to provide those students with equal access to educational opportunities and benefits.[7]

Accommodations can be wide ranging, and may include academic adjustments (such as additional time for testing) as well as accommodations in other realms (a student may need to have a service animal or may require first-floor accommodation due to inability to negotiate stairs). In a student conduct setting, students may require accommodation—for example, a blind student may need information about the student code of conduct charge and procedures prepared in Braille so that the student understands the process. Similarly, a performance put on by the institution may need to provide an American Sign Language interpreter. These are all academic adjustments or accommodations that federal law requires institutions to provide.

Notably, institutions are not obligated to grant all requests—federal law does recognize that certain actions may fundamentally alter the nature of a program, and an institution is not asked to do that. Similarly, an institution is not obligated to provide certain types of accommodations, such as a personal aide to assist with personal care. However, the institution's first response to a request for accommodation should be a willingness to identify a reasonable accommodation through an interactive process with the student, not an attempt to refuse the request. Working with an institution's disability office, legal counsel, and the area(s) of campus involved in the request often times will result in identification of an accommodation that works for

---

6. Title II of the ADA governs public universities; Title III covers private institutions.
7. Employees are similarly entitled to reasonable accommodations, but this article focuses solely on legal obligations relating to students.

all parties and provides the student with the access to which he or she is entitled.

The federal (and state) laws discussed above generally provide several enforcement mechanisms. First, institutions are required in many instances to identify one or more individuals with responsibility to ensure compliance with the law on campus. This is why most campuses have one or more individuals with responsibility over Title IX—discussed in more detail later—or Section 504/ADA, for example. Those coordinators typically have an internal complaint process that allows individuals to bring discrimination concerns forward for review. A student who believes a request for accommodation was not properly fulfilled can bring a complaint internally to have that reviewed and addressed, if necessary. Similarly, a student who believes the living environment is a hostile environment on the basis of sex could bring that to the attention of the institution, which would review the situation and act as necessary.

Students, however, are not required to use the institution's internal complaint procedures. Federal law provides that the United States Department of Education, Office for Civil Rights ("OCR") may investigate complaints of discrimination on the basis of sex, race, color, national origin, age, and disability. Some states have similar state agencies that can investigate some or all of the same matters. Sometimes students will use internal complaint processes, and if unsatisfied, will forward their concerns to OCR. Other students will file a formal complaint only with OCR. OCR's investigation process is straightforward and laid out in detail in their Case Processing Manual.[8] If you are involved in such a complaint, your institution's counsel or another office on campus will likely work with you to review the situation, respond to the OCR complaint, and recommend actions be taken to address issues raised in the complaint. During or after the OCR investigation the institution may be given an opportunity to resolve the investigation through a resolution agreement with OCR and the student. If a resolution is not offered, or is not reached, OCR may reach a conclusion that the institution is not meeting its legal obligations as a recipient of federal funding and may pursue action to end the institution's ability to continue to receive federal funding. Although this penalty is severe, and to date has not yet been used by OCR against any institution of higher education, it remains a significant penalty that emphasizes the importance of awareness of and compliance with these laws.

Finally, students have the option of pursuing litigation against the institution and/or individuals employed by the institution (in certain circumstances). A student may have brought forward an internal complaint and/or

---

8. https://www2.ed.gov/about/offices/list/ocr/docs/ocrcpm.pdf (last visited June 24, 2019).

an OCR complaint, but may not have—it is possible that litigation is the first time you or your institution learns that a student has a complaint about some aspect of his or her experience. Again, your institution's counsel will work with you and others to handle the matter.

Student affairs professionals should have a solid understanding of their institution's nondiscrimination policies. These policies will set forth the protected classifications at the institutions. Nondiscrimination policies oftentimes also indicate which individuals on campus investigate complaints of discrimination prohibited by those policies. Student affairs professionals are often the persons to whom complaints are directed, and should be well-versed in how those matters are addressed. Similarly, student affairs professionals should ensure that they and their staff receive regular, up-to-date training on nondiscrimination topics.

Another important best practice is to ensure your institution's record retention schedule is followed. If your institution finds itself the subject to claims of discrimination your institution's counsel, the investigating agency, or the Court will need copies of the complaint, the final outcome, and anything in between that relays the facts about what occurred. Having a practice of deleting emails or shredding documents once you have resolved a problem or concluded a project may not comport with your institution's records retention schedule, and may constitute a violation of a legal record-keeping requirement. Such a practice may impact your institution's ability to explain the actions it took with respect to particular issues or students. Records retention schedules typically have considered legal requirements for records retention and applicable statutes of limitation for aggrieved individuals to bring claims against the institution, and should always be followed.

II. Free Speech/Academic Freedom of Students

The First Amendment to the United States Constitution, applied to states through the Fourteenth Amendment, provides for freedom of speech. Public institutions in some states are subject to additional state constitutional or statutory provisions providing for similar or additional protections. Private institutions by contract or policy may have adopted similar protections; however, in the absence of that type of action, a private institution's actions are typically not subject to the First Amendment. Public and private institutions, however, are both subject to the Higher Education Act[9] which provides that "no student attending an institution of higher education . . . should, on the basis of participation in protected speech or protected association, be

---

9. 20 U.S.C. sec. 1011a.

excluded from participation in, be denied the benefits of, or be subjected to discrimination or official sanction. . . ."

Under First Amendment jurisprudence, some speech—not all—is protected. Certain speech has been held by the Supreme Court of the United States to be outside of the realm of protection, meaning institutions are free to prohibit it and have no obligation to allow it in any forum. Unprotected speech includes fighting words or true threats,[10] incitement to imminent lawless action that is likely to produce such action,[11] obscenity,[12] and child pornography.[13]

For other types of speech, if the Supreme Court or another court with jurisdiction over your institution has not clearly concluded that it is unprotected, the question of its legal status depends on where the speech takes place. In legal terms, this is known as "forum analysis." Determining the forum at issue is the first step in analyzing the speaker's and institution's rights and responsibilities. Campus locations generally fall into one of three distinct categories: traditional public forum, limited public forum, or nonpublic forum.[14]

A traditional public forum is an area that has traditionally been where public speech occurs. In the Supreme Court's opinion, this includes sidewalks and parks. In these locations, an institution has the least ability to regulate speech. In this forum, the viewpoint of the speaker may not be considered by an institution when imposing regulations. Practically, this means that any attempt to limit speech must not consider whether the speaker is delivering a message that aligns with the institution's values or not. An institution can, however, impose reasonable time, place, and manner restrictions that do not consider the content of the speech so long as they meet what courts call "strict scrutiny"—the regulations serve a compelling state interest and are narrowly tailored, leaving alternate routes for speech.[15]

A different area of campus may constitute a limited public forum. A limited public forum is an area the institution has opened for the purpose of speech and discussion. The institution may limit use of this forum to certain types of speakers or certain types of speech (e.g., bulletin boards, space in print publications, etc.). In these areas, the same rules as in a traditional public forum apply.[16]

---

10. *Virginia v. Black*, 538 U.S. 343 (2003) (true threat). Chaplinsky v. New Hampshire, 315 U.S. 568 (1942) (fighting words).
11. *Brandenburg v. Ohio*, 395 U.S. 444, 447 (1969).
12. *Miller v. California*, 413 U.S. 15 (1973).
13. *Osborne v. Ohio*, 495 U.S. 103 (1990).
14. *Perry Educators Association v. Perry Local Educators Association*, 460 U.S. 37 (1983).
15. *Id.*
16. *Id.*

Even at a public institution, there are areas that are simply unavailable to the public. In these nonpublic forums, an institution is able to impose the types of regulations it sees fit, subject only to review of whether those regulations are reasonable in light of the purpose of the forum. For example, the Supreme Court has concluded that a school district's internal mail system,[17] and an airport terminal,[18] are nonpublic forums.

Another area in which student affairs professionals become involved in First Amendment issues occurs in the context of student activity fees. Distribution of student activity fees at a public school is subject to the First Amendment, which provides that the distribution must not be based on the viewpoint of the student organization if those fees are mandatory.[19]

Finally, the Supreme Court has also recognized the role that social media and online speech has come to occupy in our daily lives. Recently, the Court acknowledged that "[w]hile in the past there may have been difficulty in identifying the most important places (in a spatial sense) for the exchange of views, today the answer is clear. It is cyberspace—the vast democratic forums of the Internet in general, and social media in particular."[20] The Internet and social media are the "modern public square."[21]

At times, the posts, comments, or "likes" a student shares may not align with institutional values or expectations, and may be brought to the institution's attention with a request for disciplinary action or other enforcement. How to address those issues requires analysis of a number of factors. What is the scope of the institution's code of conduct? If it covers social media, does it address the type of content at issue? Does the content threaten another individual or the institution? Or is the concern based on viewpoint of the speaker? At some institutions, certain programs have adopted additional professionalism expectations holding students to a higher standard. Upon First Amendment challenge, some have been upheld.[22]

In light of the complex jurisprudence in this area, there are several actions a student affairs professional can take to put themselves—and their institutions—in a better position to analyze these issues. First, an understanding of the institution's policies and space designations is key. What areas on your campus are traditional or limited public forums? What are the regulations that apply to those spaces? Next, understanding the specific laws that apply to your institution is critical, and this is where your institution's legal counsel can help. If you are at a public institution, your institution is

---

17. *Id.*
18. *International Society for Krishna Consciousness, Inc. v. Lee,* 505 U.S. 672 (1992).
19. *Board of Regents of the University of Wisconsin System v. Southworth,* 529 U.S. 217 (2000).
20. *Packingham v. North Carolina,* 137 S.Ct. 1730 (2017) (internal citations omitted).
21. *Id.*
22. *Eg., Yoder v. University of Louisville,* 526 Fed.Appx. 537, No. 12-5354 (6th Cir. May 15, 2013).

subject to the First Amendment principles discussed above, but that is not all. There may be additional case law from your jurisdiction that further refines the principles described above. State constitutions or laws may provide additional or different protections on speech. If you are at a private institution, what promises or commitments has your institution made regarding access, speech, and related issues?

As a student affairs professional, particularly in a public university setting, understanding when content or viewpoint of speech may be considered—and importantly, when it may not be considered—is essential. These are only a few examples of situations that you may face as a student affair professional, but demonstrate a clear understanding of the First Amendment, and your institution's policies and practices, are important.

III. Student Discipline and Due Process

Maintaining an orderly and safe campus conducive to learning and development, with attention to the legal liberties of students is an essential role for student affairs divisions within institutions of higher education. Institutions of higher education are continually contemplating and revisiting how to most effectively handle student disciplinary issues. In so doing, professionals must thoroughly understand the legal relationship between institution and student, and—for professionals working within public institutions—have a working knowledge of the rights afforded students under institutional policies and applicable laws, including the state and U.S. Constitution.

From a historical perspective, court cases from the early 1900s established a relationship positioning university administrators to supervise students as if they were standing in the position of a parent—a relationship referred to as *in loco parentis*.[23] This resulted in student affairs professionals taking an authoritarian approach to student conduct through a good part of the twentieth century. Students' rights under the U.S. Constitution were not fully considered within the disciplinary process until the 1960s following groundbreaking cases such as *Dixon v. Alabama State Board of Education* (1961), *Tinker v. Des Moines Independent Community School District* (1968), and *Goss v. Lopez* (1975) which brought focus to constitutional rights and eroded the notion of the institution standing *in loco parentis*.[24]

Specifically, the Fourteenth Amendment of the U.S. Constitution protects an individual's life, liberty, and property interests from arbitrary government action. The Supreme Court has treated an individual's interest in continued

---

23. *Gott v. Berea,* 156 Ky. 376 (1913).
24. *Dixon v. Alabama,* 294 F.2d 150 (5th Cir. 1961); *Tinker v. Des Moines Independent Community School District,* 393 U.S. 503 (1969); *Goss v. Lopez,* 419 U.S. 565 (1975).

enrollment at a public education a property interest.[25] Thus, a public institution of higher education may not deprive an individual of this pursuit by implementing serious disciplinary action without due process of law (i.e., objective, fair, nonarbitrary process).[26] Students must be given due process which, the Court in *Dixon v. Alabama* explained, requires notice and an *opportunity for a hearing* before serious disciplinary action can be taken against a student.[27] At a minimum, *notice* means that a student facing action must be adequately informed of the specific charges and, if the student denies the charges, then the student must be provided an explanation of the evidence.[28] An *opportunity for a hearing* means that the institution must provide the student the opportunity to respond to and defend against the allegations of misconduct.[29] Circuit courts have begun to recognize additional due process elements, such as an opportunity to cross examine, to be necessary in certain cases, particularly when the credibility of the accuser is at issue.[30] The decisions have stopped short of requiring institutions to provide students the right to legal counsel during the hearing, the opportunity to cross examine witnesses, or a trial by a jury of peers. Nonetheless, cases such as Dixon and Goss laid the groundwork for an adjudicatory step within a more formalized disciplinary process to ensure that Fourteenth Amendment rights of notice and an opportunity to be heard were afforded.

Another constitutional consideration emerging within the disciplinary process during the 1960s was First Amendment protections. Decisions such as *Tinker v. Des Moines Independent Community School District* (1969)[31] clarified that public institutions could not legally prohibit (or categorize as "misconduct") any conduct that would be constitutionally protected as free speech, free exercise, or assembly under the First Amendment of the U.S. Constitution. During the *in loco parentis* era, institutions were more apt to prohibit conduct that might have been protected activities under the First Amendment. Following the demise of *in loco parentis,* ensuring that constitutionally protected activity was not prohibited by campus disciplinary policies became a consideration to be carefully analyzed in reviewing the disciplinary framework.

In response to these shifts, institutions have updated approaches for addressing disciplinary issues by adopting more legalistic and procedurally comprehensive conduct systems. Such conduct systems and processes are

---

25. *Board of Curators of the University of Missouri v. Horowitz,* 435 U.S. 78 (1978); *Regents of the University of Michigan v. Ewing,* 474 U.S. 214 (1985).
26. *Dixon v. Alabama,* 294 F.2d 150 (5th Cir. 1961); *Goss v. Lopez,* 419 U.S. 565 (1975).
27. *Id.*
28. *Dixon v. Alabama,* 294 F.2d 150 (5th Cir. 1961); *Goss v. Lopez,* 419 U.S. 565 (1975).
29. *Dixon v. Alabama,* 294 F.2d 150 (5th Cir. 1961); *Goss v. Lopez,* 419 U.S. 565 (1975).
30. *Doe v. University of Cincinnati,* 872 F.3d 393 (6th Cir. 2017).
31. *Tinker v. Des Moines Independent Community School District,* 393 U.S. 503 (1969).

now typically memorialized in a comprehensive written document commonly referred to as the student code of conduct. The student code of conduct has become a vehicle for entrenching student constitutional rights into the fabric of the campus disciplinary process as well as a means of communicating expectations to students. In essence, the student code of conduct has become an agreement between student and institution supporting the notion that the student-institution relationship is now contractual in nature.[32]

Consequently, student affairs professionals must focus more attention and resources on the careful drafting of the student code of conduct to ensure it continues to meet the intended legal objectives. Legal professionals are often taking a significant role in the drafting and/or routine review of the student code of conduct. At a minimum, four broad elements are typically addressed in the student code of conduct and warrant further discussion here: (1) scope, (2) prohibited conduct, (3) adjudication, and (4) sanctions.

With regard to the scope of the student code of conduct, the document will need to answer both the *where* and the *who* in determining whether the code applies. Does the institution want or need to include both on-campus and off-campus conduct of student within its purview? Will social media activity of students be addressed as specific conduct (i.e., cyber-bullying) or rather a mode by which a student can engage in conduct otherwise prohibited under the code (i.e., threats of harm)? Will the code apply to student organizations and individual students alike? Irrespective of the institutional decision on these questions, the scope of the code will need to be carefully and clearly drafted to ensure students and organizations know if and when they are subject to it.

The code must also effectively state the what as in "What conduct is prohibited?" Here again, constitutional principles engender several requirements. In defining the prohibited conduct, the wording must not be vague, but must adequately explain or state what behavior is not permitted. If the average student cannot ascertain by reading the code what he or she should not do, a court may find that the code is impermissibly vague. The prohibited conduct must also not be overbroad so as to reach beyond the code's intent. That is, language inadvertently punishing conduct that is otherwise protected is impermissibly overbroad.

With regard to the adjudication of complaints of student code of conduct violations, all steps of this process must be clearly delineated in writing and readily available to all students. Steps in the adjudication process may include, but are not limited to intake of complaints, options for informal resolution, formal hearing procedures, list of possible sanctions, and opportunities for an appeal of a decision. Determining the most effective way to dis-

---

32. *Mangla v. Brown University,* 135 F.3d 80 (1st Cir. 1998).

seminate and educate incoming students on the student code of conduct and the disciplinary process is a critical student affairs initiative. Likewise, training of all personnel involved in the conduct process is paramount to ensure the required consistency in affording the due process rights discussed above to students.

As a student affairs professional, it is certainly worth stepping back at regular intervals to carefully consider whether your institution's process effectively promotes learning and community, prevents harm and liability, and upholds legally afforded rights. Legal considerations should not preclude professionals from broadly reflecting on whether the code of conduct and disciplinary process fully consider the moral and ethical character development of the student.[33] Do procedures serve as educational tool? Prevent reoccurrence? Promote self-reflection of the student? Reflect the values and culture of the institution? Offer reasonable protections to the university community? If overly legalistic, a student code of conduct may not provide clear expectations or definitions and may be unreasonably rigid and complicated forcing the student and institution into an unnecessarily burdensome process. Furthermore, an overly legalistic disciplinary approach may not allow the necessary flexibility for the institution and student alike by eliminating informal or diversionary resolutions and conflict resolution mechanisms, such as mediation. A broad-minded approach which involves a routine, comprehensive review of the student code of conduct and disciplinary process is prudent.

IV. Campus Safety

Institutional responsibility for maintaining a safe campus environment is driven by several legal considerations including (1) federal law/compliance mandates and (2) potential liability for damages in private civil actions (under state tort law).

Congress has established mandates under the Jeanne Clery Disclosure of Campus Security Policy and Campus Crime Statistics Act (Clery Act).[34] All public and private institutions, including branch campuses and certain locations of U.S. institutions, receiving Title IV funding are subject to the requirements.[35] The Clery Act requires that each institution disclose information about crimes occurring on and around their campuses. Specifically,

---

33. A Developmental Framework for a Code of Student Conduct: The NCHERM Group Model Code Project. Available at https://www.ncherm.org/resources/model-code-project/
34. 20 U.S.C. § 1092(f)
35. Distance education-only and foreign institutions are exempt from the Clery Act.

the 2016 edition of *The Handbook for Campus Safety and Security Reporting,* published by the U.S. Department of Education, requires institutions to:[36]

- By October 1st of each year, publish and distribute to all current students and employees, a comprehensive **Annual Security Report** (ASR) containing safety- and security-related policy statements and crime statistics. Institutions also must inform prospective students and employees about the availability of the report.
- Collect, classify, and count crime reports and crime statistics based on 1) **where** the crimes occurred (Geography), 2) **to whom** the crimes were reported (Campus Security Authorities) and 3) the **types** of crimes that were reported (identified as Clery Act crimes)
  1. Geography—Institutions must disclose statistics for reported Clery Act crimes that occur (1) on campus, (2) on public property within or immediately adjacent to the campus, and (3) in or on non-campus property owned or controlled by the institution.
  2. Campus Security Authorities (CSA)—A crime is "reported" when brought to the attention of a Campus Security Authority which includes (1) campus police, (2) non-police security personnel, (3) individuals or organizations designated by institutional policy, and (4) any officials of the institution who have *significant responsibility for student and campus activities.*
  3. Clery Act Crimes—The types of crimes that must be disclosed include (1) certain criminal offenses,[37] (2) hate crimes,[38] (3) VAWA offenses,[39] and (4) arrests and disciplinary referrals for violation of weapons, drug abuse, and liquor laws.
- Issue **timely warnings**[40] and **emergency notifications**[41]
- Provide **education** programs and campaigns (primary prevention for all incoming students and employees and ongoing prevention for students and employees).

---

36. U.S. Department of Education—Office of Postsecondary Education (2016). *The Handbook for Campus Safety and Security Reporting* available at https://www2.ed.gov/admins/lead/safety/handbook .pdf (last visited June 24, 2019).
37. Murder, sexual assault, robbery, aggravated assault, burglary, motor vehicle theft, arson as defined by the FBI's Uniform Crime Reporting Program.
38. A criminal offense that manifests evidence that the victim was intentionally selected because of the perpetrator's bias against the victim.
39. Dating Violence, Domestic Violence and Stalking (added to the Clery Act by the Violence Against Women Reauthorization Act of 2013, 34 CFR 668.46(c)(1)(iv)).
40. Warning about the occurrence of a Clery Act crime which poses an ongoing threat to students and employees.
41. Confirmation of a significant emergency or dangerous situation involving an immediate threat to the health or safety of students or employees occurring on the campus.

- Establish **disciplinary procedures** for institutional action on cases of dating violence, domestic violence, sexual assault, and stalking.
- Complete annual **web-based submission of crime statistics** to the U.S. Department of Education.
- Record all alleged criminal incidents in a **daily crime log** open for public inspection (if the institution maintains its own campus police or security department).

In addition to these requirements, all institutions with on-campus housing facilities must:

- Compile and report fire data to the federal government and publish an annual fire safety report
- Enact policies and procedures to handle reports of missing students ("disclose **missing student notification** procedures that pertain to students residing in those facilities")

An institution's failure to comply with the requirements of the Clery Act can result in significant consequences for the institution. Charged as the enforcement agency of the Clery Act, the U.S. Department of Education–Office of Postsecondary Education can issue civil fines against the institution up to $57,317 per violation, effective February 1, 2019 and adjusted annually for inflation. The agency is also empowered to limit or suspend institutional Title IV funding for violations of the Clery Act. These agency actions, along with the fact that all U.S. Department of Education Final Review Determination Reports are public records, can severely impact the financial and reputational condition of an institution.[42] Furthermore, the failure to comply with the Clery Act can be used in court to demonstrate liability of the institution in private civil actions.

As a student affairs professional, it is critical to be familiar with your individual and departmental role in executing responsibilities under the Clery Act. Because so many student affairs professionals have significant responsibility for student and campus activities, many are Campus Security Authorities requiring them to report all allegations of Clery Act crimes in their capacity as a CSA. If you are a CSA, it is vital that you know to whom, how, and when to report an incident or crime. While a CSA is not expected to know how to categorize crimes under the Clery Act, a CSA should be pre-

---

42. For example, a historic fine of over $2 million USD was levied against Pennsylvania State University after a campus crime program review found eleven violations. U.S. Department of Education, "Department of Education Levies Historic Fine Against Penn State Over Handling of Sexual Misconduct Incidents, November 3, 2016, http://content.govdelivery.com/accounts/USED /bulletins/16ff1a3 (last accessed June 24, 2019).

pared to document and promptly relay as much information as possible about crimes reported to them to allow law enforcement to effectively handle the crime and appropriately categorize it.

As a department head, it is your responsibility to know what your institution's policies say about your department's role in maintaining campus safety and meeting educational obligations under the Clery Act. You will also want to consider how your department may assist or contribute to the institution's compilation of the comprehensive Annual Security Report. With regard to the Annual Security Report, the preparation of this critical and comprehensive report that, as a best practice, should involve cross-divisional collaboration.

Another federal statute with implications for campus safety is Title IX of the Educational Amendments of 1972 (Title IX)[43] which prohibits discrimination on the basis of sex in federally assisted education programs and activities. This statute is also enforced by the U.S. Department of Education, through the Office for Civil Rights (OCR). Sex discrimination is unwelcome conduct of a sexual nature toward a student by an employee, student, or third party. Sexual harassment includes sexual violence and is a form of sex discrimination covered by Title IX. If an institution has notice of possible sexual harassment or violence against a student, it must take immediate and appropriate steps to investigate or otherwise determine what occurred and take prompt and effective steps reasonably calculated to end any harassment or violence. Title IX requires institutions to adopt and publish a policy against sex discrimination, designate a least one employee to coordinate and carry out Title IX responsibilities, and adopt grievance procedures providing prompt and equitable resolution of complaints of sex discrimination.[44]

As previously discussed, noncompliance with federal laws such as Title IX carries significant consequences, as OCR has the authority to eliminate an institution's ability to receive federal funding. Over the last several years, OCR has focused significant additional resources on investigation and enforcement of Title IX. The issue of sexual assault in the higher education environment has become a public dialogue and an ongoing institutional challenge. Thus, it is imperative student affairs professionals fully understand and are committed to the individual and departmental role in ensuring strict adherence to the procedures for prompt and equitable institutional action on cases of dating violence, domestic violence, sexual assault, and stalking.

The Clery Act and Title IX set forth requirements for notification, procedures, disclosure, and education related to campus safety. Awareness and

---

43. 20 U.S.C. § 1681 et seq.
44. U.S. Department of Education - Office for Civil Rights (2001). Revised Sexual Harassment Guidance: Harassment of Students by School Employees, Other Students, or Third Parties: Title IX.

compliance with laws and regulations promulgated by the U.S. Department of Education will aid law enforcement personnel and student affairs professionals in preventing campus crimes. A question to be considered is whether and to what extent an institution may be held responsible for monetary damages if safety on campus is compromised. Court cases in which individuals have claimed that the institution was "negligent" in upholding its duty to protect a student or employee against violent crime, provide some insight as to when an institution may be responsible/liable for damages to a victim of crime. To bring a successful civil action against an institution under the negligence theory, a claimant must meet four elements:

1. Duty–The institution owed a duty (required standard of conduct) to the individual to protect the individual from harm;
2. Breach–The institution failed to uphold the duty (neglected the required standard of conduct);
3. Causation–The institution's neglect was the proximate cause of harm to the individual; and
4. Damages–The individual was harmed in a substantial/quantifiable way.

Generally, there is no duty to protect an individual from acts of a third party unless a special relationship exists so as to trigger the duty. Thus, the critical question becomes whether the institution has a duty to protect the individual from violent crimes. Several factors will likely be considered by courts in determining whether the institution owed a special duty to the harmed individual: Where did the harm occur? Who inflicted the harm? How predictable was the harm? Was the institution positioned to be able to prevent the harm?

As there exists a wide spectrum along which the institution may be more or less likely to be held responsible, there are several rules of thumb to keep in mind when assessing which situations present an enhanced risk of responsibility. First, safety and security related to living quarters must be a priority. Next, because employees are acting on behalf of the institution, employees' mistakes or intentional wrongs are likely to be legally attributed to the institution. Thus, a thorough and judicious hiring and retention process for employees is a critical institutional function. Another important tip is a careful analysis of past safety shortfalls. Prior incidents of violence must serve as lessons to prevent future similar incidents. Finally, campus-sponsored events should be monitored with an appropriate level of oversight.

Several key strategies are commonly employed to operationalize campus safety including the implementation of campus law enforcement services, constitutionally-cognizant campus residence life professionals, and campus threat assessment teams.

While many institutions employ a security or police force to take a leadership role in advancing campus safety initiatives, campus governing boards are usually charged with setting parameters for the roles and powers to be afforded campus officers. Questions to be addressed include whether campus officers will be sworn peace officers afforded with all of the rights and responsibilities of such certification. If a non-sworn security force is contemplated, administrative decisions include whether officers will have the authority to carry weapons, make an arrest, or initiate an investigation. In the cases of a sworn force, institutions must work to clarify the relationship with local and state police forces to ensure that jurisdiction parameters are understood and mutual aid opportunities are operationalized.

Sworn campus police, as public officers, are versed in the Fourth Amendment protections against unreasonable searches and seizures. Employees of public institutions must also be cognizant that students residing in institution-sponsored housing have a reasonable expectation of privacy with the right to be free from unlawful searches or seizures. In the course of maintaining an orderly and safe campus environment, those charged with responsibility for the residential areas of campus face daily challenges in this regard. Public university housing staff are commonly presented situations in which the reported facts would seem to necessitate entry into a residence hall room. However, there are only limited circumstances in which administrators of public institutions can enter a student's premises without a search warrant. A student can provide specific consent for particular search or have provided general consent to search in their written housing agreement.[45] An administrator may also conduct an administrative search to enforce a health or safety purpose such as a fire code inspection or to address an emergency situation.[46]

Each circumstance in which a search is a contemplated by an institutional administrator should involve a fact-specific analysis. Training on the practical application of the Fourth Amendment in the student housing context is highly advisable for all residence life professionals at public institutions. It is also essential that residence life professionals and campus police undertake advanced dialogue about proper procedures for administrative searches as well as conditions meriting the engagement of law enforcement.

Another effective approach institutions apply to assist in enhancing campus safety is some version of a threat assessment model. Sometimes referred to as a Threat Assessment Team (TAT) or Behavioral Intervention Team (BIT), a cross-divisional team is convened to serve as a clearinghouse for information about person(s) from sources across campus to identify indicators

---

45. *Piazzola v. Watkins,* 442 F.2d 284 (5th Cir. 1971).
46. *Camara v. Municipal Court,* 387 U.S. 523 (1967).

of potential violence and determine the degree of threat such behaviors pose. The team takes a totality of the circumstances approach to recommend steps to manage risk. While the threat assessment model is not new—it had its origins in law enforcement profiling and evolved as a K-12 tool following the Columbine shootings—post-Virginia Tech reports and analysis illuminated the importance of formalizing the function of such groups in the higher education setting.

Membership of a TAT can vary from institution to institution but typically includes participants from departments such a law enforcement, student affairs, counseling, legal affairs, health and safety, student discipline, human resources, academic affairs, and Title IX compliance.

Not surprisingly, Virginia Tech (VT) has become a model and resource with regard to the function of the TAT on the college campus. The who, what, when, and why of the TAT along with a myriad of resources are available through a perusal of VT's Threat Assessment Team website.[47] The United States Department of Justice has also provided guidance on this front. TAT members should (1) identify persons of concern, (2) gather information and investigate, (3) assess information and the situation, and 4) manage the person and situation to reduce the overall threat and get appropriate help.[48]

If you are participating in a TAT as a regular or ad hoc participant maintain the integrity of the process by utilizing multiple collateral data sources that are credible, able to be corroborated and possess first-hand knowledge to minimize impact of bias. Also be mindful of the facts and behavior specific to the case versus personal traits

V. Privacy of Student Educational Records

Student affairs professionals come into contact on a regular basis with information about students—academic performance, conduct matters, disability status, or a host of other sensitive topics. Student affairs professionals also need an understanding of what confidentiality protections apply to what information they are able to access. Federal law applies, and institutions may have additional state laws to follow, or policies regarding access to or use of student information. Institutions receiving U.S. Department of Education funding are subject to the Family Educational Rights Privacy Act of 1974,[49]

---

47. Virginia Technological Institute—Threat Assessment. Available at http://threatassessment.vt .edu/
48. U.S. Department of Justice—Office of Community Oriented Policing Services (2012). *Campus threat assessment case studies: A training tool for investigation, evaluation, and intervention.* Available at https://ric-zai-inc.com/Publications/cops-w0693-pub.pdf
49. 20 U.S.C. § 1232g.

known as FERPA. Under FERPA, understanding what an "education re-cord" is and what your institution designates as "directory information" is important.

FERPA provides that a student's education records may not be released without the student's consent, subject to certain exceptions. Education records are records directly relating to a student and are maintained by the institution or a party acting for the institution. Some records an institution maintains, such as law enforcement records, are not education records.

Education records within an institution are to be disclosed only to school officials who have legitimate educational interests. Simply put, if to do his or her job, an employee of the institution does not need to know certain infor-mation from a student's educational record, he or she should not be given that information. For example, a student conduct administrator, for the most part, should not need to know a student's grade in a particular class. He or she may need to know the student's address and academic schedule in order to schedule and provide notice of a student conduct hearing, but does not necessarily need to know a student's academic performance. Student affairs professionals should be aware of FERPA rules when requesting information from, or disclosing information to, other institutional officials.

When sharing occurs beyond those who are employees or agents of the institution, a term known as "directory information" becomes relevant. Each institution is able to designate a category of information known as "directo-ry information." Typically, directory information includes items like email address, program of study, and date(s) of attendance. By designating cate-gories of information as "directory information" and providing notice annu-ally to students, the institution allows itself to share that information with anyone—inside or outside of the institution—without obtaining prior consent from the student subject to one caveat. The caveat is that a student may instruct the institution to not disclose any information about the student.

FERPA also provides for disclosure without prior consent in other specif-ically defined circumstances. For example, institutions may provide infor-mation to the U.S. Department of Education or state and local educational authorities; may provide certain information relating to the provision of financial aid; when necessary to protect the health or safety of the student or others; or to accrediting organizations. To be sure, there are other excep-tions, but the exceptions permitting disclosure without consent are the ex-ception rather than the rule. Student conduct administrators should always consult the institution's FERPA policy before sharing information, particu-larly before sharing information outside of the institution.

Doubtless, the daily practice of a student affairs professional introduces multifaceted considerations related to the best interest of students and the institution. Addressing these varied issues often requires consideration of the potential academic, financial, ethical, or health effects of professional decision making. However, it is imperative that student affairs professionals also take legal rights and responsibilities into account in analyzing options and solving problems. A fundamental understanding of the legal issues within areas of student civil rights, free speech, discipline, campus safety, and privacy will serve as a valuable tool for student affairs professionals. Of course, the unique nature of each institution, the dynamism of the law, and the particularities of given situations, underscore the value of specific advice from your institution's legal counsel to assist in addressing the complexities of the higher education environment.

Chapter 7

ACADEMIC INTEGRITY AND THE STUDENT AFFAIRS PROFESSIONAL

Tricia Bertram Gallant

Academic integrity may not be the foremost ethical issue on the mind of the student affairs professional, given that it primarily falls under the purview of the faculty and there are a multitude of other pressing ethical issues that fall under the typical jurisdiction of student affairs. Yet, student affairs professionals are often pulled into academic integrity matters whether by design or happenstance. In this chapter, I introduce academic integrity, overview different academic integrity systems found in higher education and the position of the student affairs professional within such systems, and discuss the different ethical and legal touchpoints at which a student affairs professional might interact with academic integrity. The chapter ends with case studies and recommendations for intentionally designing the student affairs professionals into an institutional approach to academic integrity.

OVERVIEW OF ACADEMIC INTEGRITY IN HIGHER EDUCATION

Borrowing from the International Center for Academic Integrity's (2014) Fundamental Values document, I define academic integrity as having the courage to only submit academic work that is an honest, trustworthy, responsible, respectful, and a fair representation of one's knowledge and abilities. Academic integrity is critical to fulfilling the educational institution's purpose. It is expected that when a student submits a piece of work for assessment, that work was completed according to the standards of the instructor and the university. Only the honest and fair completion of academic work enables the instructor to fairly and honestly evaluate the submitted work,

95

which enables the university to fairly and honestly certify the student met the criteria established for degree granting.

To further elucidate this concept of academic integrity, I provide examples of specific and typical academic behaviors. Writing with integrity, for example, means that a person is honest about the origins or influences on their thoughts, ideas, and words. That is, when one uses sources to construct a piece of writing (e.g., essay, paper, homework, assignment), the author discloses those sources to the reader. Writing with integrity does not mean using a particular formatting for citations, but merely the act of explicitly giving credit to the utilized sources.

Taking exams with integrity means completing an exam (or test or quiz) in accordance with the expectations and standards of the professor. If the exam is an independent exam, this means taking the exam without collaboration with others. If the exam is "closed book," this means taking the exam without aids of any kind.

Collaborating with integrity means that we are honest about the contributions of others and we fairly represent who contributed what to the project. So, for example, when students collaborate on a project or assignment but do not acknowledge that collaboration (i.e., they submit the work as if it were done independently), this is dishonest and misrepresents the student's knowledge and abilities.

A note about the subject of study is probably appropriate at this time. Although certainly integrity is expected of every member in higher education, from students to staff and faculty, this chapter is focused on the academic integrity of the students. Of course, those familiar with my work will know that I do pair the integrity of the faculty with the integrity of their students in the sense that faculty should act as they expect their students to act (e.g., with fairness, honesty, trustworthiness, responsibility, and respect). It is difficult to extricate the two from one another, but for the purpose of this chapter, the conversation about this relationship will be limited. Readers should know this is not a reflection of the author's opinion or views on the topic, but a narrowing of the focus for purely practical purposes.

Academic integrity is essential to the mission of higher education, which is, in part, to educate the next generation of scholars, professionals, and citizens. Without integrity in the work being completed by the students (and the faculty and staff), there is little reason for higher education to exist. Society depends on the integrity of the conferred degrees because these degrees are used as an initial determination that an individual is prepared for a profession, career, or job. If, *en masse,* the knowledge and abilities of higher education graduates do not match the degrees they possess, society will cease to trust colleges and universities. In fact, we have already seen the results of this disintegration of trust—in the form of external regulations and "disruption" of the education industry through establishment of alternative education institutions that are intended to respond to these shortcomings (e.g., online institutions, for-profit institutions).

If, as Sandeen (2011) argues, the mission of student affairs is "to help the institution achieve its educational mission" (p. 6), then academic integrity is also intimately tied to student affairs and the student affairs professional. This intricate link between academic integrity and student affairs will be thoroughly explored in this chapter. First, however, I will continue to overview academic integrity in higher education by delineating institutional approaches to academic integrity and their resulting academic integrity systems.

Institutional Approaches to Academic Integrity

I characterize institutional approaches to academic integrity into three camps: rule compliance, integrity, and teaching and learning (Bertram Gallant, 2008).

The rule compliance approach states the rules for behaviors and then tells people to "comply or else" (with the "or else" representing consequences for disobedience). The rule compliance approach came to fruition in the 1970s and remains popular in higher education today (more on this in the next section). Unfortunately, despite its popularity, the rule compliance approach seems to be lacking in its effectiveness. After decades of a rule compliance approach in higher education, violations of academic integrity continue to be commonplace (Bertram Gallant, 2008) and other research has found that such an approach does not work in any type of organization (Bazerman & Trensbrunsel, 2011). The rule compliance approach can have a negative impact on encouraging ethical behavior because it focuses primarily on providing extrinsic motivations for not cheating (i.e., punishments). Such motivations are situational and inconsistently applied, leading people to act according to the rules only if someone is watching or if the likelihood of detection is high. This is insufficient for academic integrity since much of the academic work (e.g., homework, paper writing) performed by students is conducted in private and the likelihood of getting caught or punished is minimal.[1] With the rule compliance approach, people do not learn how to make their own ethical decisions or act ethically even if no one is watching.

---

1. While as many as 43% of students admit to cheating at least once/year (McCabe, 2005), it is suspected (based on institutional reports) that less than 3% of the student population is reported for cheating. For example, according to public reports from UC San Diego, less than 1000 students are reported annually for cheating, which is about 3% of the population. Or, at the University of Missouri, around 200 students are reported annually for cheating, which is only about .5% of the population.

The integrity approach came to fruition in the 1990s when certain groups (e.g., Josephson Institute for Ethics and the International Center for Academic Integrity) decided that the rule compliance approach failed to have a clear impact on academic integrity and ethics education in schools. The integrity approach conveys to people that one should act ethically because it is the right thing to do. The Fundamental Values document from the International Center for Academic Integrity (2014) is an artifact of this approach as it defines integrity according to values (honesty, respect, responsibility, fairness, trustworthiness, and courage) and describes the behaviors that uphold those values. The integrity approach is built on the foundation of the Honor Code system (see next section) and is still gaining ground in higher education as universities continue to adopt the approach in response to publicized cheating "scandals" (e.g., see Harvard University).

The last approach mentioned in my 2008 book is the teaching and learning approach. The teaching and learning approach expands the focus beyond the student to the professor and the teaching and learning context. The teaching and learning approach recognizes that the ways in which the professor establishes the curriculum, articulates expectations, designs assessments, and interacts with her classroom will influence student integrity and therefore learning. The teaching and learning approach recognizes that the ways in which the institution supports (or does not support) the teaching and learning mission can also influence student behavior. The teaching and learning approach also recognizes that despite actions taken to making cheating the exception and integrity the norm, individual students will still occasionally make bad decisions under stress and pressure. Thus, the teaching and learning approach encourages institutions to leverage the cheating moment as a teachable moment. In essence, the teaching and learning approach shifts the conversation from "how do we stop students from cheating?" to "how do we best facilitate and assess student learning?"

This brief overview of academic integrity in higher education suggests that academic integrity is fundamental to the educational mission of the higher education institution even though institutional approaches to academic integrity have taken various shapes and forms over the decades. These various institutional approaches are not mutually exclusive. In fact, the teaching and learning approach borrows concepts from both the rule compliance (e.g., consequences can provide teachable moments) and integrity (e.g., clearly explicating values and expectations can be helpful) approaches. And, all three approaches have the same goal of ensuring that cheating is the exception and integrity is the norm when students are submitting academic work for credit towards a higher education credential. Yet, these approaches have led to the development of five different academic integrity systems within higher education institutions, with varied levels of involvement by student affairs professionals. And it is to this topic of academic integrity systems I now turn.

Current AI Systems in Higher Education

The three common approaches to academic integrity (rule compliance, integrity, and teaching & learning) are made manifest in different types of academic integrity systems—that is, the structures, policies, and procedures that guide academic integrity education, culture creation, and the handling of academic integrity violations. Although there are extensive variations in these systems between different institutions, each system has distinct characteristics that are shared and can be highlighted.

Traditional Honor Code

According to McCabe and Pavela (2000), a traditional honor code has the following characteristics: a student-run judicial system, an honor pledge signed by all students upon matriculation, unproctored examinations, and a prohibition against tolerating cheating by others. In traditional honor code systems, the students not only write the policies and procedures, but they create and run the structures (e.g., honor council) that deal with honor violations. The Honor Council is responsible for educating their peers about academic integrity and honor, as well as for hearing contested allegations of violations and imposing academic and other sanctions for honor violations.

The origins of the traditional honor code can be traced to the colonial college era in America when the colleges of the time co-opted the southern gentlemen's honor code used at the individual level to save face or "one's honor" (Bertram Gallant, 2008). The colleges used the honor code to redirect the students' sense of honor away from self and toward community so that it is the honor of the college, rather than the individual student, that must be protected. So, the traditional honor code really took an integrity approach to rule compliance. In other words, the colonial colleges attempted to appeal to one's individual sense of integrity or honor in order to get them to comply with the rules of the day.

The College of William & Mary argues that their honor code, established in 1735, is the original honor code.[2] The number of institutions with traditional honor codes remains small. Aside from the College of William & Mary, the most well known honor codes can be found at the military academies, University of Mary Washington, and University of Virginia. The University of Virginia provides a telling example of a traditional honor code that serves a rule compliance approach to academic integrity with their "one

2. See https://www.wm.edu/offices/deanofstudents/services/studentconduct/honorcodeandcouncils/

strike" system that enables the Honor Council to expel a student for even their first violation of academic integrity.[3]

The role of the student affairs professional in academic integrity within traditional honor code systems is minimal to nonexistent. Although traditional honor councils typically receive advisement from professors, student affairs professionals may provide some type of administrative support. In some traditional honor code schools, like University of Mary Washington, student affairs professionals are only involved in non-academic cases (like sexual assault) while the Honor Council deals with academic integrity violations and other forms of lying and stealing.

Modified Honor Code

University of Maryland is credited with creating the first modified honor code. The modified honor code differs from the traditional honor code in the following ways: administrators and/or faculty members are involved in the administration of the code and its processes; proctored exams are allowable; there is no required cheating-nontoleration clause; and, perhaps their most significant deviation from traditional honor codes is a "lighter" response to honor violations (McCabe & Pavela, 2000). Specifically, students who violate modified honor code provisions typically receive an XF for the course rather than suspension or expulsion; this transcript notation is removed if the student engages in an educational experience to learn from the violation (McCabe & Pavela, 2000).

The modified honor code of 2017 seems to be quite different than that originally conceived within the University of Maryland in the late twentieth century. Harvard University may be the most infamous university claiming to implement a modified honor code after their "cheating scandal" in 2012. According to Harvard, what defines their modified honor code is the "honor pledge" and the inclusion of students in the hearing and deciding body (formally only comprised of faculty and administrators) for contested allegations of academic integrity.[4] This is a step toward a student-run system (if that is the goal), but it definitely does not sound like a modified honor code system as designed by the University of Maryland.

As with traditional honor codes, the involvement of student affairs professionals in modified honor codes is minimal, although they may serve (in some institutions) on a joint student-staff-faculty body that hears contested

---

3. The Honor Council at the University of Virginia has implemented a new process that they call Informed Retraction. If students report themselves before being reported for cheating, they can escape expulsion but must accept an academic penalty and a two semester leave from the University. See https://news.virginia.edu/content/5-things-you-should-know-about-uvas-honor-system

4. See, for example, https://harvardmagazine.com/2013/04/toward-a-modified-honor-code

allegations of academic integrity violations. Typically, however, faculty and students are the most heavily involved players and decision-makers.

Student Conduct Office

By far the most common academic integrity system in higher education is the student conduct system that handles all forms of "student misconduct" from cheating on tests to noise violations in the residence halls and even to sexual assault and other crimes committed by students. In the student conduct system, which grew strength out of the rule compliance approach that became dominant in the 1970s, the policy and processes are primarily in the control of student affairs professionals (although student input may be included).

In the student conduct system of academic integrity, there may be no-to-minimal involvement of faculty. Faculty tend not to be included because this system casts cheating as a student conduct problem that requires a rule compliance or integrity approach, rather than a teaching and learning approach. Some institutions, however, have tried to blend the modified honor code system with the student conduct system. For example, Princeton and Stanford universities both have honor codes or pledges, but cannot be classified as either traditional or modified honor code schools given the heavy involvement and control by judicial affairs/student conduct officers. At Princeton, the student-run, student-only Honor Committee only hears cases of in-class exam cheating, but the Committee on Discipline (comprised of faculty, staff, and students) handles all other types of academic integrity violations.[5] At Stanford, violations of the honor code are handled entirely through the judicial process offered by the student affairs professionals in the Office of Community Standards,[6] although other staff, faculty, and students may be involved in the process (e.g., as advisors).

The involvement of student affairs professionals in the student conduct system is obviously extensive. The student conduct office is typically located within the student affairs division under the responsibility of a dean of students or vice-president of student affairs. The career paths of the judicial or student conduct officers who work in the student conduct office tend to trace back to other student affairs offices such as residential life or student life and development where they would have handled student conduct issues like residence hall violations or hazing. These student conduct professionals manage the office and the processes of the student conduct system, and they tend to involve other student affairs professionals (e.g., residential life direc-

---

5. See https://www.princeton.edu/honor/
6. See https://communitystandards.stanford.edu/student-conduct-process/honor-code-and-fundamental
-standard/what-happens-judicial-process

tors; student organization advisors) in the process. Faculty are typically not very involved (except to report the potential academic integrity violations) and student involvement in management and decision-making is usually minimal to none (of course, there are exceptions).

Academic Integrity Policy

Probably the least common academic integrity system in higher education institutions in American colleges and universities is, perhaps ironically, the Academic Integrity Policy (AIP) system. The AIP system reflects the teaching and learning approach and is the least common because the teaching and learning approach to academic integrity is a relatively recent phenomenon (since Bertram Gallant, 2008). The management of the AIP system typically falls under the responsibilities of a senior level academic affairs officer (e.g., provost, academic dean) rather than a senior-level student affairs officer (e.g., vice-president of student affairs) and the academic integrity policies and procedures are distinct from those that cover nonacademic conduct issues (e.g., hazing, sexual assault). For example, at Syracuse University, academic integrity is located within the Center for Learning and Student Success. At the University of Oklahoma, academic integrity is located within the office of the Provost and at the University of California, San Diego, academic integrity falls under the Dean of Undergraduate Education.

In an AIP system, the academic integrity policy is separate from the nonacademic student conduct policy and handled by different staff members, usually those with an academic or policy, rather than student affairs, background. Although not consistently found in AIP systems, there can be heavy student involvement on boards or councils or as advisors/educators. For example, the Integrity Council at the University of Oklahoma involves students as hearing officers, investigators, and adjudicators, as well as preventative educators and peer educators after a violation has occurred.[7] At the University of California, San Diego, students serve alongside faculty on the Academic Integrity Review Board (the hearing board) and also act as Integrity Peer Educators who advise students, conduct preventative education and outreach, and facilitate academic integrity training after a violation has occurred.[8]

The involvement of student affairs professionals in the AIP system ranges from nominal to non-existent. At the University of California San Diego, the deans of students are a critical part of the process to resolve allegations of academic integrity violations with the students. However, in other

---

7. See https://integrity.ou.edu/faq.html for more information. The University of Oklahoma system borrows many principles from the honor code system.
8. See http://academicintegrity.ucsd.edu for more information.

institutions (like Syracuse and University of Oklahoma), there does not appear to be a formal role for student affairs professionals to play within the academic integrity system.

Decentralized System

The last type of academic integrity system is a decentralized one with no central office or body responsible for conducting academic integrity education, responding to allegations of academic integrity violations, or managing a university-wide policy/process. In such decentralized systems, the academic departments or divisions typically handle academic integrity on their own, although sometimes violations are escalated to student affairs (especially in the case of suspensions or expulsions). Such a decentralized system allows individual faculty members to handle academic integrity violations in their classroom without any (or any significant) involvement by the broader institutional administration. The faculty member is responsible for educating their students about academic integrity, and responding to violations of academic integrity when they occur without a report to any centralized office. The upside of this approach is that academic integrity violations can be handled promptly and contextually. The downside of this approach is that different faculty will treat different violations differently, thus resulting in a lack of fairness and consistency across the campus. Another downside of the decentralized system is that student affairs professionals, who are trained to counsel students through difficult life challenges, are not involved. The final, and perhaps most impactful, downside is that a student could cheat their way to a degree because only each individual faculty member (or academic department or division) is aware of each incident of cheating.

Summary

This section defined academic integrity and then overviewed academic integrity within the higher education institution. The three approaches to academic integrity (rule compliance, integrity, and teaching and learning) all exist within higher education today and impact the ways in which academic integrity systems are designed and implemented within the institutional setting. These systems can take many forms, but I categorized them into five: traditional honor code, modified honor code, student conduct office, academic integrity policy, and decentralized. For those student affairs professionals who wish to be involved in academic integrity, it is important to understand these varied approaches and systems and how they may impact their involvement. A summary of this section is provided in Table 7.1. Next, I will dive more deeply into the ways in which student affairs professionals can be involved.

Table 7.1
ACADEMIC INTEGRITY SYSTEMS

	Traditional Honor Code	*Modified Honor Code*	*Student Conduct*	*Academic Integrity Policy*	*Decentralized*
Based on	Integrity Approach	Integrity Approach	Rule Compliance Approach	Teaching & Learning Approach	Varied (depending on faculty member)
Organizational Home	Student Government	Student Government or Student Affairs		Student Affairs	Academic Affairs Department/Units
Run by	Students	Students	Student Conduct Administrators	Academic Integrity Professionals/Faculty	Faculty
Student Involvement	High	High	Low to None	Medium to High	None
Faculty Involvement	Medium	Medium	Low to None	Medium to High	High
Student Affairs Involvement	None	Low	High	None to High	Low

STUDENT AFFAIRS PROFESSIONALS
AND ACADEMIC INTEGRITY

In this section, Dalton and Crosby's (2011) conceptual paradigms framework of the student affairs profession provides a foundation for the proposal that student affairs professionals can contribute to academic integrity in three ways: building an integrity culture, designing and implementing procedures, and developing and implementing training. After an exploration of this proposal, I drill down into some targeted student affairs functional areas (e.g., student life and development, student conduct office) to propose the specific roles they could play in helping to build the culture, ensure fair and efficient procedures, and develop in students the capacity to act with integrity.

Conceptions of Student Affairs and
the Impact on Academic Integrity

In their 2011 article, Dalton and Crosby overviewed the "four most important conceptual paradigms" (p. 4) that have guided the work of student affairs professionals over the years: student services, student development, student learning, and student success. These conceptual paradigms provide a framework by which we can understand how student affairs professionals should or could be involved in academic integrity.

Student Services Paradigm

The student services paradigm suggests that the "essential role of student affairs [is] the delivery of services enhancing the educational experiences of students" (Dalton & Crosby, 2011, p. 4). This paradigm thus supports the involvement of student affairs professionals within academic integrity systems, predominantly by filling the vacuum left by faculty members whose direct interactions with students often ends the moment their students walk out of the classroom. Student services can include offering academic support services like tutoring centers, professional skill building programs, and counseling or support centers, all of which could help students maintain academic integrity by providing the type of support needed when under stress or pressure or by teaching students the skills necessary to resist cheating temptations (e.g., leadership, critical reflection, communication).

Student Development Paradigm

The student development paradigm provided the first solid "intellectual framework for student affairs work" (Dalton & Crosby, 2011, p. 4) and was specifically tied to academic integrity by researchers such as Bill Kibler (1988, 1993a, 1993b). In this paradigm, the purpose of higher education is to facilitate student moral development by providing "opportunities to role play, to confront different social or moral perspectives, and to participate in decision-making on ethical issues" and creating an environment that offers the "necessary challenges and support to encourage new responses and developmental growth" (Kibler, 1993b, p. 11, referencing Nuss 1982). According to Kibler (1993b), a student development framework for addressing academic integrity violations includes developing an academic integrity culture, policy, and education program. Implementing such a thorough framework requires the "active participation and cooperation by academic and student affairs on all campuses" (Kibler, 1993b, p. 15) both because of the amount of work that needs to be done, but also because the framework leverages the expertise of faculty (in teaching) and of student affairs professionals (in supporting moral development). Student affairs professionals can be particularly helpful in facilitating opportunities outside of the classroom to "role play and confront different social or moral perspectives" through residential life, extracurricular programs, and student involvement organizations. Student affairs professionals (particularly those who work within student conduct) can also lend their expertise on designing and implementing fair and efficient due process procedures, as well as holding difficult conversations with students going through the adjudication process, conversations which often involve developmental issues like dealing with family or other forms of personal trauma or hardships. And finally, student affairs professionals may be able to assist with appropriate response to integrity violations that leverage the cheating moment as a teachable moment by using the cheating moment as the experiential impetus on which to practice ethical decision making.

Student Learning Paradigm

The student learning paradigm argues that "learning is . . . something larger and transformative [than development], incorporating both intellectual and personal growth and resulting in qualitative change in who a learner is" (Reason & Broido, 2011, p. 92). This paradigm "places student affairs practice in the center of the learning environment" (Reason & Broido, 2011, p. 92), thus firmly positioning student affairs professionals as partners within the academic integrity initiatives on campus. To be sure, not all of the learning and development that occurs in college occurs in the classroom or under the direction of faculty members. Student affairs departments have been critical to facilitating student learning and development for decades through such initiatives or units as career services, student leadership development opportunities (e.g., orientation leaders; residential advisors), community and cultural centers, and student life and involvement organizations. The student learning paradigm influence in academic integrity can be seen in the support of academic integrity systems that include substantial student involvement, such as in the traditional honor code, modified honor code, and AIP systems mentioned earlier. Student affairs professionals may be best poised to support the training and on boarding of students serving in these roles.

Student Success Paradigm

The student success paradigm builds on the student learning and student development paradigms to support a broader conception of student success beyond quantitative measures of academic success (i.e., GPA) to personal or transferable successes as measured by skills and experiences. In particular, the student success paradigm looks "to implement more objective measures of accountability for student outcomes as a way to document institutional effectiveness in achieving student success" (Dalton & Crosby, 2011, p. 55). A specific manifestation of the student success paradigm might be the twenty-first century re-emergence of the cocurricular record which is "intended to enhance students' learning and development, encourage the discovery and reflection of self-awareness, and foster an environment that encourages civic responsibility and engagement" (Elias & Drea, 2013, Paragraph 4). In addition to the cocurricular record, many student affairs organizations on college campuses have implemented student success coaching programs, primarily to back-fill the lack of support offered by faculty outside of the classroom. According to Dalton and Crosby (2014), student success programs are used for: "(a) Informing students about the relevant educational resources of the institution; (b) helping students to set goals; (c) mentoring students in time management; (d) assisting students in planning action; (e) providing students with observation and assessment; and (f) giving students feedback, support, and maintenance" (p. 62).

Clearly, by developing in students these skills and capacities, student success programs have the potential to greatly benefit students in upholding academic integrity.

Summary

Overall, Dalton, and Crosby (2011) argue that despite the ebb and flow of different conceptual paradigms, there has been a persistent purpose of the student affairs profession—"to provide services and programs that enhance the intellectual and ethical development of college students" (p. 6). In that vein, student affairs professionals have a significant role to play in building an academic integrity culture, designing and implementing fair and efficient procedures for handling academic integrity violation allegations, and in developing and implementing training that will support academic integrity. In this next section, I will explore the roles to be played by different types of student affairs professionals within the world of academic integrity.

Student Affairs Professionals and the Roles They Can Play

As mentioned in the previous section, there is clearly a role for student affairs professionals to play in academic integrity even though "faculty prerogatives and faculty jurisdictional sensitivities might seem to inhibit a significant student affairs professional role in regulating academic dishonesty and promoting academic integrity in the student body" (Drinan & Bertram Gallant, 2008, p. 259). Specifically, Drinan and Bertram Gallant (2008) argued that student affairs professionals might be involved in three main ways: (1) as the administrative support for an honor council or other student-run body; (2) as the judicial body that handles academic integrity violation allegations; or (3) as a support group to the academics who handle academic integrity violation allegations (p. 262). However, in this chapter, I argue that the role of student affairs professionals can move beyond providing procedural support or acting as the rule compliance or judicial officers (as in a student conduct system). Instead, I argue that the talents, skills, and interests of student affairs professionals must be harnessed in order to truly realize an institutional approach to making cheating the exception and integrity the norm.

In this section, I take a look at different areas within student affairs to examine the roles they might play in academic integrity, how those roles translate into activities or actions, and what contributions their actions might make (e.g., building an integrity culture, designing and implementing procedures, and/or developing and implementing educational programs). It is aptly noted that there lacks consistency in the organization of student affairs from college to college, so not every role or unit I explore will fall under student affairs in every institution and it is also likely that I may have neglected to include an important student affairs unit that can be found in the reader's institution. However, it is my hope that the exploration here will provide a basis by which institutions could explore their own student affairs professionals and the roles that they could possibly play in academic integrity.

Table 7.2
THE ROLES OF DIFFERENT STUDENT AFFAIRS
PROFESSIONALS IN ACADEMIC INTEGRITY

	Building an Integrity Culture	Designing & Implementing Procedures	Developing & Implementing Training
Admissions	√		
New Student Orientation	√		√
Residential Life	√		√
Success Coaching/Tutoring	√		√
Counseling/Psychological Services/Wellness	√		√
Student Conduct Office	√	√	√
Student Life & Development	√	√	√
Career Services	√		

Admissions

Student affairs professionals who work in admissions have much to con-tribute to building an academic integrity culture. It is through the admissions office that prospective students first develop an interpretation of the campus culture and a sense of what really matters to the campus. Including acade-mic integrity/fundamental values messages in admissions materials sends a signal to students that they should only apply to the institution if they intend on putting honor or integrity above all else (see Figure 7.1. Caltech Undergraduate Admissions). Asking students to provide an example of how they have demonstrated integrity in their life, either in written statements or admissions interviews, conveys to students that it is their responsibility to uphold integrity. And finally, having students sign an integrity agreement/honor code in order to be admitted into the institution completes the integrity messaging that only admissions can deliver.

Caltech Undergraduate Admissions

Explore   Apply   Afford   Visit   Inquire

Honor Code

At the heart of Caltech is its Honor Code, the principle that has guided and defined campus life since Caltech's earliest days. It states, "No member of the Caltech community shall take unfair advantage of any other member of the Caltech community." This code of ethics guides the entire campus community of students, staff, and faculty.

It's a simple idea with far-reaching implications. It means, for instance, that Caltech students are routinely given 24-hour access to labs, workshops, and other facilities on campus.

Collaboration

The Honor Code establishes a community of trust. Another important elemental principle is collaboration. The life of a Techer relies heavily on teamwork, mirroring the scientific world. When you do academic work at Caltech, it is assumed that you'll have not only the guidance of a faculty team that is second to none but also the support of your classmates as you tackle your assignments.

Collaboration is a way of life at Caltech. In fact, most problem sets are assigned with the understanding that students will work together to solve the problems—sometimes including ones that no one is even sure are solvable. At Caltech, students find themselves among their intellectual equals, and hours of discussion, argument, and perhaps even late-night pizza can lead to an understanding of concepts fundamental to the advancement of science and friendships that will last a lifetime.

Related Pages

History

Honor Code

Figure 7.1.

New Student Orientation

Student affairs professionals working in new student orientation programs can also play a significant role in building an integrity culture and facilitating activities that provide academic integrity training to the new students. In building the culture, new student orientation can continue the messaging that began in the admissions process by asking institutional leadership, faculty, and student orientation leaders to speak to the critical role integrity plays within the institution. According to McCabe, Trevino, and Butterfield (2001),

> When they hear the president, a dean, or an orientation leader talk about the scholarly enterprise and the importance of never representing the work of someone else as their own . . . [students] internalize this message to some degree and begin their college experience with a positive attitude about the need for academic integrity, in spite of their experience with cheating in high school. (p. 230)

This messaging can be reinforced when student affairs professionals organize and implement an honor/integrity pledge signing ceremony during orientation (as done at, for example, Vanderbilt University, University of Mary Washington, College of William & Mary).

Student affairs professionals can also provide student development training to their student orientation leaders to equip them with the skills to engage new students in discussions and role plays about academic integrity. Research has shown that peers' perceptions of cheating have a great impact on academic integrity (see, for example, McCabe & Trevino, 1997; McCabe, Trevino & Butterfield, 1999) and presentations by peers on the subject matter can be viewed positively (Zivcakova et al., 2014). Thus, when we train student orientation leaders to convey a disapproval of cheating and an encouragement of integrity/honor, this can be highly effective in building an integrity culture. Peer led discussions/role-plays can also help new students develop the knowledge and awareness necessary to act with integrity once their classes begin (see Appendix 1 for example scenarios, activities, and discussion questions). A nice compliment to this training would be to provide students with a guide for making good ethical decisions when they face academic integrity dilemmas throughout their education.

Residential Life

Professional residential life staff can continue the work begun by admissions and the new student orientation professionals in building an integrity culture and providing academic integrity training to students. Student affairs staff can ensure that integrity/honor messaging is predominantly displayed throughout the residential areas, specifically targeting common areas where students might gather to study or complete academic assignments. This messaging can take the form of integrity or honor pledge plaques to remind students of the pledge they made during orientation or posters that more creatively convey to students to think about integrity when making any decision about academic work (see www.academicintegrity.org for example posters from a variety of institutions).

Of course, student leaders in residential life (e.g., RAs, Dons) can be similarly trained as orientation leaders to convey disapproval of cheating and facilitate learning about academic integrity. Student residential life staff can be rewarded for hosting programs/workshops to teach academic integrity skills (by using the resources in Appendix 1), showcasing available resources on campus that exist to help students, or by holding skill building sessions on related skills like time and stress management.

Beyond providing constant integrity messaging and education, residential life staff can train their student leaders to recognize dangerous behaviors in their residents and intervene when they see them. This not only role models for residents that it is possible to take action in the face of ethical wrongdoings, but may also serve to prevent residents from violating academic integrity (or other university) standards. With such bystander intervention training, residential life student leaders will have the awareness, knowledge and skills to be able to intervene when they hear conversations about potential cheating or interrupt students whom they see engaging in cheating or other undesirable behaviors (e.g., hate or bias incidents, sexual assault).[9]

Success Coaching

Student affairs professionals who work as success coaches can play a significant role in student development and learning around academic integrity. Success coaching is a relatively new phenomenon, following programs like orientation, welcome weeks, and First Year Experience (FYE) that originated out of the recognized need that institutions must "create a climate of support that helps new students to succeed, and encourages them to become committed to practices that promote their success" (Dalton & Crosby, 2014, p. 60). Academic integrity must be one of those practices that students are coached into adopting given that true success (as defined by learning, knowledge, and skill development, rather than by GPA or degree attainment) is dependent on integrity. One could even argue that success coaching professionals are integral to academic integrity even if the only goal is student retention, which seems to be the main argument for coaching programs (Dalton & Crosby, 2014). If students violate academic integrity and, as a result, fail a course or are suspended or dismissed, there are obvious threats to retention. So, how can success coach professionals help?

First, I propose that success coaches can teach students the skills and practices needed to succeed academically with integrity. There are multiple student driven factors that can lead to academic integrity violations, such as having a performance (versus mastery) orientation and poor meta-cognitive skills (Bertram Gallant, 2017). Student success coaches can make a concerted effort to reinforce in their students the attitudes that lead to mastery orientation by continually reorienting their students to learning and knowledge acquisition when they hear them worried about grades or course completion. Student success coaches can also engage their students in practices that will build their meta-cognitive skills, that is, "self-awareness of the knowledge they have, the knowledge they need, and how they can develop new knowl-

---

9. See http://academicintegrity.ucsd.edu/take-action/prevent-cheating/excel-with-integrity-bit_students.pdf for the Bystander Intervention Training (BIT) used at the University of California San Diego.

edge" (Bertram Gallant, 2017, p. 89). For example, when students comment on poor academic performance or an inability to understand the course material, success coaches can facilitate self-reflection to raise awareness of the practices that facilitate material mastery and those that do not. Student success coaches can then guide students toward conscientiously adopting and rejecting certain practices. When students have stronger meta-cognitive skills, they are more likely to manage their time with accuracy, reducing the likelihood that they will cheat under stress and pressure.

Students are also more likely to cheat if they perceive poor instruction (Bertram Gallant, 2017) and success coaches may be in the best position to hear such complaints from students. Thus, success coaches can also benefit from Bystander Intervention Training so they become able to identify such cheating motivations and are more comfortable intervening in response. For example, when a student complains about a class, the materials, or the instructor, a success coach should hear those as potential warning signals that the student may be feeling unmotivated to learn or master the material and thus more likely to do whatever it takes to get through the course. In such cases, success coaches can greatly serve the student and academic integrity by helping the student see where they have some choice and control over the situation, which can reduce the likelihood of resorting to cheating (Bertram Gallant, 2017). By coaching the student through good ethical decision making, the success coach can not only prevent a stressed and pressured student from engaging in an academic integrity violation, but build in the student life-long habits and skills that will serve them well as students and professionals.

Counseling/Psychological Services/Health & Wellness

Student affairs professionals who serve in health and wellness roles may also have a critical role to play in academic integrity. Mental health, physical health, and relationship problems (among any other number of health and wellness issues) are known risk factors for cheating (Murdock & Anderman, 2006). Therefore, health and wellness professionals can counter these risk factors by providing students with avenues and strategies for maintaining health and wellness. In addition, these professionals can be asked to provide services to students in order to enhance the likelihood that the student can learn and experience personal development after a violation has occurred. Counselors and psychologists can also help train faculty and staff to hold difficult conversations with students about potential academic integrity violations and to identify any potential students of concern during or after these conversations.

Student Life & Development

In many institutions, there is at least one unit responsible for student involvement and student development. This unit may advise student organizations, offer legal or other professional advice to students, run events and gathering spaces, and/or offer extracurricular/training opportunities to develop needed competencies (e.g., leadership, communication, teamwork). Student affairs professionals in such units can be beneficial partners in building an integrity culture and designing and implementing training. For example, those professionals advising student organizations could encourage the students to incorporate the International Center for Academic Integrity's (2014) Fundamental Values (the courage to be honest, respectful, responsible, fair, and trustworthy) within their constitutions and/or behavioral guidelines. Those professionals with expertise in training and development could partner with faculty, other student affairs professionals, and student leaders to develop and implement training around these values, particularly around ethical decision making when faced with an ethical wrong (e.g., someone cheating) or an ethical dilemma (a conflict between a right and a right). The student development professionals could also be asked to help honor councils and academic integrity offices train their student leaders to run processes, advise their peers, and make critical and important decisions about academic integrity violations.

Career Services

The professionals in career services are critical partners in building an integrity culture and developing and implementing training. First, our career services partners help prepare students for the world of work in which integrity is a highly valued quality or skill (Hart, 2006, 2013) and a lack of integrity is a top reason why new college hires are disciplined or fired (Gardner, 2007). Thus, institutions with any type of academic integrity system should involve career services professionals in a campaign to raise student awareness about the importance of integrity. Career services professionals could, for example, invite employers to campus to talk to students about the critical role that integrity and ethics play in the workplace. Career services could develop a career services code of integrity that students are expected to follow when they are using their services. For example, the code could state that students are expected to be honest in all of their job search materials (e.g., cover letters, resumes, and interviews), be responsible to arrive at job interviews early or on time, and be respectful by only accepting job offers that you intend to take. Finally, career services professionals could reinforce the integrity message by incorporating ethics and integrity into their job search related trainings (e.g., cover letter and resume writing; interviewing skills).

Student Conduct Professionals

As mentioned earlier, student conduct professionals are often directly involved in the handling of academic integrity violation allegations because the student conduct office is the office charged with handling student conduct procedural and disciplinary issues (Alschuler & Blimling, 1995; Cole & McCabe, 1996). And, viewing academic integrity as a student conduct (or rule compliance issue) rather than a teaching and learning issue, it is still quite common in institutions today. However, this focus on rule compliance is receding within the student conduct professional world; this is perhaps best exemplified by the naming shift from "student judicial officers" to "student conduct professionals" which began about 2008 (see Schrage & Giacomini, 2009). This shift in focus is also exemplified by the slow emergence of the restorative justice approach to conduct violations, which takes a developmental and learning (rather than punitive) approach (Schrage & Giacomini, 2009). In institutions with student conduct systems, then, student conduct professionals should look to involve an increasing variety of student affairs professionals in addition to more faculty and students if they wish to continue the trend away from rule compliance and toward a teaching and learning approach.

For other institutions that have an honor code, modified honor code, academic integrity or decentralized system, however, the involvement of student conduct professionals may be nonexistent. The extent of the inclusion of student conduct professionals in the building of an integrity culture, designing and implementing policy and procedures, and developing and implementing training will then vary from institution, but their expertise in fair and efficient procedural methods for resolving allegations could be leveraged. For institutions that have a system other than a student conduct system, student conduct professionals could be asked to provide representation on a procedural or policy committee so that the involved others (e.g., faculty, students) could benefit from their expertise in due process, rules of evidence, and/or conflict resolution. The honor council, academic integrity body or the faculty could also partner with student conduct professionals on building an integrity culture, launching a campaign to raise student awareness about the importance of acting with integrity within the community. Community members across campus, including student conduct professionals, could work together to reinforce the values and build awareness among students (faculty and staff) on why it is important to build the capacity for exercising the courage to act honestly, respectfully, responsibly, fairly, and trustworthy in all that they do. For students, this definition of integrity can be applied to their academic work, as well as the issues with which student conduct professionals deal—personal and dating relationships, fraternity and sorority behaviors, interactions with campus staff and units, residential life behaviors, and so on. A campus-wide campaign about integrity that is not distinct to academics could help build a stronger integrity culture and teach students that integrity is a life-long practice.

Summary

In this section, I used Dalton and Crosby's conceptions of the student affairs profession to lay the foundation for the ways in which student affairs professionals might be involved with academic integrity. The student services, student development, student learning, and student success conceptual paradigms all point to a persistent purpose of the student affairs profession, which is to contribute to the "intellectual and ethical development of college students" (Dalton & Crosby, 2011, p. 6). And this, I argue, means that student affairs professionals have a significant role to play in building an academic integrity culture, designing and implementing fair and efficient procedures for handling academic integrity violation allegations, and developing and implementing training that will support academic integrity. To help illustrate this, I explored various functional areas of student affairs and the ways in which those professionals might contribute to academic integrity on any campus. In this next section, I will explore the legal and ethical issues with which student affairs professionals should be aware if they are going to get involved in academic integrity.

ETHICAL (& LEGAL) ISSUES INVOLVED IN ACADEMIC INTEGRITY

It would be inappropriate to end a chapter on academic integrity without first speaking to the ethical and legal issues of which any professional should be aware before getting involved in academic integrity. While academic integrity may be primarily a teaching and learning issue, if the institution issues any disciplinary actions (e.g., probation, suspension, expulsion) in response to academic integrity violations, the courts will treat "academic dishonesty as a disciplinary rather than an academic offense" (Pavela, 1997, p. 106) and expect institutional adherence to certain basic legal principles. Thus, in this section, I will overview three basic legal issues with which student affairs professionals should be aware and then I will advise on three main ethical issues in which student affairs professionals may become entangled if involved with academic integrity.

Legal Issues

There are three main legal requirements with which student affairs professionals should be familiar if they are going to be directly involved in academic integrity and especially if they are involved in the resolution of academic integrity violation allegations. One will be familiar (FERPA), while the other two may not be. It is important to note here that I am not an attorney and the opinions offered here are my own and are not intended as legal advice. All student affairs professionals involved in academic integrity at their institution should seek the advice from their institutional colleagues delegated to provide institutional guidance on the following three issues.

Family Educational Rights & Privacy Act (FERPA)

The Family Education Rights and Privacy Act (FERPA) "is a Federal law that protects the privacy of student education records" (U.S. Department of Education, n.d.). In higher education institutions, where the majority of students are 18 years of age or older, this means that faculty, staff, and students involved in academic integrity violation allegations cannot disclose to parents (or any other person) a student's involvement in an allegation or any record of a violation that may exist, at least not without that student's consent. It is advisable that institutions have a standard form that can be provided to students who would like to give an institutional representative consent to speak with parents (or others) about their academic integrity case. This form should be filled out and signed by the student and kept on file in case of disagreement or misunderstanding.

To handle situations in which this consent is not provided, student affairs professionals (and others involved in academic integrity) must be given training on how to protect student education records while still providing parents (and others) information that will meet both legal requirements as well as parental concerns. For example, faculty and staff can be trained to talk to parents generally about academic integrity, the process for resolving allegations, and the assistance available to students who are going through the process. Parents can be directed to online resources and frequently asked questions. It can also be good practice to inform the student that their parent was enquiring and offer to the student the opportunity to provide consent if they so wish to. Student affairs professionals should know to have students complete the consent form even for the attorneys who have been hired to represent them; a letter from an attorney claiming to represent a student can be forwarded to the student with a request that they fill out the consent form if they want the institution to include the attorney in communications. Even when consent is officially provided by the student, it may also be appropriate to continue to include the student in all communications, rather than speaking directly with the parent or attorney without the student's involvement.

FERPA also means that institutions should think carefully about who within the university has a legitimate "educational need to know" about a student's academic integrity violation allegation or the violation itself. That is, one needs to consider if the knowledge is necessary for the other person to: perform their duties or responsibilities, advise the student, educate the student, or make decisions on behalf of the institution. For example, even if student affairs professionals are involved in building an integrity culture or implementing training, there may not be an "educational need" for them to know about a particular student's involvement in an academic integrity violation. A person considering hiring a student may not have an "educational need" to know about the student's history, unless they have disclosed to the student that their disciplinary record may be checked as part of the hiring process. A faculty member wanting to know if the student has ever been previously disciplined for an academic integrity violation before they report the student for a violation may not have an "educational need" to know that information. So, before releasing information protected by FERPA (and you should check with your institution on what that information will be), always ask yourself "is there a legitimate educational need for this person to know this about the student's record of academic integrity violation(s)?".

Decision-Making Standard

When decisions are made about a student's involvement in an academic integrity violation, the institution needs to use a standard to ensure fairness and consistency across cases. Most people are probably familiar with the beyond a reasonable doubt standard, the standard used in criminal court and on television crime dramas. However, this is not the standard expected to be used within educational institutions because it is considered "too demanding" for consideration of student conduct or academic integrity issues (Stoner & Lowery, 2004). Instead, institutions usually choose from one of two other standards - clear and convincing or a preponderance of the evidence. Pavela (1997) recommends that institutions adopt the clear and convincing standard as a middle ground between beyond a reasonable doubt and a preponderance of the evidence because the clear and convincing standard requires the institution to meet a higher burden of proof without being overly demanding or burdensome. However, preponderance of the evidence is by far the most commonly applied within higher education institutions (Stoner & Lowery, 2004), especially with respect to academic integrity violation allegations. Preponderance of the evidence still lays the burden of proof on the institution but on a "more likely than not" standard. In other words, the institution has to present sufficient evidence to the decision makers that it is "more likely than not" that the student violated academic integrity standards or policies. If there is insufficient evidence, the institution should not hold the student responsible.

There is one more common question about decision-making standards I will address here: should intention to cheat be taken into consideration when deciding responsibility for academic integrity violations? If "intentionality" is written into the policy (as suggested by, for example, Pavela, 1997), then decision makers should consider intent in their decision making. However, if intent is absent from institutional policy definitions of cheating or plagiarism than decision makers do not need to consider that factor. Unfortunately, Lee (2013) found that there lacks consistency across institutional policies on the inclusion of "intent". I found that even the two most cited "model" codes of conduct are inconsistent—Pavela (1997) clearly defines academic dishonesty as intentional acts, while Stoner and Lowery (2004) do not mention intent at all.

In her review of court cases, Lee (2013) states that clear evidence of intent does not seem to be required by the courts, even in cases where the institution mentions intent in their policies. The question of intent, whether to include in an institutional policy or not, is one with which institutions should wrestle, stake a claim, and then ensure that those involved in deciding academic integrity cases follow that policy (i.e., consider intent if the policy states it as a requirement and not consider intent if the policy does not). Pavela (1997) makes one last important point on this topic—"requiring a showing of intent is not to be confused with excusing students who claim they were unaware of the rules" (p. 105). The claim "I didn't intend (or mean) to" is the most common claim given by students going through an academic integrity violation allegation process. However, a determination of "intent" (if it is required by institutional policy) should be made on the basis of facts and evidence, not on students' claims.

Due Process

The U.S. court system has been clear that due process must be provided when educational institutions impose disciplinary actions (especially those actions that result in separation from the University) for academic integrity violations. Beyond such basic due process rights, "public colleges and universities retain reasonable flexibility in the application of student due process standards "(Buchanan & Beckham, 2006, p. 102). Basic due process is defined as "the right to notice" and "the right to be heard." "Right to notice" means that the student is notified of the allegation (i.e., what they are accused of) and "right to be heard" means that they are "afforded the opportunity to respond to the charges, to explain his or her conduct, and to defend against the allegations of misconduct" (Buchanan & Beckham, 2006, p. 102). Generally, the courts have decided that due process does not require an "evidentiary hearing" in which the student is afforded the opportunity for counsel, to bring in witnesses, to present evidence, or to cross-examine the witnesses (Lee, 2013).

What can confuse the situation within the realm of "academic integrity" is the distinction some courts have made between the due processes necessary for resolving academic qualification disputes (e.g., dismissal for failure to meet academic requirements as determined by the faculty) and the due process necessary for resolving disputes about academic conduct. Generally speaking, the courts have decided that sanctioning a student for an academic integrity violation is more akin to sanctioning a student for nonacademic misconduct (i.e., disciplinary issue) and less like sanctioning a student for their failure to reach academic standards (Buchanan & Beckham, 2006; Lee, 2013). The latter is a result "subjective and evaluative" decisions by knowledgeable disciplinary experts regarding a student's "present competency," while the former requires evidence, perhaps witnesses, and a "neutral decision-maker" to make a "careful and deliberate" decision about "past actions" (Kibler, Nuss, Paterson, & Pavela, 1988, p. 38). Thus, it is usually advisable that colleges and universities follow nonacademic misconduct resolution best practices for handling allegations of academic integrity violations, at least when there are disciplinary actions that follow from an allegation.

If the institution allows faculty members to treat academic integrity violations as academic matters (that is, the outcome of a violation is a grade penalty only), then it could be that less elaborate processes are necessary. However, the downside of this approach is that grade penalties are poor deterrents of future academic integrity violations (Kibler et al., 1988) and a lack of centralized record keeping by the institution will mean that the teachable moment of an integrity violation is not leveraged and a student could really cheat their way through to the awarding of the degree.

Those interested in better understanding due process or the appropriate procedures for resolving academic integrity violation allegations should consult with the references in this section, along with Pavela's (1997) model code of academic integrity. In the meantime, these are the general due process principles that can be kept in mind by student affairs professionals who are asked to advise their institution on this matter:

- All suspected incidents of academic integrity violations should be reported to a centralized system/process for appropriate record keeping and monitoring.

- The institution should have a written and publicly available policy and procedures for handling allegations of academic integrity violations.
- Students should receive a written notification (email is fine if that is the official means of communication for the institution) that they have been alleged with a violation.
- Students should receive an opportunity to be heard by an impartial party regarding the allegation.
- As the seriousness of the disciplinary action increases (e.g., from warning to dismissal), it may be appropriate to expand the extent of due process afforded to the student. In particular, it may not be necessary to afford the same due process to students not facing separation as those facing separation (Kibler et al., 1988). For example, the "right to be heard" for students not facing separation could be as simple as talking with a neutral party who has the authority to decide if the violation occurred or not (Lee, 2013). While for a student facing separation, the "right to be heard" may take the form of some sort of formal hearing during which they have the chance to review the evidence ahead of time, present witnesses, and evidence, and ask questions of those alleging the violation, as well as an opportunity to appeal the findings of the hearing board (Kibler et al., 1988; Lee, 2013).
- Students afforded a formal hearing should receive advanced notice of the date, time, and location of the hearing, as well as a chance to review evidence ahead of the hearing (Kibler et al., 1988).
- If there is a formal hearing, there should be some recording of the hearing (written or audio) that can be accessed by the student afterwards (Kibler et al., 1988).
- Students who admit to violating academic integrity need not be afforded due process beyond the right to notice and right to be heard (Lee, 2013).
- It is advisable to provide the students with at least one appeal process, whether that is to appeal the decision, the sanctions imposed, or both.
- Whatever procedure and policy the institution has for handling academic integrity violations, the institution should follow them and if they do not they should afford the student another chance to go through the process.

Ethical Issues

While those directly involved in academic integrity processes and policies should be aware of the above legal issues, other student affairs professionals may face some ethical issues as they interface with students and faculty around the issue of academic integrity. Although the range and extent of ethical issues cannot be predicted, this section covers three of the most common I have seen over the last decade of practice.

Getting Involved at the Request of the Student

Student affairs professionals who mentor, coach, supervise, or advise students may be drawn into the academic integrity violation resolution process at the request of their students. Students who have been alleged with an academic integrity violation may ask for counsel or perhaps even for a character witness. This can present the student affairs professional with an ethical issue because they feel drawn to help the student they know while at the same time, respecting the university's processes for resolving such allegations. It may be important at this point to recognize that the student you know as a good, hard working, dedicated, and engaged student can also be a student who made a bad decision under stress and pressure. Research studies provide sufficient evidence that most people will cheat just a little bit when given the "right" opportunity and circumstances (see Ariely, 2013 for just one good explanation). Thus, most institutional processes to resolve academic integrity violation allegations do not consider "character witnesses" as relevant parties to the process. It is important to remember that the institution is not accusing your student of being a "bad person," rather it is being alleged that their actions violated academic integrity standards.

In academic integrity processes, the student affairs professional can support the student best by not getting directly involved, but instead pointing the student toward the resources that exist to help them through the process, including the policy or honor code document itself. It can be tempting to intervene—to call the office in charge or faculty member involved to talk to them on behalf of your student, but this temptation should be resisted. Part of the learning and development experience for the student is managing this process themselves, as it will not be the last time in their life that they have to deal with institutional processes and systems under difficult circumstances. Providing emotional support is helpful, but making promises or stepping in as a surrogate may not be. Of course, ethical and professional judgment is needed to make this determination on a case-by-case basis.

Moving from Bystander to Active Agent

As a student affairs professional, you may find yourself in a position where you are able to prevent students from engaging in an academic integrity violation. For example, as a Residential Life employee, you may overhear a group of students working together on what was to have been an individual assignment. Or, as a Success Coach, you may realize that your student is under a significant amount of stress with two papers due in one week that have not even been drafted. A timely intervention at times like these may make a tremendous and significant difference in your student's life. Yet, often, human beings are hesitant to get involved if it feels like we are inappropriately intervening or intervening without a full understanding. We lack the skills and tools for getting involved, so we look the other way—we become bystanders. Overhearing or seeing an academic integrity violation in action, or detecting the signs that may lead to an integrity violation (e.g., stress, lack of progress on an assignment), are key ethical touchpoints for the student affairs professional. Do I, or do I not, get involved? What do I say? How will they react? I recommend using UCSD's Bystander Intervention Training (BIT) Model for guidance in such situations. The first ethical touchpoint in moving from bystander to active agent is even recognizing that you are facing an ethical situation for which you have the responsibility of acting. Using the BIT tests (in particular, the values and standards tests) will be particularly helpful in assessing the situation.

Determining the best course of action through the BIT model may be itself sufficiently difficult, but acting on the best course of action takes the most courage. People in such situations often feel torn between conflicting values, otherwise known as "ethical dilemmas" (Kidder, 2009). Kidder talks about four sets of values that are most often in conflict in such ethical dilemmas. Looking through the lens of student affairs and academic integrity, here are some examples:

- If I know about an actual academic integrity violation and I report the student, I am upholding *justice* but it is also right to have *mercy* for the student and not report the violation.
- If I think students might be considering violating academic integrity, it is right to act on behalf of the *community* to prevent the violation, but it is also right to allow *individuals* to make their own decision.
- If a student has confided in me that they cheated by plagiarizing their last assignment, it is right to tell the *truth* and report the student, but it is also right to be *loyal* to the student by keeping their confidence.
- If I see a potential academic integrity violation in progress in the residential halls, it is right to act in the *short-term* to stop the violation from occurring, but it is also right to protect the *long-term* relationship I have with the students by not interfering.

As Kidder (2009) notes, these dilemmas constructed in our minds are often false; that is, there is usually a third option that can be chosen that upholds both values at the same time. The key for the student affairs professional in acting to prevent academic integrity violations from occurring is to understand that the best choice for action is to choose "both and" and to examine the situation for the possibility of the "both and." For example, in the first situation above, what action will uphold justice and mercy? One possibility is that I recognize my duty to justice to report the violation, but I can uphold mercy by speaking with the student first, showing them compassion, and volunteering to support them throughout the process. In the third situation, what action will uphold truth and loyalty? One possibility is that I truthfully tell the student that I disapprove of their action and have an ethical and professional obligation to uphold the integrity of the institution but maintain loyalty by giving the student a chance to report themselves for the plagiarism and by supporting the student throughout the process. The main point is that student affairs professionals should be prepared to step in and act in situations in order to prevent academic integrity violations from happening or to respond when they have already occurred.

Helping Students Make Ethical Decisions

The third ethical touchpoint for the student affairs professionals involved (directly or indirectly) in academic integrity might be the implicit responsibility to help students make ethical decisions. This is related to the bystander touchpoint above which calls on the student affairs professional to make and act on an ethical decision; in this case, it is to coach or train the student in making ethical decisions. Student affairs professionals can do this in many ways, including incorporating ethical decision-making training into their existing training programs (e.g., new student orientation, mandatory training for student organization officers, student worker training) or offering training to students through a Student Life & Development Office, for example. Training students to make good ethical decisions can serve to prevent academic integrity violations from occurring because it equips students with the knowledge and techniques they can use when they are under stress and pressure to make decisions about completing academic assessments with or without integrity. Such training can also remind students of the importance of integrity and ethics to themselves and their community. When moving from bystander to active agent, the student affairs professional can also step in as an ethical decision-making coach to walk a student through the process toward a good ethical decision.

The BIT Model mentioned earlier could be used as a simple way to train students to begin to develop their ethical sensitivity, that is, their ability to recognize an ethical issue when they see one. Students could be presented with ethical scenarios or case studies and be engaged in a facilitated walk through the resolution of those cases using the BIT model. The benefit of the BIT model is that it requires students to think about the fundamental academic integrity values (i.e., honesty, respect, responsibility, fairness, trust-worthiness, and courage) as well as the institutional standards for academic integrity. Thus, using the BIT in training delivers what would otherwise be passive information in an active delivery fashion.

Some student affairs professionals reading this chapter may be interested in developing a more elaborate training program on ethical decision making and acting. In that case, I recommend that they consult with ethics experts on campus and look into the research on teaching ethical reasoning or decision-making.[10] For those who are interested in designing ethical decision-making training, I recommend adhering to the following key principles:

- Training should occur for no less than 4 but no more than 12 weeks of instruction at 2 hours per week (Clarkeburn Downey & Matthew, 2002; Gray & Gibbons, 2007; Schlaefli, Rest & Thoma, 1985; Trevino, 1992). Improvement in ethical sensitivity may be achievable in 3 weeks, but at least 6 weeks is needed to help students develop ethical reasoning skills.
- Training is best delivered through active learning techniques such as team-based learning (TBL) or problem-based learning (PBL) because "small groups can positively nurture student motivation towards developing their ethical and moral skills" and "generate a sense of belonging and shared experience, which can nurture motivation and enjoyment in learning" (Clarkeburn et al., 2002, p. 68; Gray & Gibbons, 2007; and Self, Wolinski & Baldwin, 1989 also advocate small groups).
- Student leaders can be trained to facilitate small learning groups and "analyze and clarify" student confusion about ethics and to help them make decisions according to ethics, rather than other factors (Clarkeburn et al., 2002, pp. 70–71).
- A supportive and safe environment for learning is critical "for spurring growth in moral reasoning" (Mayhew & King, 2008, p. 36)
- Face-to-face, rather than online, learning is preferred because social interaction is necessary and integral to ethical decision making (Antes et al., 2009).
- Storytelling (e.g., of times when one has encountered and solved an ethical issue) can be beneficial because storytelling "impacts students in ways that arouse curiosity and a desire to engage in dialogue and often leads to personal insight" (Sims & Felton, 2005, p. 41).

---

10. For a ready-made program on acting ethically, I recommend the Giving Voice to Values (GVV) Curriculum which is freely available online and can be found at http://www.darden.virginia.edu/ibis/initiatives/giving-voice-to-values/. The GVV Curriculum begins with the premise that people can identify when they should act ethically, but they lack the skills and strategies to do so. The GVV curriculum teaches people the skills to respond to ethical situations that they encounter.

- Reflections and discussions about actual experiences with ethics (preferably from a service-learning, work, or study situation) enable the "processing of experience" (Sims & Felton, 2005, p. 44; also supported by Schlaefli, et al., 1985).
- Case studies that are relevant to real-life situations and experiences of the students and their potential future profession should be used as a basis for discussion and practice in resolving (Clarkeburn, 2002; Clarkeburn et al., 2002; Gray & Gibbs, 2007; Oddo, 1997; O'Neil, 1998; Ritter, 2006; Schlaefli, et al., 1985; Sims & Felton, 2005).
- Values clarification exercises in which students identify, examine, "critically appraise" and apply their ethical values to a situation (Felton & Sims, 2005; Nonis & Swift, 2001; Oddo, 1997) can help them "reflect on the way in which their reasoning, actions, and decisions are affected by their values" (Gray & Gibbons, 2007, p. 223). This is important because otherwise students do not learn how to "deal with value conflicts" that will inevitably arise (Felton & Sims, 2005, p. 389) or begin to understand the complexity of ethical situations and the "moral conflicts" that naturally occur.

Summary

In this section on the ethical and legal issues of academic integrity, I reviewed just some of the concepts or situations with which student affairs professionals might interact. To be sure, any student affairs professional directly or indirectly involved in the process of resolving academic integrity violation allegations should be very familiar with the legal concepts of FERPA, due process, and standards for decision making. Those professionals who are involved in academic integrity processes should take steps to connect with the legal and process experts on their campus to ensure that they are up-to-date on any legal or institutional standards to be followed.

Student affairs professionals may also encounter many ethical issues related to academic integrity but these are more difficult to identify as they are constructed within specific contexts and situations. However, I identified three that I have commonly seen arise in my years of experience in the field. These ethical issues arise for student affairs professionals because of their extensive involvement with students as advisers, supervisors, mentors, and even as residential neighbors. When students ask for help in the process or when student affairs professionals see or overhear potential or actual integrity violations, ethical decisions need to be made before engaging in the situation. If training on ethical decision-making is lacking on campus, student affairs professionals could consider getting involved and helping to build an integrity culture in this way.

SUMMARY AND RECOMMENDATIONS

The purpose of this chapter is to explore academic integrity in higher education and the ways in which student affairs professionals are, and are not, involved with academic integrity. To do this, I first provided an overview of academic integrity in higher education, the typical institutional approaches to academic integrity, and the five different academic integrity systems that may manifest those approaches. Then, I explored the purpose of student affairs within higher education and what that purpose means for student affairs involvement in academic integrity. I specifically examined the roles that different types of student affairs professionals (e.g., residential life officers) can play in their own institutions with respect to helping to build an integrity culture, develop and implement procedures, and develop and implement academic integrity training. Finally, I reflected on the ethical and legal issues with which student affairs professionals should be aware if they are indirectly or directly involved with academic integrity.

The exploration undertaken in this chapter demonstrates that it is beneficial and wise to involve student affairs professionals in academic integrity for several reasons. First, student affairs professionals have contact and relationships with students outside of the classroom, which is where students do much of their academic work (e.g., writing papers, completing homework) and encounter many temptations and opportunities to cheat. Thus, student affairs professionals are bound to overhear or see potential or actual academic integrity violations of which faculty may not be aware and it is their ethical imperative to get involved to prevent or stop the cheating from happening. Also, student affairs professionals (along with faculty) must act to role model ethical standards and practices because students will learn from observation.

Second, building a culture of integrity requires the involvement of everyone within the institution, including student affairs professionals. Because of their multiple touchpoints with students outside of the classroom, student affairs professionals have opportunities to deliver the academic integrity message, opportunities that are not often available to faculty. To be sure, these messages should be developed with faculty to ensure that they are academically grounded, but the involvement of all campus members is needed if a culture of integrity is truly to be built.

Third, student affairs professionals have the expertise in areas that can be helpful to the management of the integrity policy and processes. Student conduct professionals have expertise in the legal concepts that must be taken into consideration when designing policies and processes, and many student affairs professionals have expertise in counseling students and helping them to resolve challenging or difficult situations (such as being alleged with an academic integrity violation).

In summary, it is recommended that higher education institutions consider the ways in which student affairs professionals can be integrated into academic integrity specifically to help build an integrity culture, develop and implement fair and efficient policies and procedures, and develop and implement academic integrity training to the students.

CASE STUDIES

1. The Residential Life Office wants to know if the applicants to Residential Assistant (RA) positions have a history of academic integrity violations before the applicants are hired.
   a. Is this an ethical or legal issue?
      i. If yes, what is the issue and how do you know?
   b. If you were asked for this information, how would you respond?
   c. Are there mechanisms that could be put in place that would allow Residential Life access to this information?
2. Career Services has been asked by an employer to disclose the academic and non-academic conduct record of every student who is coming to their employment information session.
   a. Is this an ethical or legal issue?
      i. If yes, what is the issue and how do you know?
   b. If you were asked for this information, how would you respond in order to maintain good relations with the employer?
3. A faculty member who suspects a student cheated in their class is asking all of the faculty in their department if the student cheated in their classes. The instructor wants to know this before deciding if they are going to report the student per University policy (the instructor doesn't want to report the student if it's their "first time").
   a. Is this an ethical or legal issue?
      i. If yes, what is the issue and how do you know?
   b. If you were advising a faculty member who was being asked this question by another faculty member, what advice would you give them?
   c. What role could a student affairs professional play in preventing a situation like this from occurring?
4. An athletics director finds out that one of their athletes has been reported for an academic integrity violation. The Director calls the faculty to find out more about the allegation.
   a. Is this an ethical or legal issue?
      i. If yes, what is the issue and how do you know?
   b. What are your ideas for how the faculty member could respond?

c. If you were the supervisor of the Athletics Director and you found out about this after it happened, what would you say to the Director?

    i. What about to the faculty member?

5. A success coach is working with a student who expresses significant distress and anxiety over an 11-page paper that is due in 8 days. The success coach works with the student on breaking down the task and connecting to appropriate resources on campus who can help (e.g., writing center, the course instructor, the course TA). The coach schedules another meeting for 2 days hence. When the coach and student meet again in 2 days, the student is not stressed at all—in fact, the student is all smiles! When the coach asks "What progress have you made on your paper since we last spoke?" the student responds—"oh, don't worry about that. I've got it all under control."

a. What might be going on here?

b. What question(s) should the coach ask next?

6. An RA is walking by a group of residents when they are overheard saying "did you all know that all of the professor's past answer keys are posted on CourseHero? I have an account; do you want to all contribute dollars so I can download for us to study from?". Using UCSD's BIT document, determine:

a. Is there an ethical issue the RA needs to address?

    i. If yes, what is it and how do you know it's an ethical issue?

b. What are the RAs IDEAs for acting?

c. What is the best right IDEA to act on?

d. What may stop the RA from acting on the best right IDEA?

    i. How as a supervisor, mentor or coach to the RAs could you help them act in situations like this?

7. A faculty member considering students on the wait-list for admittance into the class calls the Student Conduct Office (SCO) to find out which of the students (if any) have prior academic integrity violations or unresolved academic integrity violation allegations. Using UCSD's BIT document, determine:

a. Is this an ethical or legal issue for the SCO?

    i. If yes, what is it and how do you know?

b. What are the SCO's IDEAs for acting?

c. What is the best right IDEA to act on?

d. Script out what the SCO could say to the faculty member to maintain a good relationship and trust with the instructor (so the instructor continues to be concerned about academic integrity in the future)

REFERENCES

Alschuler, A. S., & Blimling, G. S. (1995). Curbing epidemic cheating through systemic change. *College Teaching, 43*(4), 123–125.

Antes, A. L., Murphy, S. T., Waples, E. P., Mumford, M. D., Brown, R. P., Connelly, S., & Davenport, L.D. (2009). A meta-analysis of ethics instruction effectiveness in the sciences. *Ethics & Behavior, 19*(5), 379–402.

Ariely, D. (2013). *The (honest) truth about dishonesty-Especially ourselves.* New York: HarperCollins.

Bazerman, M. H., & Tenbrunsel, A. E. (2011). *Blind spots: Why we fail to do what's right and what to do about it.* Princeton, NJ: Princeton University Press.

Bertram Gallant, T. (2008). *Academic integrity in the twenty-first century: A teaching & learning imperative.* San Francisco: Jossey-Bass.

Bertram Gallant, T. (2017) Academic integrity as a teaching & learning issue: From theory to practice. *Theory Into Practice, 56*(2), 88–94.

Buchanan, J. N., & Beckham, J. C. (2006). A comprehensive academic honor policy for students: Ensuring due process, promoting academic integrity, and involving faculty. *Journal of College & University Law, 33*(1), 97–119.

Clarkeburn, H. (2002). A test for ethical sensitivity in science. *Journal of Moral Education, 31*(4), 439–453.

Clarkeburn, H., Downie, J. R., & Matthew, B. (2002). Impact of an ethics programme in a life sciences curriculum. *Teaching in Higher Education, 7*(1), 65–79.

Cole, S., & McCabe, D. L. (1996). Issues in academic integrity. *New Directions for Student Services, 73*(Spring), 67–77.

Dalton, J. C., & Crosby, P. C. (2011). A profession in search of a mission: Is there an enduring purpose for student affairs in U.S. higher education? *Journal of College and Character, 12*(4), 1–7.

Dalton, J. C., & Crosby, P. C. (2014) The power of personal coaching: Helping first-year students to connect and commit in college. *Journal of College and Character, 15*(2), 59–66.

Drinan, P., & Bertram Gallant, T. (2008). Academic integrity: Models, case studies, and strategies. In J. M. Lancaster & D. M. Waryold (Eds.), *Student conduct practice: The complete guide for student affairs professionals* (pp. 258–278). Sterling, VA: Stylus.

Elias, K., & Drea, C. (2013). The cocurricular record: Enhancing a post-secondary education. *College Quarterly, 16*(1). Retrieved March 22, 2018 from https://files.eric.ed.gov/fulltext/EJ1016461.pdf

Felton, E. L., & Sims, R. R. (2005). Teaching business ethics: Targeted outputs. *Journal of Business Ethics, 60*(4), 377–391.

Gardner, P. (2007). Moving up or moving out of the company? Factors that influence the promoting or firing of new college hires. *Collegiate Employment Research Institute, Michigan State University.* Retrieved December 5, 2017 from http://ceri.msu.edu/publications/pdf/brief1-07.pdf

Gray, M., & Gibbons, J. (2007). There are no answers, only choices: Teaching ethical decision making in social work. *Australian Social Work, 60*(2), 222–238.

Hart, P. D. (2006). *How should colleges prepare students to succeed in today's global economy?* Retrieved December 5, 2017 from www.aacu.org/leap/documents/Re8097 abcombined.pdf

Hart, P. D. (2013). It takes more than a major: Employer priorities for college learning and student success. *Liberal Education, Spring,* 22–29.

International Center for Academic Integrity. (2014). Fundamental values. Retrieved December 5, 2017 from http://www.academicintegrity.org/icai/assets/Revised_FV_2014.pdf

Kibler, W. L. (1993a). Academic dishonesty: A student development dilemma. *NASPA Journal, 30*(4), 252–267.

Kibler, W. L. (1993b). A framework for addressing academic dishonesty from a student development perspective. *NASPA Journal, 31*(1), 8–18.

Kibler, W. L., Nuss, E. M., Paterson, B. G., & Pavela, G. (1988). *Academic integrity and student development: Legal issues, policy perspectives.* Asheville, NC: College Administration Publications.

Kidder, R. M. (2009). *How good people make tough choices: Resolving the dilemma of ethical living.* New York: HarperCollins.

Lee, B. A. (2013). Judicial review of student challenges to academic misconduct sanctions. *Journal of College & University Law, 39*(3), 511–539.

Mayhew, M. J., & King, P. (2008). How curricular content and pedagogical strategies affect moral reasoning development in college students. *Journal of Moral Education, 37*(1), 17–40.

McCabe, D. L. (2005). Cheating among college and university students: A North American perspective. *International Journal for Educational Integrity, 1*(1), 1–11.

McCabe, D. L., & Pavela, G. (2000). Some good news about academic integrity. *Change: The Magazine of Higher Learning, 32*(5), 32–38.

McCabe, D. L., & Trevino, L. K. (1997). Individual and contextual influences on academic dishonesty: A multi campus investigation. *Research in Higher Education, 38*(3), 379–396.

McCabe, D. L., Trevino, L. K., & Butterfield, K. D. (1999). Academic integrity in honor code and non-honor code environments. *The Journal of Higher Education, 70*(2), 211–234.

McCabe, D. L., Trevino, L. K., & Butterfield, K. D. (2001). Cheating in academic institutions: A decade of research. *Ethics & Behavior, 11*(3), 219–232.

Murdock, T. B., & Anderman, E. M. (2006). Motivational perspectives on student cheating: Toward an integrated model of academic dishonesty. *Educational Psychologist, 41*(3), 129–145.

Nonis, S., & Swift, C. O. (2001). Personal value profiles and ethical business decisions. *Journal of Education for Business, 70*(5), 251–257.

Nuss, E. M. (1982). *Undergraduate moral development and academic dishonesty* (doctoral dissertation. University of Maryland, 1981). *Dissertation Abstracts International, 42*(8), 3463A.

Oddo, A. R. (1997). A framework for teaching business ethics. *Journal of Business Ethics, 16*(3), 293–297.

O'Neill, P. (1998). Teaching ethics: The utility of the CPA code. *Canadian Psychology, 39,* 194–201.

Pavela, G. (1997). Applying the power of association on campus: A model code of academic integrity. *Journal of College and University Law, 24*(1), 97–118.

Reason, R. D., & Broido, E. M. (2011). Philosophies and values. In J. H. Schuh, S. R. Jones, S. R. Harper and Associates (Eds.), *Student services: A handbook for the profession* (5th ed) (pp. 80–95). San Francisco: Jossey-Bass.

Ritter, B. A. (2006). Can business ethics be trained? A study of the ethical decision-making process in business students. *Journal of Business Ethics, 68,* 153–164.

Sandeen, A. (2011) Does student affairs have an enduring mission? *Journal of College and Character, 12*(4), 1–8.

Schlaefli, A., Rest, J. R., & Thoma, S. J. (1985). Does moral education improve moral judgement? A meta-analysis of intervention studies using the defining issues test. *Review of Educational Research, 3,* 319–352.

Schrage, J. M., & Giacomini, N. G. (2009). *Reframing campus conflict: Student conduct practice through a social justice lens.* Sterling, VA: Stylus.

Self, D. J., Wolinsky, D. C., & Baldwin, D. C. J. (1989). The effect of teaching medical ethics to medical students' moral reasoning. *Academic Medicine, 64,* 755–759.

Sims, R. R., & Felton, E. L. (2005). Successfully teaching ethics for effective learning. *College Teaching Methods & Styles Journal, 1*(3), 31–48.

Stoner, E. N., & Lowery, J. W. (2004). Navigating past the spirit of insubordination: A twenty-first century model student conduct code with a model hearing script, *Journal of College & University Law, 31*(1), 1–78.

Trevino, L. K. (1992). Moral reasoning and business ethics: Implications for research, education and management. *Journal of Business Ethics, 11,* 445–459.

U.S. Department of Education. (nd). *Family Educational Rights and Privacy Act (FERPA).* Retrieved December 5, 2017 from https://www2.ed.gov/policy/gen/guid/fpco/ferpa/index.html

Zivcakova, L., Wood, E., Forsyth, G., Zivcak, M., Shapiro, J., Coulas, A., . . . Angardi, V. (2014). Investigating perceptions of students to a peer-based academic integrity presentation provided by residence dons. *Journal of Academic Ethics, 12*(2), 89–99.

Appendix 1

ACADEMIC INTEGRITY DISCUSSION TOPICS & ROLE PLAY SCENARIOS FOR ORIENTATION LEADERS (OLs) & RESIDENT ASSISTANTS (RAs)

1. Your friend asks to see the paper you wrote for a class last term. How do you maintain honor/integrity in this scenario?
2. You give your friend a paper you previously wrote for another class. Is this cheating? Why or why not?
   a. If you decide it's cheating, what do you say to your friend or do to prevent either of you from engaging in an honor/integrity violation?
3. You are working on an individual assignment for a class when a classmate approaches you to ask for help. What do you say?
4. You and your 3 friends decide to form a study group for a difficult class you're all enrolled in. You meet up to work on individual assignments for the class so that you have immediate help if you need it. One night, a group member proposes that the group splits up the current assignment so you all get it done faster. Is this cheating? Why or why not?
   a. If you decide it's cheating, what do you say to your group or do to prevent an honor/integrity violation?
5. A friend tells you about a website that will edit your papers for you to improve your grade. How do you figure out if using the website services upholds honor/integrity or not?
6. You go to the writing center for help on one of your essays. Is this cheating? Why or why not?
   a. Why is going to a writing center different than going to an editing service you found online?
7. According to the International Center for Academic Integrity (ICAI), academic integrity is the courage to be honest, respectful, responsible, fair, and trustworthy in all your academic work, even when it is difficult. What kind of behaviors will uphold these values and what kind of behaviors would undermine them?
8. Did you notice cheating in your high school?
   a. If yes, did it bother you? Why? Did you ever do anything about it? Why or why not?
   b. If no, why do you think that was?
9. What strategies do you personally use to ensure that you do your academic work with integrity/honor?
   a. Send students on a scavenger hunt to determine what resources on campus might exist to help them develop their strategies or find new ones
10. Have students practice telling a friend "no" or denying their cheating request (e.g., "I need your paper because I forgot to write mine") in various role plays.

Chapter 8

DESIGNING A COLLECTIVE, ETHICAL, AND EQUITABLE STUDENT SUCCESS CULTURE IN HISPANIC-SERVING INSTITUTIONS

Patricia L. Farrell-Cole and José A. Cabrales

Interpreting Paulo Freire's words in his infamous book, *Pedagogy of the Oppressed* (1970), Tim Monreal said: "Education is never a neutral process, it is a political process. This political act can never be divorced from pedagogy. Education is specifically designed and taught to serve a political agenda" (2015, p. 1).

In 2012, the Washington Post declared, "the accountability movement has arrived in higher education" (de Vise, para. 1). Trust in the public higher education system by diverse stakeholders has dwindled over time due to the inefficiencies and unresponsiveness of institutions (Complete College America, 2012) resulting in low student success rates, increased tuition costs, and student indebtedness (NASBO, 2013). The recession of the late 2000s (Miao, 2012; The Pew Charitable Trusts, 2015) and the need for highly educated workers (Jones, 2014; Miao, 2012) spearheaded much of the state and national accountability movement (Jones, 2014; NASBO, 2013).

Postsecondary education institutions distinguish the political process and agenda as a double-edged sword. Public postsecondary education institutions rely on federal and state funding for operations and student financial aid, but prior to the accountability movement, institutional leadership exercised independence for the most part on how to utilize the funding and operate an institution based on its mission. The political agenda was amplified during the recession, with policymakers imposing reciprocity of public postsecondary institutions through different accountability metrics, such as increasing the number of undergraduate student completers. Or in other words, policymakers started calling for institutions to grow the human capital in the United States (Carnevale & Strohl, 2010; Russell, 2011).

This chapter is dedicated to Hispanic Serving Institutions (HSIs). HSIs are an integral piece of the political agenda and the number of HSIs is growing; yet funding for HSIs has not kept pace (HACU, 2017; Nellum & Valle, 2015). The Federal definition of a Hispanic-Serving Institution is an institution that has an enrollment of 25% or greater Latino/a full-time equivalent students (U.S. Department of Education, n.d.). In 1994 there were 189 HSIs, including public, nonprofit, and for-profit institutions. By 2015, there were 472 HSIs, including 209 public two-year and 105 public four-year institutions, and more than 300 institutions that are emerging as HSIs based on enrollment numbers (Excelencia in Education, 2017). The majority, or 81% of the current HSIs, are located in five states—California, Florida, New Mexico, New York, and Texas—and Puerto Rico. The emerging HSIs are painting a picture of a more diverse United States as the 300 emerging HSIs are located across 35 states and D.C. (García & Taylor, 2017).

Latinos/as[1] are now the nation's largest ethnic or racial minority in the U.S., and the percentage of Latinos/as are increasing more than any other segment of the U.S. population. The Latino/a population grew 50% between 2000 and 2012, and by 2017, Latinos/as comprised 17.6% of the U.S. population (Colby & Ortman, 2015). HSIs educated 64% of all Latinos/as in postsecondary education (Excelencia in Education, 2017), and the number of HSIs will continue to grow based on these population estimates (Western Interstate Commission for Higher Education (WICHE), 2017).

Consequently, HSIs will take on greater importance for fulfilling the human capital political agenda. As Myers stated in his book, *Immigrants and boomers: Forging a new social contract for the future of America,* "the reality is that the nation's ability to remain competitive in the modern economy is indeed contingent upon increasing the educational attainment of Latinos" (2007, p. 2).

The achievement of the students attending HSIs varies, but HSIs vary, too. Like Predominantly White Institutions (PWIs), HSIs are diverse with the majority of HSIs being public and offering associate degrees. Other factors that make HSIs diverse include its institutional culture and climate, the number of students it serves, its financial context, the community where it is located and the citizens it serves (García, 2017b; Nuñez, Crisp, & Elizondo, 2016).

There is no one formula to improve the success of all students at HSIs. Each institution must know the students and the communities it serves, and develop strategies and plans that complement the political realities (Baldwin,

1. The U.S. Office of Management and Budget (OMB) defines "Hispanic or Latino" as a person of Cuban, Mexican, Puerto Rican, South or Central American, or other Spanish culture or origin regardless of race. We use Latino/a unless the author or organization has used Hispanic, Latinx, or Raza.

Bensimon, Dowd, & Kleiman, 2011). In this chapter, we explore the question: What does it mean creating and upholding a culture of ethical practice at HSIs in a time when institutions are under political scrutiny for college completion and success? This chapter will examine this question by providing the readers a combined practice-based framework for HSIs to utilize and then, we highlight a few of the critical mission-focused realities that HSIs are encountering. The realities or issues sections also includes tangible HSI examples based on the framework along with questions for institutional leaders, faculty, and staff, and their external stakeholders to use in shepherding and fulfilling their HSI's mission and vision. But, first, we address what it means to be an Hispanic Serving Institution.

WHAT DOES IT MEAN TO BE A HISPANIC-SERVING INSTITUTION?

In a September 2017, *Inside Higher Education* article, Salvador Vidal-Ortiz wrote on his rage regarding diversity and what it means to postsecondary education. He addressed the issue of PWIs becoming HSIs through its enrollment of 25% or more Hispanic students "makes those institutions less accountable to diversity, as they are academic models by the act of surpassing 'quota numbers, but they continue to instill a consumption of difference (or the showcasing of their nonwhite students for the benefit of the institution without addressing inherent inequalities" (para. 8).

Vidal-Ortiz went on to address issues with administration and faculty not wanting to understand students' challenges and concerns, and "contemporary hypocrisy that aims to be 'inclusive'; giving a visual sense to the invisibility of white dominance" across the institution including curriculum, expectations, and behavior (2017, para. 13). HSIs, especially institutions whose enrollments have changed from predominantly white to Latino/a over time, must take Vidal-Ortiz's words to heart and transform its current culture. We argue that it is imperative for HSIs to move from cognitive dissonance to a culture of collective impact across the institution and community to ensure student completion and success.

A culture of collective impact requires HSIs to step back and be thoughtful and purposeful in asking questions about the institution's mission, beliefs, and values. We utilize Schein's definition of culture in this chapter. Culture is a set of social norms, structures, processes, artifacts, and procedures that guide the behavior of the HSI (Schein, 2004). Schein (2004) goes on to state that culture is a social and ever-changing phenomenon. For HSIs that want to be successful, there is a need for HSI leadership, faculty, and staff to continuously evaluate its culture because culture is being enacted upon every day and is created by their interactions with others inside and outside the institution. As Vidal-Ortiz (2017) noted, leadership behavior is critical in creating an HSI culture that has the inclusivity of Latino/a students at the forefront as opposed to the political agenda being front and center.

Garcia (2017a) developed a typology of HSI organizational identities based on the notion that postsecondary education institutions are complex and diverse. Her typology is grounded in both the political agenda emphasizing the organizational measures of Latinxs success on one axis and the organizational culture that facilitates outcomes for Latinxs on the other (see Table 8.1). The organizational culture encapsulates the "deeply embedded assumptions and values" of the HSI (2017a, p. 121S). We introduce García's typology of HSIs because our goal is to explore ways that HSIs can become a *Latinx-serving* institution through a collective impact framework. Her definition for a *Latinx-serving* institution is, "enrolls 25% or more Latinx students, produces an equitable number of legitimized outcomes, and enacts a culture that is educationally enhancing and welcoming" (García, 2017a, p. 122S). A *Latinx-serving* institution is located in the high identity box for organizational outcomes for Latinx and the *high* identity box, where the organizational culture reflects the Latinx students and community. This is in contrast to a *Latinx-enrolling* institution, which enrolls the minimum percentage of Latinx students, but does not "produce an equitable numbers of legitimized outcomes for Latinx students and does not have an organizational culture for supporting Latinxs on campus (García, 2017a, p. 121S).

To be a successful *Latinx-serving institution,* García and others, like Vidal-Ortiz, argue that HSIs need to "decolonize" from a PWI and create its own identity that is socially constructed through institutional and cultural perspectives (García, 2017a). If HSIs frame college access and success of Latinos/as in the context of economic or accountability terms, this "may render the moral and social justice implications invisible" (Malcolm, Bensimon,

Table 8.1
TYPOLOGY OF HISPANIC-SERVING INSTITUTION
ORGANIZATIONAL IDENTITIES

		Low	High
Organizational	*High*	Latinx-Producing	Latinx-Serving
Outcomes for	*Low*	Latinx-Enrolling	Latinx-Enhancing
Latinxs			
		Low	High

Organizational Culture Reflects Latinxs

& Dávila, 2010, p. 2). It is imperative that institutions work towards a collective good for improving college completion rates by analyzing the culture of the institution. The analysis should focus on the social construction of the variables studied, and what the definitions mean based on the historical interpretation of the definitions and how they impact success (Morfin, Perez, Parker, et al., 2006). The vision, mission, and value statements, which include the defined variables, express the spirit of the institution; therefore, the voices and experiences of those whom the institution serves—students and community—are central and legitimate to the success of the institution, the students, and community. The students should not have to conform to the white values or norms in order to achieve; hence, it is critical that HSI administrators and faculty become more cognizant of the experiences, languages, and cultures of the diverse students on their campus; and then, collectively work to make changes to the perceptions, values, practices, and policies that hinder their success (Patton, McEwen, Rendón, & Howard-Hamilton, 2007).

Guiding Questions: What does it mean to be an Hispanic-Serving Institution?
- What does it mean now that our institution is a HSI as opposed to a PWI?
- What is our current identity? What do we need to change about our identity to be an effective, thriving, and successful HSI?
- What does it mean to be a HSI based on our sector and our Carnegie classification?
- What does it meant to "serve" Latino/a students?

CREATING AN ETHICAL FRAMEWORK FOR STUDENT SUCCESS

Ethics is derived from the Greek term ethos and is defined as "characteristic spirit of a culture, era, or community as manifested in its attitudes and aspirations" (Oxford English Dictionary, n.d.). The mission of an institution is to express the spirit of the institution and due to the history of the beginning of our public institutions; white privilege culture permeates, even within an HSI. As the number of HSIs and Latino/a students continues to increase, HSIs have to determine what it means to be *Latinx-serving* (García, 2017a). HSIs were organizationally built as PWIs, thus, their missions are historical of PWIs, which "plagues HSIs, inhibiting their ability to fully serve Raza students from enrollment through graduation" (García, 2017a, p. 2).

HSIs are facing several tensions or realities, which could challenge or have unintended consequences on ethical standards. We focus in on some of these realities, including the changing demographics, college readiness, accountability, and scarce resources. Consequently, it is decisive for institutional leaders to spend time and effort collectively working with internal and external stakeholders on developing a successful Hispanic-Serving Institution. This is not easy work nor will transformation occur overnight. Next, we discuss a practice-based framework that connects the institution to the community, which is important for Latino/a culture and how identity is socially constructed (García, 2017b) and then, we illustrate how one HSI has utilized the framework.

COLLECTIVE IMPACT

Collective impact is the coming together of a group of influential leaders from different sectors of the institution and community to develop "a common agenda for solving a specific social problem" (Kania & Kramer, 2011, p. 37). For HSIs, the social problem is understanding the community, the educational pathway, the students the institution serves, and altering the mission and culture to being an HSI. The collective impact group needs to recognize and acknowledge the history and oppression of marginalized populations, and how the former PWI and its mission and organizational structure and composition will suppress Latino/a success, individually and community-wide (García, 2017a; Hurtado, Alvarez, Buillermo-Wann, Cueller, & Arellano, 2012). Another aspect of an HSI that ties to the history of PWIs is the "deficit mindset" that collective impact can address, but only when a diverse group of institutional and community leaders come together and work on a common agenda. Artze-Vega (cited in Morris, 2017) states: "I think Latino students deserve validation for all of the assets that they bring to our institutions . . . we will never get rid of deficit model thinking and discourse, unless we counter with asset-based discourse and thinking in a very explicit way" (para. 9).

For collective impact initiatives to be effective, Kania and Kramer (2011) found that the initiative needs to have a "centralized infrastructure, staff, and a structured process leading to a common agenda, shared measurement, continuous communication, and mutually reinforcing activities among all participants" (p. 38). All participants need to have a shared vision for change, one that includes a common understanding of the problem and a joint approach to solving the issue(s) through agreed upon actions. The group also needs to understand that student success is one part of a larger system; so fixing one part of the student success puzzle will not ensure success in the long run. There has to be a collective investment in understanding all aspects of the students and communities the institutions serve, including behaviors, culture, processes, laws, programs, and more. It is a complex system; no one organization, however innovative or powerful, can accomplish the agenda alone.

The collective impact participants, or institutional and community leaders, are critical to the effectiveness and sustainability of the initiative. We share the Unidos Project as an example of a flourishing collective impact initiative to illustrate how an HSI is approaching its mission with the community.

Unidos Project in Albuquerque, New Mexico

The Unidos Project in Albuquerque, New Mexico uses a collective impact model and adapted their state's culture, values, and a community organizing approach (De León, Brito-Asenap, & Gomez-Chavez, 2015). Led by team members at the University of New Mexico and a community organizer/liaison, Unidos's mission is to increase Latino student success in Albuquerque, New Mexico through community and institutional engagement. In addition, the team approaches collective impact through a familial lens. Before beginning meetings, time is provided to (re)connect with colleagues, acknowledge their work, and on many occasions, share a meal. Just as important to their work, Unidos tailors the collective partnership to New Mexico's history, using an *Acequia* model. "The *Acequia* is a centuries old irrigation water delivery system native to New Mexico that was brought from Spain and is still used in many former Spanish colonies in the Americas" (De León, Brito-Asenap, & Gomez-Chavez, 2015, p. 12).

Similar to student success, with the support from the community, water is able to flow freely throughout the *acequia*. There are four different points where the community (i.e., P-12, higher education, community-based organizations, policy makers, workforce, and advocacy organizations), also called strategy groups, come together to assure the students flow freely through their educational pathway:

> ***Abriendo La Compuerta*** (opening the gate) is a term used to describe opening the gate to allow the water to flow freely. The Opening the Gate Strategy Group's focus was on providing access and ensuring that greater numbers of students were graduating and entering postsecondary adequately prepared and could transition easily from K-12 to postsecondary.
>
> ***Aumentando La Corriente*** (increasing the flow) Strategy Group engaged in work to help students and families understand the transformational power of education. They worked to strengthen the role of caring adults through mentorship and family engagement; support more positive youth leadership devel-

opment opportunities; introduce students to careers attainable through higher education; assess and provide opportunities for students to improve their workforce skills; and continually assess the local and regional economic environment for job opportunities.

Recuperando La Corriente or reclaiming the flow, worked on bringing students back who had dropped out or stopped out to complete their High School Equivalency Diplomas or their credential or degree programs.

La Limpia is the fourth strategy and refers to a highly structured system requiring the community to come together and remove debris and other barriers from the Acequia madre (main water channel) so that water can flow freely and without obstruction. This strategy group's work entails identifying and removing institutional barriers that perpetuate disparities through inequity, exclusion and institutional racism. (De León, Brito-Asenap, & Gomez-Chavez, 2015, p. 13)

A unique trait of this collaborative work is the inclusion of a community organizer/liaison. The community liaison uses community-organizing strategies to bring together key members of the community that would be able to execute activities in each of the four strategies. Prior to identifying, which community members would participate in each strategy, the community organizer/liaison convened the community leaders to identify all of the community resources that contribute to student and community success, also known as asset mapping. More clearly described, asset mapping is a community driven process that identifies and mobilizes existing community assets (Kretzmann & McKnight, 1993). Asset Based Community Development (Kretzmann & McKnight, 1993) builds on assets already found in individuals, community organizations, and associations. Those assets are then matched with people or groups that have similar interests or goals, much like the four strategies highlighted in the acequia model.

The Unidos Project collaborates with over 80 community, policy, and institutional partners and the community-organizing model enhances and aligns with the collective impact model. Early on, the institution determined the key community leaders or influencers in and out of the institution who had experience, knowledge, and influence on the issue. To fully participate in this collective impact work, these individuals needed to relinquish their individual or organization agendas to support a collective means to the issue of student and institutional success (De León, Brito-Asenap, & Gomez-Chavez, 2015).

The Unidos Project identified five common threads for Latino student success through their community model (De León, Brito-Asenap, & Gomez-Chavez, 2015):

- **Articulate a Common Vision**—Similar to collective impact, articulating a clear common vision or agenda with measurable outcomes allowed for the opportunity to engage a diverse cadre of partners that were committed to the vision.
- **Understand Whom You Are Serving**—The population you intend to serve is important to consider, particularly in a cultural and community context. Unidos used the *Acequia* model as a pathway because it reflected their community's history and collaborative effort. In addition, they used data to amplify the need for such collective effort.
- **Identify Partners**—Partnerships develop through organic relationships and commitment to a common goal. It is critical to not force partnerships as it can cause a barrier in the flow of water through the Acequia or student success efforts.
- **Work Effectively and Collaboratively with Partners**—Unidos identified a community organizer/liaison to facilitate the strategy groups. The liaison was integral to the effort because they were a trusted member of the community. In addition, because of the liaison's familiarity with the history of the community and her previous roles throughout the community, she was able to match the strengths of the partners to the appropriate strategy group.
- **View the Community as an Asset**—Viewing the community in an asset-based perspective is important because it allows the opportunity for success and investment.
- **Scale Efforts**—At every point of success in these collaborative efforts, it is important to always ask how these efforts can be scaled. Whether it is engaging policymakers to further the message of student success through policy or engaging the workforce to invest in the community, scaling efforts can have a further reach to impact students and the community. (p.22)

Overall, the Unidos Project led a community effort engaging partners across different sectors. Rather than having a top-down partnership, community partners are able to use their strengths to improve Latino student success.

To be effective in collective impact efforts the initiative "must live with the paradox of combining intentionality and emergence" (Kania & Kramer, 2013, para. 53). The intentionality comes from the group having a shared vision and a common agenda, while emergence evolves through their collective efforts of gathering and analyzing the data, listening and learning from each other, and working together towards the shared vision.

However, collaboration does not just happen when you put people in one room or around a table. As illustrated in the Unidos Project, effective collaboration is about building trust, *confianza,* and there must be an intentional effort to build it by getting members to own their own and understand others' motivations, interests, concerns, and leadership styles (Schmitz,

2014). By committing to the individuals involved and whom they represent, it is essential for the initiative to operationalize the proposed outcomes (e.g., Latino student success, college completion, etc.) for the collective community, along with how to measure the initiative's success based on the outcomes. The proposed outcomes should be attentive to student success goals and the data needed to evaluate the goals. The group should also be motivated to evaluate how well the individuals, and the groups they represent, are working together to meet the student success goals.

HSI advocates argue for HSIs to decolonize; meaning that HSIs need to work on regenerating local knowledges, epistemologies, and ways of life (Ritskes, 2012) from a PWI. As Paulo Freire stated, "How is it possible for us to work in a community without feeling the spirit of the culture that has been there for many years, without trying to understand the soul of the culture? We cannot interfere in this culture. Without understanding the soul of the culture we just invade the culture" (Horton & Freire, 1990, p. 131).

Guiding Questions: How does our institution use Collective Impact to be a successful Latinx-Serving Institution?
- What are the assets—strengths and resources—of our community?
- Who are the essential leaders from the institution—academics, student affairs, institutional research—to be part of the advisory group?
- Whom from the community is essential (e.g., p. 12, healthcare, church, community groups)?
- How do we work together?
  - Leadership
  - Communications
  - Decision making
  - Share and learn from one another
  - Accountability
  - Transparency
- What is our agenda and goals for the 1-, 3- and 5-years?
- How do we inform, involve, and gather buy-in from members of the institution, local communities, and political leaders?

Collective impact efforts require the engagement of multiple community partners. As a part of these types of efforts, it is important to gauge the local and national contexts of students' educational pathways. The next section of the chapter will address the realities of higher education and these questions.

TODAY'S HIGHER EDUCATION REALITY

Public postsecondary education institutions are facing numerous demands, which could have unintended consequences on institutional values and principles, especially at HSIs. In the rest of this section, we illustrate the pressures or realities HSIs are encountering, including college readiness, accountability, and scarce resources. The realities we discuss are dependent on the state in which the institution is located, along with the type of degrees the institution offers, and the population the institution serves. Throughout the section, we also include some best practices and examples for collective impact initiatives to consider.

College Readiness

Policymakers are not only concerned about high school graduation rates; they are also troubled by the college readiness of high school graduates. Definitions vary on what college readiness means, and the definitions vary primarily by state. Achieve (2009), which works with many states on improving K-12 outcomes, bases college readiness on the content knowledge and skills high school graduates need to possess in English and mathematics, including, but not limited to, reading, writing communications, teamwork, critical thinking, and problem solving.

Many students are underprepared for college-level work, illustrating a disconnect between K-12 and postsecondary education. Anywhere between 28% to 40% of all first-time undergraduates enroll in at least one remedial course, and approximately 41% of Latino/a students require remediation compared to 31% of white students. Remediation for community college students surpasses the 50% mark (National Conference of State Legislatures, 2017) for the highest income group and greater than 75% of students in the lowest income group (Chen & Simone, 2016). For Latino/a students, 75% take a remedial course (Chen & Simone, 2016). This data is especially important for Hispanic-Serving community colleges because Latino/a students are more likely to attend impoverished K-12 schools with inexperienced teachers and high leadership turnover (Field, 2017).

Another aspect of college readiness are the college entrance assessment exams, ACT and SAT. Both tests have developed college and career readiness benchmarks. For college readiness, ACT assesses a student on the acquisition of the knowledge and skills needed to enroll and succeed in credit-bearing first-year courses without the need for remediation (ACT, 2017). SAT defines college-readiness similarly and both have set benchmarks to determine overall readiness.

The 2017 ACT and SAT data illustrate the inequities of K-12 education. Thirty-nine percent of all ACT test takers met the ACT College Readiness Benchmarks in at least three of the four core subject areas (English, math, reading, and science), but the majority of underserved students met only one or none of the benchmarks. Of the students who took the SAT, 46% met or exceeded the college readiness benchmarks in math, reading and writing. But, again, of the 46% of the students who met or exceeded the benchmarks, inequities exist across race and ethnicity (59% white, 31% Hispanics/Latinx, 20% blacks, and 70% Asians).

ACT recognizes that underserved students, such as Hispanic, low-income, and first-generation students, are "less likely to have access to high-quality educational and career planning and resources" (ACT, 2017, p. 1). Whereas, SAT states in its report, "It is important to note that college readiness is a continuum—students scoring below the SAT benchmarks can still be successful in college, especially with additional practice and perseverance" (SAT, 2017, para. 8). This statement, along with the college assessment tests and college course remediation data illuminates the disconnect between K-12 and higher education communities.

Hence, it is an ethical imperative for postsecondary institutions to work with its communities through collective impact initiatives for student success. Remediation is costly both for the student and the institution. Remedial students are more likely to drop out of college without a degree, and less than 50% complete remedial courses. At community colleges, less than 25% of students taking remedial classes earn a certificate or degree within eight years (NCSL, 2017).

An example of a collective impact initiative that is an integral part of the community, including K-12 and higher education is the Santa Ana Partnership. In 2011, the Santa Ana Partnership, which formed over 30 years ago, embarked on a collective impact effort through the Lumina Foundation that included their founding members, Santa Ana Unified School District, California State University Fullerton, University of California at Irvine and several community, workforce, policy, advocacy, and philanthropic partners. The partnership's main goal is to have at least one college degree/credential in each Santa Ana household (Santa Ana Partnership, 2011c). There are several components to the partnership that begin as early as kindergarten through the *kinder caminata,* an event that introduces and exposes children to college at a very young age (Lumina Foundation, 2014). As students progress through their academic pathway, they are able to sign college-going pledges at the sixth grade level, committing their intent to attend college. The middle school staff plans weekly college days and college visits. During high school, there are coordinated outreach efforts and college bound activities for students and parents led by a network of high school and outreach staff from the founding partners, Santa Ana College, CSU Fullerton, and UC Irvine (Santa Ana *Adelante,* 2011c). A critical component of the college-going process in Santa Ana is the role of parents. The Santa Ana Partnership is also home of *Padres Promotores de la Educación* (Parents Promoting Education). *Padres Promotores de la Educación* targets parents who are disconnected from their kids' learning for different reasons, such as language, immigration status, time, and/or a basic misunderstanding of the education system. As a signature initiative, the *Padres Promotores* program provides parent-to-parent counseling on topics ranging from academics to college preparation (Lumina Foundation, 2014). Both the engagement of parents and the involvement of community and institutional partners are critical in the readiness of Latino/a students.

Another example illustrating the collaboration between leaders from postsecondary education and K-12 is the Project Mentoring to Achieve Latino Educational Success (MALES) in Texas. Drs. Sáenz and Ponjuan founded Project MALES in 2010, with the goal of creating a college-going culture for young Latino males. The program targets students who will complete high school, but are unsure about attending college, and matches them to role models. The role models are current college students and include males and females. They found that some male students relate better to a female role model because their role models at home are women. The program focuses on academics, but more importantly, it focuses on the soft skills they will need to succeed in college and life. For example, Dr. Sáenz noted that the mentors focus on how Latino males can cope with failure: "Latino boys, who are traditionally given a position of privilege in the family, aren't being raised to be as resilient as Latina girls. At the first sign of failure, they tend to throw in the towel . . . they'd rather go out and be a breadwinner" (Field, 2017, para. 17).

In 2013, Project MALES expanded its reach across Texas through collaborations with two- and four-year institutions and public school districts. Embracing the philosophy of collective impact, the goals for the new Texas Education Consortium for Male Students of Color are to annually hold two Consortium meetings and a male student leadership summit; to nurture research-based, male-focused programs at each institution; and to publicize the Consortium's research and evaluation findings through a resource center and other online tools (Project MALES, n.d.).

HSIs must take their designations seriously and work with community partners and across the institution through a collective impact model to insure the achievement of K-12 and college-going Latina/o students. An article in *The Chronicle of Higher Education,* Dr. Saenz stated:

If these students don't graduate from college in higher numbers than the current crop of young Latinos, there won't be enough educated workers to fill the high-skilled jobs left vacant by retiring baby boomers. In foregoing college, young Latino men may be consigning themselves to a 'permanent underclass.' (cited in Fields, 2017, para. 12)

Guiding Questions:

- How can we learn more about our K-12 students, their lives, and their needs to be successful?
- Who are our K-12 students?
- How well are our K-12 schools doing on state and national assessments by grade level, subject, and student demographics (e.g., socioeconomic, race/ethnicity, gender)?
- How are our K-12 students being prepared for college?
- Who are our K-12 administrators and teachers?
- What are the students' classroom experiences?
- What are the students' out-of-classroom experiences and activities?
- What are the students' out-of-school experiences?
- What are the social and family support systems for these students?
- What are the economic factors that affect these students?
- What are the coping processes students use in and out of school?
- How can we collaborate with K-12 on meeting the student and school needs so the students are successful?

Student Demographics

The foundational data for any collective impact initiative are student demographics. The group must comprehend and take into consideration the students that are enrolling in their postsecondary education institutions. Today's students are diverse and their story is important to understand for collective impact initiatives to be effective. Differential enrollment growth is expected by specific student characteristics, including their age, where they are enrolling, and their type of enrollment.

In the next few pages, we provide a little insight into who these students are through the lens of traditional, nontraditional, and transfer students. The data we cite are from national databases; hence, the data provides a general picture of the students across the U.S. Collective impact groups need to work with the HSIs institutional researchers on obtaining data on their area of impact, which may be the entire state or one local district or metropolitan area.

First, however, we need to understand who our K-12 students are. The number of high school students and graduates by state has been and will continue to change over time. Many states will experience an upsurge in the number of students and graduates, but what is more important, several states will experience a transformation of whom the students are by race and ethnicity. Significant growth of high school graduates will take place in Texas, Florida, and California, and the predominant increases will be in the number of Latino/a students and graduates (Western Interstate Commission for Higher Education (WICHE), 2016). The number of Latino/a public high school graduates will increase 50% through about 2025; however, their lower than average graduation rates will impact college-going trajectories and the economy (WICHE, 2016). To provide a little more context, the percentage of Latino/a students enrolled in elementary school (grades 1 to 8) rose from 14.1% in 1996 to 25.0% in 2016, and the percentage of Latino/a high school students increased from 13.2% in 1996 to 23.7% in 2016 (Bauman, 2017).

Now, we provide a national context of who our students are and will be in postsecondary education. In 2014, 11.8 million 18- to 24-year-old students were enrolled in postsecondary institutions. This number is estimated to increase to 13.3 million by 2025. As for students 25 years or older, 8.2 million were enrolled in postsecondary institutions in 2014 and the projected number for 2025 is 9.7 million; thus, a greater than 15% increase for this age group (NCES, 2017).

More white students enroll in four-year public institutions (45.9%) than Hispanics (36.3%) and blacks (36.6%), while more Hispanics (50.8%) attend public community colleges compared to 35.6% of white and 48.5% black students (Shapiro et al., 2017, April).

The student enrollment data are revealing because it illustrates that greater than 60% attended full-time and 38% attended part-time (NCES, 2017). In following the 2010 cohort of students who enrolled in postsecondary education, the National Student Clearinghouse (NSC) found that Latino/a students mixed their enrollment status, from part-time to full-time and vice versa, over the course of six years. Sixty-three percent mixed their enrollment, while only 29% enrolled full-time. In comparison, white students enrollment over the six years (2010-2016) was 42.9% full-time and 50.9% mixed between part- and full-time status (Shapiro et al., 2017, April).

Next, we concentrate specifically on students who enrolled in postsecondary education directly out of high school (traditional) or later in life (nontraditional), and those who transfer from community colleges to four-year public universities. These demographics are significant for understanding the Latino/a communities because there are three variables that are not as transparent for Latino/a students. First, only 15% of Hispanics ages 25 to 29 have a bachelor's degree or higher. Second, approximately 50% of Hispanic undergraduate students attend two-year institutions compared to 39% of all undergraduates. And lastly, they are significantly less likely to have student debt (Krogstad, 2016).

Traditional Age Students

In 2015, 2.1 million or 69% of high school graduates enrolled directly in college. The college enrollment rate for Latino/a students increased from 49% in 2000 to 67% in 2015, while the rate for white students was at 70% in 2015 compared to 65% in 2000. However, the enrollment rate for black high school graduates stayed comparable at 56% (NCES, 2017). As for the six-year graduation rate of traditional aged students entering postsecondary education in 2009, 53.5% of Latino/a, 63.2% of white, and 40.9% of black students received a postsecondary credential (NCES, 2017).

Even though the National Center for Education Statistics (NCES) does disaggregate family income data by students' race and ethnicity, it is important to note the postsecondary institution enrollment differences by family income. The rate for traditional-aged students enrolling in two- and four-year postsecondary institutions from high-income families was 83% compared with 63% for students from middle- and low-income families (NCES, 2017).

Considering male and female enrollments, data shows that black and Hispanic males have a lower percentage of postsecondary enrollment than their female peers (WICHE, 2017). One-third or fewer Latino/a and black males between 18 and 24 years of age are enrolled in postsecondary education in recent years. And once enrolled, Latino/a and black males are 8 to 10% less likely to attain a bachelor's degree within six years than their female counterparts, and 9% to 10% less likely to attain an associate's degree or certificate. This is important to note because these populations' postsecondary completion rates are already significantly below the national average. Black and Latino/a 18- to 24-year-old males are also disproportionately more likely to be incarcerated than the general population, further impacting their educational and labor force opportunities and contributions (WICHE, 2017).

Nontraditional Students

The number of students 25 and older enrolled in postsecondary institutions is estimated to increase by at least 15% by 2025. The percentage of part-time students is also projected to increase 16% between 2014 and 2025 from 7.8 million to 9.0 million (NCES, 2017).

Guiding Questions:
- Who are our traditional students?
- How many credits do our traditional students enroll in each semester and overtime?
- How well are our students—socioeconomic, race/ethnicity, gender—doing in their first-year courses? Developmental education courses?
- How well do we make them feel part of the institution? What is the institutional climate for our students?
- Is there a "sophomore slump"? If so, why?
- What are the cultural context and family expectations that should be considered?
- What are the students' classroom experiences?
- What are the students' out of classroom experiences and activities?
- What are the students' out of school experiences?
- What are the social and family support systems for these students?
- What are the economic factors that affect these students?
- What are the coping processes students use in and out of school?
- What other supports can we provide, in- and out-of-class, for our students to feel part of the institution and be successful?

In considering the increased enrollments, the most important attribute is the enrollment of students 25 years and older students by race/ethnicity. The percentage of Latino/a students is projected to increase 32% (3.2 million in 2014 and 4.2 million in 2025) and students who are two or more races is estimated to increase 37% (642,000 in 2014 and 880,000 in 2025). This is compared to 3% and 22% increase for white and black students, respectively (NCES, 2017).

The increase in the number of Latino/a students is important to note because 33% of Hispanics 25 years and older have not completed high school and only 15.5% have at least a bachelor's degree (HACU, 2017). Research denotes that Latino/a students primarily attend community colleges, enroll part-time, and attend later in life. A significant portion will also need remediation in one or more subjects, specifically math, reading, and writing (HACU, 2017).

Accordingly, many of our Latinos/as students are considered nontraditional based on a definition by National Association of Orientation, Transfer, and Retention (NODA, 2017). We have already revealed that students who are 25 years and older or attend part-time are nontraditional students. Other attributes of a nontraditional student include (one or more demographics):

- attends part-time
- pursues a nondegree
- is a readmit or stopped out and re-entered
- is a commuter
- is a veteran
- is an adult learner (25 years and over)
- is learning online or by distance
- is working full-time while enrolled
- has dependents other than a spouse/partner
- does not have a high school diploma (completed a GED or equivalent or did not finish high school)

The data shows that nontraditional students have lower postsecondary education completion rates than traditional students. Thirty-three percent of Latino/a students 25 years or older received a degree within six years, while 41.9% of white students 25 years or older accomplished the same goal. For nontraditional aged Latino/a students (the other 67%), 54.0% were not enrolled and 13.2% were still enrolled after six years. In comparison, 48.9% of nontraditional aged white students were not enrolled and 9.1% were still enrolled after six years (NCES, 2017). The reasons for lower attainment rates include amount of time to degree by attending part-time, financial resources, and academic preparedness (Shapiro et al., 2013).

Research studies have also found that nontraditional students have different needs, such as course offering flexibility, more course offerings in their major, and multiple options for financial aid and billing (Ruffalo Noel Levitz, 2017). With nontraditional students' needs and barriers in mind, collective impact initiatives should research, discuss and implement practices that will aid students with completing their degrees. Education Commission of the States (ECS, 2016) provides a few recommendations for postsecondary education institutions:

- Restructure financial aid policies for equity across students
- Provide multiple avenues to award credit, such as prior learning assessments, competency-based education, and online courses
- Require student supports at institutions, such as advising
- Create degree maps or guided pathways
- Offer courses in multiple formats and days/times

In light of this growing student population, states have introduced or enacted legislation providing student supports for adults. For example, in 2012, Florida enacted a bill, which included a program to recruit, recover, and retain adult learners. This bill also established the Florida Virtual Campus to provide access to online student and library support services. Its success has evolved to the Complete Florida initiative, offering a virtual campus; thus, providing "students with the freedom to learn, to dream, to achieve their goals" (Complete Florida, 2013, para. 1).

Guiding Questions:
- Who are our nontraditional students?
- How well are our nontraditional students doing in their courses (based on the nontraditional student variables)? Remedial courses?
- How can we learn more about our nontraditional students, their lives, and their needs to be successful?
- What communities and schools do our nontraditional students come from?
- How well are the nontraditional students prepared for college?
- What are the cultural context and family expectations that should be considered?
- How well do we make them feel part of the institution? What is the institutional climate for nontraditional students?
- What are these students' classroom experiences?
- What are these students' out-of-classroom experiences and activities?
- What are these students' out-of-school experiences?
- What are the social and family support systems for these students?
- What are the economic factors that affect these students?
- What are the coping processes students use in and out of school?
- What other supports can we provide, in- and out-of-class, for our students to feel part of the institution and be successful?
- How can we collaborate with community organizations, etc., on nontraditional student success?

Transfer Students

More than 80% of community college students desire a bachelor's degree (Collins, 2017). While these students indicate they want to earn a bachelor's degree or higher, only 33% of these students transfer to a four-year institution within six years (Jenkins & Fink, 2016). And of the 33% of the community college students who transfer to a four-year institution, only 42% complete a bachelor's degree within six years. In considering the entire cohort enrolling in a community college, only 14% earn a bachelor's degree (Jenkins & Fink, 2016).

A key indicator of success is whether or not a student is enrolled full- or part-time. In 2015-16, nine million undergraduates were enrolled in community colleges and of those nine million students; over five million were enrolled part-time (NCES, 2017). Research indicates that transfer students who enrolled full-time were 80% more likely to attain a bachelor's degree six years after transfer. However, only 55% of students who mixed their enrollment between part- and full-time and 25% of students who enrolled exclusively part-time attained a bachelor's degree (Shapiro et al., 2013).

Enrollments of Latino/a students at two-year institutions are high; however, the rate of transfer to four-year institutions is low (NCES, 2015). And for those who transfer to a four-year institution, the percentage receiving a bachelor's degree range from 45% for high socioeconomic status to 36% for lower socioeconomic status (Shapiro et al., 2017, September). Transfer students are a vital part of the HSIs' mission and culture, meaning that the institution provides a sense of belonging and helps the students recognize success through their educational development.

With the pressure to increase human capital, many institutions and states have realized that they need to gain a better understanding for why students are not transferring to pursue a four-year degree and why those who do transfer do not complete their bachelor's degree. As stated in the NSC report, "Far from achieving its promise, the transfer process ends up wasting student and taxpayer resources. Worse, it stifles human potential" (Shapiro et al., 2017, September, p. 1). Collective impact initiatives need to have a comprehensive understanding of the policies, practices, and culture for successful transfer and completion. Researchers have identified challenges in the student transfer process, and best practices have been developed by several national centers and organizations (Community College Research Center (CCRC) at Teachers College, Jobs for the Future, and National Student Clearinghouse). A few examples include:

- **Advising.** Advising is critical at community colleges. In today's world, advising is not only helping a student register for classes; advising is helping students find their career goals, what program (2-year and 4-year transfer) works best to meet or align with their goals, help them work through issues that non-traditional or first-generation students may encounter, work through financial resources necessary to meet their goals, and discuss employment opportunities (Collins, 2017).

Institutions should create monitoring functions and utilize advisers to provide frequent feedback and intervene when appropriate (Shapiro et al., 2017c). Two other practices include having (1) advisers from 4-year universities be located on community college campuses and available virtually, and (2) dedicated advisers for transfer students.

- **Transfer articulation agreements.** Articulation agreements are formal transfer agreements that can originate at the state level or between a two- and four-year institution. The agreement documents the transfer policies for a specific academic program or bachelor's degree (ECS, 2014).
- **College pathways.** Community colleges develop clear programmatic pathways for degree programs so students know the specific courses they need to take and when. Four-year institutions should work with its feeder community colleges to create major-specific program maps for students' successful transfer and completion (Bailey, Smith, Jaggars, & Jenkins, 2015).
- **Financial aid.** Analyze and be equitable in offering transfer students financial aid (Shapiro et al., 2017c).

Santa Ana Partnership and College Access and Success

College readiness is a mere fraction of what the Santa Ana Partnership does for the community. Through participation in Santa Ana *¡Adelante!*, students who graduate from a Santa Ana Unified School District (SAUSD), enroll at Santa Ana College (a two-year public institution), and complete all academic and transfer requirements, will be admitted to its partner four-year institutions, UC Irvine or CSU Fullerton (*Excelencia in Education,* 2016). In addition, *¡Adelante!* pays for SAUSD graduates' first year of college and provides them a laptop for their studies at Santa Ana College. High school graduates who choose to participate in *¡Adelante!* sign a pledge to complete components of the program that include:

- Attending one Santa Ana *¡Adelante!* Transfer Orientation
- Completing an educational plan during the first semester
- Enroll in a minimum of 12 college units each semester
- Submit financial aid and scholarship documents each year
- Participate in college fairs, university field trips, and other transfer activities whenever possible
- Participate in tutoring & support services as needed
- Make a transfer plan appointment—fall of second year of enrollment
- Apply for participation in the Mentor Program the year before transferring to the University

- Apply to university one year in advance to transferring (Santa Ana *Adelante,* 2011b)

Overall, Santa Ana *¡Adelante!* has had several successful outcomes through its coordination with the Santa Ana Partnership and has been acknowledged for its work through *Excelencia in Education's Growing What Works Database* (2016). Some of these outcomes include: a 74% increase in FAFSA completion from 2011 to 2015; during the same timeframe, a 78% increase in the number of associate degrees, certificates, and transfers; and in the last four years, 323 *¡Adelante!* students have transferred to partner institutions (*Excelencia in Education,* 2016).

Guiding Questions:
- Who are our transfer students by demographic characteristics?
- When are they transferring to our institution (e.g., number of credits, degree)?
- What is the process they go through to transfer to our institution?
- How do they feel about navigating the process?
- How well are our nontraditional students doing in their courses?
- How can we learn more about our transfer students, their lives, and their needs to be successful?
- What communities and schools do our transfer students come from?
- How well are the transfer students prepared for a four-year institution?
- What are the cultural context and family expectations that should be considered
- How well do we make them feel part of the institution? What is the institutional climate for transfer students?
- What are these students' classroom experiences?
- What are these students' out-of-classroom experiences and activities?
- What are these students' out-of-school experiences?
- What are the social and family support systems for these students?
- What are the economic factors that affect these students?
- What are the coping processes students use in and out of school?
- What other supports can we provide, in- and out-of-class, for our students to feel part of the institution and be successful?
- How can we collaborate with community organizations, etc., on nontraditional student success?

Accountability

The tension between state policymakers and higher education leaders increased during the recession. Policymakers realized the need for increased human capital for economic development in the states, and along with lower appropriations, started implementing various accountability measures on public higher education institutions (Jones, 2014, Miao, 2012). Public higher education leaders, who were not used to accountability measures, argued for increased appropriations, which could offset rising tuition costs and the need for specialized programs to help students succeed. Several state legislative bodies implemented dashboards or performance funding for accountability and transparency of public higher education institutions (Doughtery et al., 2016; Jones, 2014; Miao, 2012). As discussed further in the next few pages, the dashboards or funding formulas vary by state, and in some states, the institution's mission or student population that it serves is considered in the equation for success and increased appropriations (NCSL, 2015; Tandberg & Hillman, 2014).

College Dashboards

The overarching political reality causing stress and apprehension for HSIs is accountability and transparency. In today's world, students are understood to be consumers, purchasing a degree for a job (Martinez-Saenz & Schoonover, 2014). Or in other words, students are part of the political agenda to increase human capital. Each student is a number as shown on an institution's profile or scorecard, or federal or state government's dashboard. These profiles illustrate how well an institution is doing in such areas as undergraduate access, retention, financial aid, and persistence. We provide two examples of web-based dashboards, both painting pictures of who is attending a specific institution in aggregate (or compare institutions) by different accountability metrics, such as percentage of students by gender and race/ethnicity, retention and graduation rates, average costs and financial aid, and average salaries and debt after graduation.

The scorecards or profiles were created to make institutions more accountable to its constituents and for institutions to be transparent, especially regarding costs and financial aid. One can learn about the students who attend the institution, such as the racial, ethnic and socioeconomic diversity of the student body and the average financial aid received by students, including student loan debt and future average earnings. The primary issue is that the scorecard paints a generic picture of the institution and its students, and the word "scorecard" also suggests a competition of institutions within a market-driven economy.

U.S. Department of Education's College Scorecard: In President Obama's 2013 State of the Union address, he stated that the administration would release a College Scorecard for families and students can compare and learn about postsecondary education institutions based on specific criteria (Duncan, 2013).

https://collegescorecard.ed.gov/

Education Trust's College Results Online (CRO): The CRO database allows users to learn about high-performing institutions and compare institutions based on graduation rates, net price, and other pertinent information (Ed Trust, 2018).

http://www.collegeresults.org

Institution administrators and policymakers need to be cognizant that single or aggregated variables do not paint a genuine picture or provide a realistic explanation for what is occurring at an HSI. The data from the profiles or scorecards are examples of where collective impact initiatives can begin; to understand the data that is being reported to the public and how well the institutions are doing according to the stated accountability metrics.

Outcomes-Based Funding

One factor that further exacerbates the funding issues are that HSIs are significantly underfunded. HSIs largest revenue sources are federal, state, and local funding. Revenue from private giving and endowments represented a smaller percentage of revenue raised by HSIs than revenue raised at other institutions (Nellum & Valle, 2015). The revenues hide per-student inequities at HSIs due to the communities the HSI resides in and the students it serves, resulting in dependence on federal and state support. This dependency makes HSIs vulnerable to the economy and government investment in higher education.

Change in higher education is usually slow due to the governance structures, and with scarce resources at the state level and the pressing need for an educated citizenry, many state policymakers have realized the need to change the public higher education funding formula from input to outcome (Jones, 2014). More than 30 states utilize performance funding for higher education and several more are seriously considering it (Doughtery et al., 2016). As few examples of states providing incentive funding include Florida, Indiana, Ohio, Oklahoma, Pennsylvania, Tennessee, and Washington. These states provide incentive funding based on performance or outcome indicators such as course completion, time to degree, transfer rates, the number of degrees awarded, or the number of low-income and minority graduates (NCSL, 2015).

As stated earlier, Florida is one of five states with the majority of HSIs, and its State University System of Florida implemented performance-based funding in the 2014–15 academic year. The development of the metrics began in the fall of 2012 and included university presidents, provosts, boards of trustees, and other stakeholders. Ten metrics, or outcomes, were created in several different areas, such as academic progress, completion, and post-baccalaureate employment and wages (see Table 8.2). Like the web-based dashboards, state governments or systems offices are transparent with the funding by providing web-based information on which institutions are doing well and receiving more funding and those institutions that are lagging and not receiving full or partial funding (State University System of Florida example: http://www.flbog.edu/board/office/budget/).

Many institutions across the nation are implementing student success strategies to increase college completion and to assure that they are doing the best they can to progress and grow, particularly along different performance metrics. Some of the strategies include redesigning bottleneck courses where students are not succeeding in a timely fashion. These courses are the prerequisites to other courses, and usually involve large enrollments with little support and concerns about pedagogical rigor (Education Advisory Board (EAB), 2010).

Other student success strategies include monitoring the number of credits students are accumulating along their pathway that may impact their time to degree. For example, Florida International University (FIU) has been successful in their efforts to redesign math courses, like algebra. In 2009, the passing percentage rates among students enrolled in algebra were 30%; how-

Table 8.2

STATE UNIVERSITY SYSTEM OF FLORIDA PERFORMANCE-FUNDING METRICS

1. Percent of Bachelor's Graduates Employed (Earning $25,000+) or Continuing their Education
2. Median Wages of Bachelor's Graduates Employed Full-time
3. Average Cost to the Student (Net Tuition per 120 Credit Hours)
4. Six Year Graduation Rate (Full-time and Part-time FTIC)
5. Academic Progress Rate (2nd Year Retention with GPA Above 2.0)
6. Bachelor's Degrees Awarded in Areas of Strategic Emphasis
7. University Access Rate (Percent of Undergraduates with a Pell-grant)
8. a. Graduate Degrees Awarded in Areas of Strategic Emphasis
8. b. Freshman in Top 10% of Graduating High School Class—for NCF only
9. Board of Governors Choice - Percent of Bachelor's Degrees without Excess Hours
10. Board of Trustees Choice

ever, through redesigning the course, the passing percentage rate skyrocketed to 69% in 2015. From an institutional perspective, shifts in the way courses are taught and redesigned take an immense amount of commitment and buy-in from faculty and administrators. The intentionality behind course redesign has positively contributed to the academic progress that the performance-based metrics call for in Florida.

Another way FIU is addressing progress in its performance metrics is through providing more attention to career education. Between the 2013-2014 and 2014-2015 academic years, the university experienced a 0.3 percentage point change, from 68.6% to 69% in the percent employed or enrolled one year after graduation. However, during that same timeframe, the greatest gains were found in the median wages of bachelor's graduates employed full-time one year after graduation that increased 3.7 percentage points from $37,400 to $38,800 (FIU Board of Governors Annual Report, 2016). In general, career education is housed in a student affairs division; however, there is a movement in higher education where career education is moving toward the auspices of academic affairs. The intent is to infuse career education as soon as students step onto campus and begin their educational pathway. This prevents the transactional relationship of reviewing resumes and job searching toward the end of the students' tenure at the institution.

We close this section stating that outcome-based state funding formulas should reward institutions that serve the students they are intended to serve. With the abundance of data on the students, the communities they come from, and program success, there is a need to tailor accountability and funding formulas to institutional missions and the students the institution serves as opposed to the one-size-fits all data dashboard or funding formulas (Abdul-Alim, 2017).

Guiding Questions:
1. How much state support is allocated to performance-based funding?
2. What is the political context at the federal and state level? How is it shaping the response on campus?
3. How does state performance-based funding impact institutions that serve Latinos/a students?
4. How equitable are the funding metrics across state institutions?
5. What metrics are missing that are important to HSIs?
6. Does the funding and metrics affect who the institution serves?
7. Within the current political and social environment, is the institution serving the community and fulfilling its needs?

Scarce Resources

State Funding

While increasing higher education attainment continues to be a priority of state governors and legislatures, the state fiscal landscape has changed dramatically in recent years. Even with a recovering economy, the fiscal environment for state higher education support is expected to be very different and much more constrained compared to past decades. State expenditures and revenues are growing, but more slowly than they have in past economic recoveries. It is a trend that is expected to persist, of which, many analysts are calling the "new normal" (Doyle & Delaney, 2009). As revenues grow slowly, the demand for funding continues to rise in a number of high-priority program areas, such as Medicaid and infrastructure. As a result, competition for state funds for public postsecondary education institutions will continue to be stifled, leaving support for these institutions' funding unalterably different from the past (NACUBO, 2013). This statement is especially important with the implementation of performance-funding in many of the states.

Public postsecondary education institution leaders have experienced fluctuating state support over time based on state tax income, which political party is in charge, and other competing state budget items. Overall, appropriations have increased over time, but average public postsecondary education appropriations support per student has not kept up with the increasing number of postsecondary students enrolled, pensions, healthcare costs, salaries, and specialized programs. These different factors impact tuition and financial aid. It is generally understood that state funding for higher education acts as the "balance wheel" during economic downturns with funding reductions typically greater than reductions in other budget areas. In part, this is because higher education funding reductions can be offset (in whole or in part) with money from tuition increases (NACUBO, 2013).

Tuition

Students often look at the published tuition and fees for a postsecondary institution as an indicator of affordability. However, they need to include room and board, books and supplies, transportation, and other living expenses. What students pay is the net price; the full cost of attendance minus expected financial aid (TICAS, 2015). In 2017, the average student debt was over $27,000 and it varied significantly by state (www.debt.org) due to state commitment or appropriations to postsecondary education.

Debt is also cultural, and Latino/a students are significantly less likely to have student debt (Krogstad, 2016). And for many students and their families, it is difficult to understand why tuition continues to increase and how to pay for college. Students and families are caught in the crossfire between state appropriations, college financing, financial aid, state performance accountability measures, colleges' responses to state performance accountability measures (e.g., new programs and resources), and their own financial resources.

Federal Funding

Approximately half of the Latino/a undergraduate students attend two-year institutions (Nellum & Valle, 2015) and HSIs primarily serve students who need remediation and embedded support to persist and graduate. HSIs primarily rely on federal, state, and local revenue sources, and the shares of revenue from federal and state sources were lower than at PWIs (Nellum & Valle, 2015). HSIs also have limited ability to raise tuition due to the financial backgrounds and the culture of the Latino/a population the institution serves. Therefore, revenue is critical to an HSIs success and sustainability (García & Taylor, 2017); however, factoring only federal funding, HSIs receive less than 70 cents for every dollar going to all other institutions, per student (HACU, 2017). This is critical to acknowledge because federal investment has also been decreasing due to the increasing number of HSIs competing for federal funding (Nellum & Valle, 2015).

The 1998 reauthorization of the Higher Education Act (HEA) was amended to include Title V, Part A for HSIs (Nellum & Valle, 2015). The Federal Developing Hispanic Serving Institution was enacted to provide more equitable funding to HSIs by providing grants to expand educational opportunities for, and improve the education attainment of Latino/a students (Nellum & Valle, 2015). The grants enable HSIs to "expand and enhance the academic offerings, program quality, faculty quality, and institutional stability" of HSIs (U.S. Department of Education, 2017, Purpose). In 2017, one of the new Title V competitive preference priorities focused on developing and enhancing articulation agreements and/or support programs to facilitate successful transfer from two-year to four-year institutions (U.S. Department of Education, 2017).

As previously mentioned, due to the increasing number of HSIs and enrollment growth in HSIs, Title V has not been able to keep pace with these increases. For example, in fiscal year 2010, HSIs received over $116 million in Title V new and continuing development and cooperative grants, but by 2015, HSIs received approximately $100 million (US Department of Education, 2017). The decline in available funding is likely to continue, intensifying funding inequities across public postsecondary institutions (Nellum & Valle, 2015), forcing HSIs to provide educational programming with limited resources, which can impact student success (Malcom, Bensimon, & Dávila, 2010).

Guiding Questions:
1. What is the state political and fiscal environment and how does it affect our institution's appropriations?
2. Where are Title V funds being spent at our institution?
3. With the competitiveness of Title V funding, what other resources are allocated to serving Latino/a students?
4. With limited resources, how does the institution underwrite programs that serve Latino/a students?
5. How do we engage with the community to support our student success efforts?

Conclusion

Despite the realities facing HSIs, HSIs can contribute significantly to the economic success of its community and state by collectively and intentionally working with its internal and external stakeholders. It is not easy work, especially transforming a PWI culture that is steeped in tradition and rules, but it can be done through collective impact initiatives; thus, shepherding the HSI towards meeting its mission and vision.

To be successful, HSIs must listen and build empathy with the people it serving. The institution must do this within the context of the political agenda and not allow the political agenda to set a precedent for the effort. Large-scale social or institutional change success has to come from better collective efforts and coordination rather than from isolated interventions.

> To succeed long-term, there must be more attention paid to the culture. Culture is created through shared values, expectations, and goals. These must be built intentionally, transparently, and evolve with the project. Collective impact efforts that focus on building an effective culture will achieve greater and more enduring change. (Schmitz, 2014, para. 24)

This is especially true for HSIs, whose "identity is socially constructed through both institutional and cultural perspectives" (García, 2017, p. 126S).

> *We are paradigms of our own values, advertisements of our own ethics.*
> Toni Morrison (as cited in Schwartz, 2002, p. 4)

REFERENCES

Abdul-Alim, J. (2017, October 10). Spellings: Affordability is families' No. 1 concern regarding college. *Diverse Education.* Retrieved from http://diverseeducation .com/article/102880/

Achieve, Inc. (2009). *What is college- and career-ready?* Retrieved from https://www .achieve.org/what-college-and-career-ready

ACT (2017). *The condition of college and career readiness 2017.* Retrieved from http://www.act.org/content/act/en/research/condition-of-college-and-career -readiness-2017.html

Bailey, T., Smith Jaggars, S., & Jenkins, D. (2015, April). What we know about guided pathways. Retrieved from https://ccrc.tc.columbia.edu/publications/what -we-know-about-guided-pathways-packet.html

Baldwin, C., Bensimon, E. M., Dowd, A. C., & Kleiman, L., (2011). Measure student success. *Special Issues: Institutional Effectiveness, New Directions for Community Colleges,* no. 153, pp. 75–88.

Bauman, K. (2017, August 28). School enrollment of the Hispanic population: Two decades of growth. *U.S. Census Blog.* Retrieved from https://www.census.gov /newsroom/blogs/random-samplings/2017/08/school_enrollmentof.html

Carnevale, A., & Strohl, J. (2010). How increasing college access is increasing inequality. *Rewarding strivers: Helping low-income students success in college. Center of education and the workforce,* Washington, DC: Georgetown University:. https://www.luminafoundation.org/resources/how-increasing-college-access-is -increasing-inequality

Chen, X., & Simone, S., (2016, September). Remedial Coursetaking at U.S. Public 2- and 4-Year Institutions: Scope, Experiences, and Outcomes. Statistical Analysis Report. National Center for Education Statistics, U.S. Department of Education. Retrieved from https://nces.ed.gov/pubs2016/2016405.pdf

Colby, S. L., & Ortman, J. M., (2015, March). Projections of the size and composition of the U.S. Population: 2014 to 2060 population estimates and projections current population. *Current Population Reports,* U.S. Census Bureau. Retrieved from https://www.census.gov/content/dam/Census/library/publications/2015 /demo/p25-1143.pdf

Collins, M. L., (2017, August 1). Maximizing mobility. *Inside Higher Education.* Retrieved from https://www.insidehighered.com/views/2017/08/01/new-data -can-help-increase-low-income-students-economic-mobility-essay

Complete College America (CCA). (2012). Retrieved from http://www.complete college.org/about/

Complete Florida. (2013). Retrieved from https://www.completeflorida.org/about-us

De León, J., Brito-Asenap, T., & Gomez-Chavez, J. (2015). *Community organizing on behalf of Latino student success: A case study of the Unidos Project in New Mexico.* Washington, D.C.: Excelencia in Education.

De Vise, Daniel. (2012, May 16). College accountability: A closer look. *Washington Post.* Retrieved from https://www.washingtonpost.com/blogs/college-inc/post /college-accountability-a-closer-look/2012/03/16/gIQAECG7GS_blog.html ?utm_term=.3f9c4502e907

Doughtery, K. J., Jones, S. M., Lahr, H., Natow, R. S., Pheatt, L., & Reddy, V. (2016). *Performance Funding for Higher Education.* Baltimore: John Hopkins Press.

Doyle, W. R., & Delaney, J. A., (2009, July-August). Higher education funding: The new normal. *Change: The Magazine of Higher Learning, 41*(4), 60–62.

Duncan, A. (2013, February 13). *Obama Administration launches college scorecard.* Retrieved from https://obamawhitehouse.archives.gov/blog/2013/02/13/obama -administration-launches-college-scorecard

Educational Advisory Board (EAB). (2016). *Promoting timely degree completion: Reconciling student choice and the four-year graduation imperative.* Retrieved from http://enrollmentmanagement.oregonstate.edu/sites/enrollmentmanagement.o regonstate.edu/files/promoting_timely_degree_completion.pdf

Education Commission of the States. (2016, August 3). *27 is the new 18: Adult students on the rise.* https://www.ecs.org/27-is-the-new-18-adult-students-on-the-rise/

Education Commission of the States. (2014, May). *Transfer and articulation–All state profiles.* Retrieved from http://ecs.force.com/mbdata/mbprofallRT?Rep =TA14A

Excelencia in Education. (2016). *Growing what works database* [Santa Ana ¡Adelante!]. Retrieved from: http://www.edexcelencia.org/program/santa-ana-%C2 %A1adelante

Excelencia in Education. (2017). *Hispanic serving institutions.* Retrieved from https: //www.edexcelencia.org/research/hispanic-serving-institutions-hsis

Field, K. (2017, July 2). Building Latino male achievement. *The Chronicle of Higher Education.* Retrieved from https://www.chronicle.com/article/Building-Latino-Male/240474

Florida International University (FIU). (2016). *2015–2016 Annual accountability report: Florida International University.* Retrieved from https://aim.fiu.edu/BOG/FIU _2016_Annual_Report.pdf

García, A. G. (2017a). Decolonizing Hispanic-serving institutions (HSIs): A frame-work for organizing, *Journal of Hispanic Higher Education,* 1–16. DOI: 10.1177/1538192717734289

García, A. G. (2017b, April). Defined by outcomes or culture? Constructing an orga-nizational identity for Hispanic-Serving Institutions, *American Educational Research Journal 54*(1S), 111S–134S. DOI: 10.3102/00028312166669779.

García, A. G., & Taylor, M. (2017, September 18). A closer look at Hispanic-Serving Institutions. *Higher education today: A blog by American Council on Education.* Retrieved from https://www.higheredtoday.org

Hispanic Association of Colleges and Universities. (2017). *2017 Fact sheet: Hispanic higher education and HSIs.* Retrieved from https://www.hacu.net/images/hacu /OPAI/2017_HSI_FactSheet.pdf

Horton, M., & Freire, P. (1990). *We make the road by walking.* Philadelphia: Temple University Press.

Hurtado, S., Alvarez, C., Guillermo-Wann, C., Cuellar, M., & Arellano, L. (2012). A model for diverse learning environments: The scholarship on creating and assessing conditions for student success. In M. B. Paulsen (Ed.), *Higher education: Handbook of theory and research, 27,* 41–122. New York, NY: Springer.

Jenkins, D., & Fink, J. (2016, January). Tracking transfer new measures of institutional and state effectiveness in helping community college students attain bachelor's degrees. Community College Research Center, Teachers College, Columbia University. Retrieved from https://ccrc.tc.columbia.edu/media/k2/attachments/tracking-transfer-institutional-state-effectiveness.pdf

Jones, D. (2014, July/August). The unanswered question: How will we pay for aggressive attainment goals? *Change: The Magazine of Higher Learning*, 16–25.

Kania, J., & Kramer, M. (2011, Winter). Collective impact. *Stanford Social Innovation Review: Informing and Inspiring Leaders of Social Change*. Retrieved from https://ssir.org/articles/entry/collective_impact

Kania, J., & Kramer, M. (2013, January 21). Embracing emergence: How collective impact addresses complexity. *Stanford Social Innovation Review: Informing and Inspiring Leaders of Social Change*. Retrieved from https://ssir.org/articles/entry/embracing_emergence_how_collective_impact_addresses_complexity

Kretzmann, J. P., & McKnight, J. L. (1993). *Building communities from the inside out: A path toward finding and mobilizing a community's assets*. Evanston, IL: Institute for Policy Research.

Krogstad, J. M. (2016, July 28). 5 facts about Latinos and education. *FastTank: News in the Numbers*. Pew Research Center. Retrieved from http://www.pewresearch.org/fact-tank/2016/07/28/5-facts-about-latinos-and-education/

Lumina Foundation. (2014). *Lumina Foundation Focus*. Retrieved from http://focus.luminafoundation.org/archives/summer2014/

Malcom, L. E., Bensimon, E. M., and Dávila, B. (2010, Winter). (Re)Constructing Hispanic-serving institutions: Moving beyond numbers toward student success. *EP3: Education, Policy and Practice Perspectives*. Retrieved from https://cue.usc.edu/files/2016/01/CUE-policy-brief_Malcom_Bensimon_Davila_Reconstructing-HSIs.pdf

Martinez-Saenz, M., & Schoover, S., Jr. (2014, November-December). Resisting the "student-as-consumer" metaphor, *Academe, 100*(6). Retrieved from https://www.aaup.org/article/resisting-student-consumer-metaphor#.Wm0XOojwY2w

Miao, K. (2012, August 7). *Performance-based funding of higher education*. Center for American Progress. Retrieved from https://www.americanprogress.org/issues/education-postsecondary/reports/2012/08/07/12036/performance-based-funding-of-higher-education/

Monreal, T. (2015, August 15). From a Teacher Blog. Retrieved from https://medium.com/from-a-teacher/8-quotes-of-education-wisdom-from-paulo-freire-s-pedagogy-of-the-oppressed-1cc5891bcfc5

Morfin, O. J., Perez, V. H., Parker, L., Lynn, M., & Arrona, J. (2006). Hiding the politically obvious: A critical race theory preview of diversity as racial neutrality in higher education, *Educational Policy, 20*(1), 249–270.

Morris, C. (2017, October 8). Accelerating Latino Success in Postsecondary Education is Focus of *Excelencia*. Obtained from http://diverseeducation.com/article/102728/?utm_campaign=DIV1710%20DAILY%20NEWSLETTER%20OCT9&utm_medium=email&utm_source=Eloqua

Myers, D. (2007). *Immigrants and boomers: Forging a new social contract for the ruture of America*. New York: Russell Sage.

National Association for Orientation, Transfer, and Retention in Higher Education (NODA). (n.d.). *Nontraditoinal Student Populations.* Retrieved from http://www .nodaweb.org/?page=network_non_trad

National Association of State Budget Officers (NASBO). (2013, May 15). *Financing Higher Education: The Need for a New Approach.* Retrieved from https://higher logicdownload.s3.amazonaws.com/NASBO/0f09ced0-449d-4c11-b787-10505 cd90bb9/UploadedImages/Issue%20Briefs%20/Financing%20Higher%20 Education-The%20Need%20for%20a%20New%20Approach.pdf

National Center for Education Statistics. (2017, March). Immediate college enrollment rates. *The Condition of Higher Education.* Retrieved from https://nces.ed.gov /programs/coe/indicator_cpa.asp

National Conference of State Legislators. (2015). *Performance-based funding for higher education.* Retrieved from http://www.ncsl.org/research/education/performance-funding.aspx

National Conference of State Legislators. (2017). *Reforming remedial education.* Obtained at http://www.ncsl.org/research/education/improving-college-completion -reforming-remedial.aspx

Nellum, C. J., & Valle, K. (2015, September). Government investment in public Hispanic-Serving Institutions. *American Council on Education Center for Policy Research and Strategy Issue Brief: Minority-Serving Institution Series.* Retrieved from http://www.acenet.edu/news-room/Documents/Government-Investment-in -Public-Hispanic-Serving-Institutions.pdf

Nuñez, A., Crisp, G., & Elizondo, D. (2016, January/February). Mapping Hispanic-serving institutions: A typology of institutional diversity. *The Journal of Higher Education, 87*(1), pp. 55–83.

Oxford Dictionary. (n.d.). Ethics definition. Retrieved from https://en.oxford dictionaries.com/definition/ethics

Patton, L. D., McEwen, M., Rendon, L., & Howard-Hamilton, M. F. (2007). Critical race perceptives on theory in student affairs. *Responding to the Realities of Race on Campus,* New Directions for Student Services, no. 120, pp. 39–53.

Project MALES. (n.d.). *Project males: Mentoring to achieve Latino educational success.* Retrieved from http://diversity.utexas.edu/projectmales/

Ritskes, E. (2012, September 21). What is decolonization and why does it matter? *Intercontinental Cry.* Center for World Indigenous Studies. Retrieved from https: //intercontinentalcry.org/what-is-decolonization-and-why-does-it-matter/

Ruffalo Noel Levitz. (2017). *Effective practices report for student success, retention, and completion.* Retrieved from http://learn.ruffalonl.com/rs/395-EOG-977/images /Student_Success_Report_1.0.pdf

Santa Ana *Adelante.* (2011a). *Santa Ana ¡Adelante! Partnership pledge.* Retrieved from https://sac.edu/StudentServices/SantaAnaAdelante/Documents/Partnership %20Pledge%20Revised.pdf

Santa Ana *Adelante.* (2011b). *Santa Ana ¡Adelante! College completion pledge.* Retrieved from https://www.sac.edu/StudentServices/SantaAnaAdelante/Documents /College%20Completion%20Pledge.pdf

Santa Ana Partnership. (2011c). *Santa Ana ¡Adelante! Latino student success grant.* Retrieved from https://sac.edu/Accreditation/2014SelfEval/IIID_Evidence /IIID-27.LuminaDocuments.pdf

SAT. (2017). *Class of 2017 SAT Results.* Retrieved from https://reports.college-board.org/sat-suite-program-results/class-2017-results

Shapiro, D., Dundar, A., Ziskin, M., Chiang, Y., Chen, J., Harrell, A., & Torres, V. (2013, July). *Baccalaureate attainment: A national view of the postsecondary outcomes of students who transfer from two-year to four-year institutions (Signature Report No. 5).* Herndon, VA: National Student Clearinghouse Research Center.

Shapiro, D., Dundar, A., Huie, F., Wakhungu, P., Yuan, X., Nathan, A., & Hwang, Y. W. (2017, September). *Tracking transfer: Measures of effectiveness in helping community college students to complete bachelor's eegrees (Signature Report No. 13).* Herndon, VA: National Student Clearinghouse Research Center.

Shapiro, D., Dundar, A., Huie, F., Wakhungu, P., Yuan, X., Nathan, A., & Hwang, Y. W. (2017, April). *A national view of student attainment rates by race and ethnicity—Fall 2010 cohort (Signature Report No. 12b).* Herndon, VA: National Student Clearinghouse Research Center.

Schein, E. H., (2004). *Organizational culture and leadership.* San Francisco: Jossey-Bass.

Schmitz, P. (2014, October 22). The culture of collective impact. *HuffPost blog.* https://www.huffingtonpost.com/paul-schmitz/the-culture-of-collective_b _6025536.html

Schwartz, A. J. (2002, Summer). Introduction. *Association of American Colleges & Universities Peer Review,* 4(4). Retrieved from https://www.aacu.org/publications -research/periodicals/introduction

State University System of Florida. (n.d.). *Performance-based funding model.* Retrieved from http://www.flbog.edu/board/office/budget/performance_funding.php

The Education Trust. (2018). College Results Online, www.collegeresults.org

The Institute for College Access & Success (TICAS). (n.d.). https://ticas.org

The Pew Charitable Trusts. (2015, June). Federal and state funding of higher education: A changing landscape, *A Chartbook.* Retrieved from http://www .pewtrusts.org/en/research-and-analysis/issue-briefs/2015/06/federal-and-state -funding-of-higher-education

U.S. Department of Education. (n.d.). *Developing Hispanic-serving institutions program— Title V.* Retrieved from https://www2.ed.gov/programs/idueshsi/definition.html

U.S. Department of Education. (2017). *Title V request for proposals.* Retrieved from https://www2.ed.gov/programs/idueshsi/index.html

Vidal-Ortiz, S. (2017, September 22). Latinx in academe. *Inside Higher Education.* Retrieved from https://www.insidehighered.com/advice/2017/09/22/scholar -describes-his-rage-about-diversity-work-campuses-essay

Western Interstate Commission on Higher Education (WICHE). (2016). *Knocking at the college door: Big change with high school graduates through the 2030s.* Retrieved from www.wiche.edu/knocking

Western Interstate Commission on Higher Education (WICHE). (2017, September). Impact and implications: Projects of male & female high school graduates. *WICHE Insights.* Retrieved from https://knocking.wiche.edu/reports/2017/09 /projections-of-male-and-female-graduates

Chapter 9

ETHICAL VIGNETTES AND CASE STUDIES

Tamara Hullender and Margaret Partlo

This chapter presents cases with inherent ethical dilemmas representative of the myriad situations that student affairs professionals face daily. As institutions accommodate an ever-increasing range of student interests and embrace diverse student populations, it is important to consider the ethically-charged issues and situations that challenge the personal ethical frameworks of individuals and require ever-increasing finesse and cultural, legal, and ethical understandings. Law and policy attempt to frame the behavior and responses of professionals; however, not all situations can be clearly defined and often fall into gray areas in which actions and reactions do not neatly fit into statute and rule. Situations often require ethical decision making, perspective taking, and complex analysis.

Although law, policy, and organizational codes of ethics exist to guide student affairs professionals, understanding how to apply these requires considerable skill, experience, and subtlety. Where does the law begin and end? How can policy address the nuance of human behavior and interaction? Which consequences are unavoidable and which ones are extreme in any given situation? Can blame truly be attributed to a student or are situations more complicated than policy can address? Student affairs professionals work in environments and situations rife with competing tensions and ill-defined problems. Within the student affairs profession resides an inherent responsibility for individuals to recognize and report ethical violations.

The following vignettes present seven real-world cases that invite analysis and discussion on the ethical and legal dilemmas presented. Vignettes were crafted with consideration of the complexity of the student affairs profession and offer a means for reflection on practice, values, abilities, and strengths necessary to the work. Additional care was taken to offer opportunities for deconstruction of the vignette as well as perspective taking, ethical decision making, and application of the principals of beneficence and harm avoidance. Resources are included to guide analysis; however, the following questions are offered for consideration:

- What ethical issues are identifiable within the case?
- What resources and association or organizational guidelines might be helpful?
- With whom should the professional consult, if anyone?
- Does the case present ethical violations that must be reported?
- What potential courses of action could be taken and what consequences do each present?

As you reflect on these vignettes, keep in mind the ethical principles of "doing no harm" and acting in the best interest of others. Have these principles prevailed in each vignette? How can the professional involved remained grounded in these principles and perhaps remedy any previous lack of adherence to them?

He Said, She Said

Jaylen recently accepted his first student affairs position: Title IX Coordinator at a small public college. His first order of business was working with the parents of a male student accused of exposing himself to a female student in her dorm room. Although the case had already gone through the college's judicial process, under the direction of the Director of Student Affairs, the parents of the accused disagreed vehemently with the outcome.

The Director's transcripts on the proceeding were extensive. Jaylen noted that there were a number of students in the room, both male and female, who were playing video games, talking, or working on homework. According to the accuser, the male student had harassed her while she attempted to complete an assignment. She had rebuffed him earlier that day when he had proposed they go out together. She stated, however, that she had not refused firmly, but had used her assignment as an excuse. When he arrived later with a group of her friends, he took the opportunity to ask her out again that evening when she finished her assignment. She had made additional excuses, hoping he would pick up on her cues, but he continued to press for her to agree. Her statement then detailed that he had exposed himself to her. At this point, she said she yelled at him to leave and the male student and his friend both left the room and did not return.

The accused student's story was similar, but different. He readily admitted to asking the accuser out, both earlier in the day and at her dorm room. To him, she was simply playing hard to get. Every interaction was friendly and received with laughter, smiles, and joking around, as far as he remembered. He related that she had firmly told him that she was not interested and he had left; no yelling, and nothing inappropriate had happened. The first he'd heard that he was in trouble was at 2:00 am when the campus police picked him up at his dorm room across campus. They questioned him on an alleged sexual assault, which he vehemently denied, noting that many witnesses were there to corroborate his recollection of the evening's events.

To Jaylen's surprise, the Director of Student Affairs had not questioned any of the other students present in the dorm room when the alleged incident had occurred. Instead, the Director ruled in favor of the accuser and the male student was required to write three papers on sexual harassment, complete an online sexual assault course, and refrain from all contact with the accuser on threat of expulsion. Three weeks later, the young man's parents were calling for redress and taking their story to the press. The verdict was improperly decided, they charged, because none of the students who witnessed the alleged incident were questioned. Just days prior to Jaylen's arrival, they called to meet with the "the person in charge." Sidestepping the meeting, the Director instructed the staff to schedule the appointment with the new Title IX Coordinator when he arrived. The appointment was scheduled for Jaylen's first week of employment. With little time to prepare to meet with the accused parents, and reporters calling daily to his office, Jaylen knew his actions would be scrutinized. What course of action should he take?

Maria

Dr. Yakubi is a new professor in the business department at a small private liberal arts college. The move from a large research university, where he had spent eight years, presented opportunity to develop stronger connections to his department, colleagues, and his students. He was also able to create programming more easily in the absence of the glacial-paced curricular process at his previous institution. His first endeavor had sailed through the approval process: fully paid study abroad internships to the top five students in the business and entrepreneurship program, through the generous support of grant funding from alumni. Although such a program would mean more work for him, he reveled in the knowledge that his students would have a transformative experience likely to place them at a significant advantage in the job market upon graduation.

Maria, a phenomenal student who, despite her disadvantaged home life, was selected to participate in Dr. Yakubi's abroad internship. Receiving the full scholarship associated with the opportunity felt like a reward for her hard work and sacrifice while in the first two years of the business program. Her excitement doubled when her best friend and classmate, Nicole, was also selected. The two young women decided to live together while intern-ing at a top international company in Europe. They quickly finalized their housing and travel arrangements.

Maria's mother, however, had serious concerns about her daughter living so far from home. Maria had been diagnosed with a severe mental disorder three years ago. Her disorder completely managed with medication, Maria never applied for college counseling or support services, and she feared the stigma generally associated with mental illness. Maria assured her mother that everything would be fine and that she would talk with the program director, Dr. Yakubi; however, she did not discuss the issue with him, nor did she share information about her disorder with Nicole.

Maria and Nicole moved into their new apartment abroad and began their internship experience, excited to finally apply their education to the real world. They enjoyed short weekend trips together and both immediate-ly realized the benefit of being abroad with a friend. After a long weekend in Spain, Maria discovered that her medication was missing. She immedi-ately called her mother who suggested that she see a local doctor and attempt to refill her medication. Maria easily received a medication prescription and was relieved to report to her mother that everything was resolved. Within two weeks, however, Nicole noticed significant changes in Maria's behavior.

Maria adamantly expressed that her internship coworkers were not happy with her or the work she was doing. Her coworkers, she insisted, were talking about her behind her back, and she was sure that one of them was undermining her to the internship supervisor. Nicole repeatedly attempted to reassure Maria. There was no real evidence to support Maria's claims, nor had there been a specific incident. She suggested that Maria was either inse-cure about her abilities, or that they were both starting to feel homesick. Maria's roommate proposed that they go to a club after work to unwind, relax, and have some fun. That evening the girls consumed several alcoholic drinks and had a great time enjoying the club culture and talking with a group of local college students.

On the walk home, Maria verbally attacked Nicole, accusing her of con-tributing to the talk at work, and inferred that, perhaps, Nicole was the undermining colleague. Her state of agitation increased, and Nicole become more than upset at the accusations; she realized that something was terribly wrong with Maria. Back at the apartment, as Maria paced the kitchen, Nicole noticed a pill bottle had fallen out the handbag her friend had tossed on the chair. She surreptitiously picked it up and researched the medication and its uses.

Dr. Yakubi received a phone call in the middle of the night from Maria's distraught mother. Nicole had called her: Maria was in trouble and the local doctor had given her daughter the wrong medication. Assuming Dr. Yakubi was aware of Maria's condition, her mother discussed in detail Maria's disorder and the potential for Maria to harm herself or others. Without first-hand knowledge of Maria's condition, and aware that legalities protected his student, Dr. Yakubi, 4000 miles away, wondered what he could possibly do.

Double Jeopardy

As Samar walked out of the local police station, he reflected on what had happened yesterday. A student athlete at the small private college on the other side of town, he was aware that he was an anomaly to the local population. As the son of first-generation immigrants from a Middle Eastern country, he had grown up in a large metropolitan city known for its high crime and homicide rates. Run-ins with the law were commonplace where Samar came from, but he had worked hard in school and earned the scholarship that brought him to this institution. Although he often felt like an outsider in this small town, it was different from home and he considered it safe and quiet. As a result, he had learned to let his guard down on campus and while moving about in the community.

Because it was fall break, Samar's cousin Omar had arrived on campus for a visit. Omar was always looking for adventure, usually in the form of something illegal or daring. The small town and campus presented a challenge that Omar could not resist. Omar talked Samar into stopping by the local gas station to pick up some drinks and snacks. While at the store, Omar grabbed a beer and handed it to Samar and encouraged him to put it in his pocket. Samar put the beer back in the cooler, picked out a bag of chips and two sodas, paid for his items, and walked out of the store. Omar followed. As Omar and Samar returned to the college residence, Omar removed an ice-cold beer from his jacket pocket. A surprised Samar laughed and the two enjoyed their snacks, watched a football game, and then joined some of Samar's friends at the fraternity house for an evening of games and hanging out.

Working at the small college meant wearing several hats for Lindsay. She enjoyed her job as both student involvement coordinator and student conduct officer; she rarely had to convene conduct panels and mostly planned events for students, keeping them connected to each other and the campus community. Samar's run-in with the local police was troubling. In the five years she had been at the college, few students had been arrested in town. Samar's phone call from the town's lock-up yesterday was the first for Lindsay, and he was on his way to her office now. His claims of discriminatory actions by the local police, profiling him because of his ethnicity, as well as his insistence on his innocence concerned her. Samar had been in trouble once, but the skirmish was minor. He and his roommate had scuffled over typical issues that roommates often have. Words had become heated, one had pushed the other, and the residential hall assistant had intervened. Both young men had been disciplined, but that was two years ago. Samar's academic and athletic record were clean. His grades could be higher, but he was passing his classes. On the soccer field, he was a starter and known as an exemplary teammate. How had this student been arrested for shoplifting and resisting an officer? The college would consider it a second offense, punishable by expulsion, no exceptions. Given the minor nature of the first disciplinary action, Lindsay felt uneasy about the potential outcome of the upcoming meeting with Samar.

Samar fretted the details of the prior evening as he approached the campus administrative office building. The owner of the gas station believed he had stolen the beer that Omar had lifted. The scene at the fraternity house replayed in his head. Asking the officers for an explanation was completely within his rights, but the officers had taken offense and when he refused to lay down on the ground, things had really gone wrong. Samar touched his left side where the sting of the Taser remained. He had not refused the officer's order, he simply asked for more information. Sure, he had been nervous and perhaps that appeared to be defiance, but he had not stolen anything. Once down on the ground, the officers had placed him in handcuffs, and, as he tried to stand, used the Taser again.

The entire scene seemed like a nightmare and had quickly escalated, regardless of how he had tried to explain and cooperate. At the police station, Samar was shown the gas station surveillance video. Due to the angle of the camera, the video did not record Samar returning the beer to the cooler nor did it capture Omar placing one in his pocket. Samar had spent the night in the county lock-up and he would be reporting before the local magistrate next week. Meeting with Lindsay in the Office of Student Conduct might at least keep him in college, Samar hoped. Surely the college's "two strikes and you're out" rule would not apply in this case. What should Lindsay do?

Called to Serve

In the aftermath of a major hurricane, the governor has activated 24,000 National Guard members. For Alecia, an assistant director of student services at a mid-sized state university, the National Guard activation signaled more than relief for hurricane victims; she now faced the questions of a concerned group of students who serve in the National Guard. National Guard-connected students begin trickling in to her service center as soon as the office opens the day after the governor's announcement. Unfamiliar with campus policy on National Guard activation, Alecia consults the bulletin and, to her surprise, discovers that there is no stated policy on military-connected absences. Responding to students will require further investigation.

Nick and Kelsey, National Guard members and classmates in the same biology section, have approached their professor to inform her of their impending activation in just two days' time. Her response is troubling: special consideration of their absences will not be granted. With only three weeks left in the semester, both students currently have excellent grades. Both Nick and Kelsey are informed that they will be held to their biology professor's attendance policy: three absences, excused or unexcused, results in a failing grade. Nick and Kelsey respectfully listen and attempt to explain the circumstances of their upcoming absence, but the professor refuses to offer concessions. Confused and facing a rapidly approaching deployment date, they appeal to Alecia for assistance.

Through her quick research, Alecia learns that under the Uniformed Services Employment and Reemployment Rights Act (USERRA) ensures that members of the armed forces are protected in their civilian jobs. Upon returning from a period of service, the law enforces reinstatement with the seniority, status, and rate of pay equivalent to continuous employment without interruption. National Guard and Reserve Members who are students are not guaranteed the same rights; few protections for military-connected students are spelled out in statute or policy. A military-connected student who is called up to active duty is guaranteed the right of readmission under the Higher Education Opportunity Act, but this applies only if the institution participates in Title IV federal financial aid programs and makes no mentions of how to address service-related absences and their impact on course credit. Additionally, National Guard members are unique in that they serve both national and state missions. Federal protections only apply when the member is mobilized for national emergencies, when activated for state-level service, members are subjected to state law, if such protection has been enacted. In a state without specific protections for National Guard or military reserve students, and no corresponding university policy, Alecia realizes that, in the cases of Nick, Kelsey, and their comrades, the dispensation of attendance policies and resulting course grades or credit are completely at the discretion of faculty members.

Alecia fears that the impending deployment deadline, just two days away, leaves her little time to intervene on behalf of the National Guard students involved in hurricane relief efforts. Failing the students, who have completed all other course requirements in an exemplary manner, seems unfair. Their reason for the absence is outside their realm of control and is precipitated by the fulfillment of much-needed service to the state's suffering residents. Additionally, failing their courses will create a financial burden to several of the National Guard members who used Federal Tuition Assistance benefits to pay their tuition. Receiving a grade lower than a C for any course paid through the Federal Tuition Assistance program results in recoupment of those costs from the member's military pay account. Allowing the National Guard students to lose both course credit and tuition dollars is too much for Alecia to allow, but what can she do?

Anonymity Isn't Always Anonymous

Matias, a Greek Life coordinator at a mid-sized university contemplates how he might assist a fraternity member in trouble. The usual complaints from the local community that arose each semester were generally minor issues of parties that became a nuisance. The good done by fraternity and sorority members outweighed the bad; therefore, community members were welcoming to Greek life students. Last night's incident involved a near-death emergency room visit, an underage drinking violation, a police report, and a highly involved fraternity member was cited for a misdemeanor.

Brandon enjoyed living at the fraternity's new house and the comradery that fraternity membership offered. In particular, his leadership for the fraternity's big brother program was a point of pride for him. He credited his leadership position as the determining factor in landing an internship at a prestigious law firm next semester, his senior year. Now all that was in jeopardy. Anonymous reporting of alcohol-related issues to campus police was purported to protect individuals—both those who make the report and those who may have had too much to drink. From Brandon's perspective, the reporting system had failed him.

Hoping to ensure that no student suffered from alcohol poisoning, campus officials had instituted a no-fault, alcohol-related reporting system. Students were encouraged to call campus police and report any suspected alcohol poisoning, even for under-aged victims, allowing adequate medical response to occur and preventing a campus tragedy. The campus policy promised anonymity for the reporting student, and pledged that no student who reported an incident in good faith would be punished or face legal consequences. Somehow, campus was not following through on that promise to Brandon.

Brandon did not expect his girlfriend Gabbi, an 18-year-old, first-year student, to stop by the fraternity house yesterday. Of course, his fraternity brothers had let her in the house to wait for Brandon to return from his study session at the library. When the wait became long, and Gabbi had not been able to reach Brandon by text, she looked around for a snack. The cinnamon flavored alcohol had been too interesting to resist, and within an hour, the fifth was empty. Brandon had found her unconscious on the kitchen floor, the empty bottle nearby. Afraid that Gabbi had ingested too much alcohol, he had called campus police immediately, relieved to know that she would receive appropriate care and he would be protected as well.

When the ambulance arrived, however, so did the local police. Gabbi was transported to the hospital and was doing better today. Unexpectedly, Brandon had been charged with a misdemeanor: contributing to the delinquency of a minor and furnishing alcohol to a minor. If found guilty, he faced a $2,500 fine and up to one year in jail. In addition, he had just heard that the fraternity might also lose their charter due to the incident. At the minimum, they faced a probation of their charter and many of the fraternity brothers were blaming Brandon for the consequences of Gabbi's behavior. Seeking Matias' support was the only course of action that Brandon could think of. Surely the college would stand up for him, especially since he had followed through and reported Gabbi's condition. His anonymity and protection from consequences had been promised. What should Matias do?

Standardized Testing and Diverse Students

Dr. Kimberly Walton mulls over the data received from the university's institutional researchers on enrollment in the teacher education courses. Just as she suspected, many students of color completed the introduction to education course; however, very few students of color are represented in the capstone school-based internship. The department's efforts to recruit more diverse students to the teacher education program appeared to be successful; the number of students of color enrolling in the introductory course had increased fivefold over the past three years. Retaining them to graduation, however, was simply not happening. Further investigation appeared necessary to determine the point at which students of color were leaving the teacher education program.

The teacher education program faculty worked diligently in the past few years to ensure the program met accreditation standards and state requirements. The state's basic skills requirement, demonstrated on the college entrance exam, continued to present a significant challenge for some students. At first glance, the passing score didn't seem too challenging; students were to score at the 50th percentile nationwide, thus demonstrating an average ability in math, reading, and grammar. Dr. Walton suspected, however, that the program's typical student was incapable of achieving that score. The majority of the teacher candidates came from inner-city or rural settings and attended either poorly funded urban schools or small understaffed rural schools. While some of the rural students seemed to be able to meet the testing requirement, more of the urban students remained unable to do so.

Antoinette, a sophomore pursuing an elementary education degree, nervously opens the email from the testing service. Yet again, her math score is not high enough to meet the state's basic skills requirement for teacher candidates. When she arrived at State University, she was aware that her scores on the college entrance exam were lower; however, she didn't understand the impact those scores would have on her ability to pursue her dream of becoming a teacher. Growing up in the inner-city, the local schools consistently received poor ratings on state department of education metrics, but this school was the only option available to her family. The university's bridge program for inner-city students had been her ticket to college; however, the quality of her secondary education continued to hold her back as she attempted to complete her postsecondary studies. Antoinette decides to make an appointment with the professor of her introductory education course, Dr. Walton.

Dr. Walton's further research confirms her suspicion: students of color are leaving the teacher education program because they cannot meet the testing requirement. The institutional research report revealed that less than 20% of students of color who complete the introductory education course persist to the capstone internship and obtain a teaching certificate compared to more than 80% of white students who complete. She is dismayed that the data clearly demonstrates that students of color change their majors because they do not meet the testing requirement. Dr. Walton notes that Antoinette has emailed and would like to talk about her college entrance exam scores. Antoinette has been one of the most promising educators in the introductory class. Dr. Walton wonders how she might advise Antoinette, given all that she now understands about the disparity between diverse candidates in the teacher education program.

Financial and Family Responsibilities

Meg has worked her way through college for the past four years. As the only child of a disabled veteran, she felt fortunate to have a little assistance from her father's old GI Bill. Without another family member to help, she found herself increasingly involved in providing direct care to her father last semester, making it impossible for her to continue her part-time job at the college bookstore. As she approached the end of the spring semester, with an outstanding account at the university, the hold on her account prevents her from completing her fall registration for the two required courses necessary prior to her final semester internship to receive her marketing degree.

With just two weeks remaining in the semester, Meg's father takes a turn for the worse, and she must arrange hospice care for him. She consults with her professors and decides to spend the remainder of the semester with her father. Her professors express their understanding and make arrangements for her to receive incomplete grades with one year to complete the work. Meg's distress for her father overshadows her concern about incomplete college classes, outstanding tuition bills, and registration problems. She leaves campus for the summer, during which her father passes away.

Returning to campus as the fall semester begins, Meg has yet to solve her registration issues, but hopes for a new opportunity to move forward after her father's death. The hold on her account remains active and she is still unable to register for two required courses left in her program. Meg fears the courses may be full by now; classes began two days ago. Additionally, she must also complete the three classes that are unfinished from spring. She has found a new job at a local restaurant; however, she is behind on most of her bills. With only two semesters left in her degree, she is determined to finish and, perhaps, obtain a decent marketing job. On the advice of a professor, Meg reaches out to Jason, the College of Business success coach.

In his third year as a success coach, Jason is well-versed in connecting students to campus resources, equipping them with study skills and time management strategies, and guiding them in academic, personal, financial, and ethical decision making. He listens to Meg's concerns, and together they prioritize her most pressing concern: finances. Tapping into the campus emergency fund allowed Jason to assist Meg in paying her electric bill and get the power company to turn on the lights at her apartment. Lifting the hold on her outstanding campus account would require research into what was happening, especially because she received a steady GI Bill payment, had adequate loan funds, and surely qualified for a maximum Pell Grant.

Pell Grants are awarded to students with demonstrated significant financial needs. The amount awarded is based on expected family contribution and the cost of attendance, and the student's enrollment intensity. Full-time students, like Meg, receive larger amounts than half-time students do. The cost of attendance at the state university, Meg's family situation, and her full-time student status qualified Meg for the maximum Pell Grant each semester of enrollment as she pursued her first bachelor's degree.

In the student account system, Jason sees that the GI Bill payment has been processed each semester and her loan payments are also on time; the Pell Grant, however, has posted to her account and then been removed every semester. Strangely, the Pell Grant was not being applied to her account balance. Because her account has perpetually had a hold on it, Meg typically obtained additional loan funds or personally paid each semester so she could register for classes. Consequently, she registered each semester during the late registration period, after classes had begun. The cycle of paying her account late and registering late meant that she appeared to not be enrolled in the university at the time the Pell Grant funds posted. The funds were then returned, unnoticed by the university financial aid officials.

Jason realizes that the university has not accurately tracked Meg's account, and therefore, she has never received the Pell Grant funds awarded to her. With only two semesters left to complete her degree, Meg has taken additional loans and made personal payments that would have been covered by her Pell Grant, had the university noticed the glitch. Jason reflects on all that Meg has done to maintain her grades, complete assignments, work a part-time job, and care for a terminally ill family member. Determined to assist her, Jason wonders, what can the university do?

The vignettes presented in this chapter demonstrate the complexity of the student affairs profession. Many resources are available to assist in negotiating the ethical and moral obligations inherent to student affairs. Each institution presents specialized assistance, such as Title IX coordinators, legal counsel, and offices of civil rights. Additionally, professional associations and licensure boards maintain codes of ethics, ethics councils, and prepare resources to assist professionals facing ethical decisions. These resources also assist individuals to recognize and report ethical violations, a necessary and required element of the work.

RECOMMENDED RESOURCES

Ethical Decision-Making Processes

ACPA: College Student Educators International. (n.d.). Ethics standards and practices. Retrieved from: www.myacpa.org/ethics (2018, January 8).

ACPA: College Student Educators International. (n.d.). Ethical Principles and Standards. Retrieved from http://www.myacpa.org/sites/default/files/Ethical _Principles_Standards.pdf (2018, January 16).

ACPA/NASPA. (n.d.). Professional competencies Rubrics. Retrieved from https: //www.naspa.org/images/uploads/main/ACPA_NASPA_Professional_Competency _Rubrics_Full.pdf (2018, January 16).

ACPA/NASPA. (n.d.). Professional Competency Areas for Student Affairs Educators. Retrieved from https://www.naspa.org/images/uploads/main/ACPA _NASPA_Professional_Competencies_FINAL.pdf (2018, January 16).

Fried, J. (2003). Ethical Standards and Principles. In S. Komives, D. Woodward & Associates (Eds.), *Student services: A handbook for the profession* (4th ed.). San Francisco: Josey-Bass, 107–127.

Ford, R. C., & Richardson, W. D. (2013). Ethical decision making: A review of the empirical literature. In *Citation classics from the Journal of Business Ethics* (pp. 19–44). Netherlands: Springer.

Herlihy, B., & Corey, G. (2014). *ACA ethical standards casebook.* Alexandria, VA: John Wiley & Sons.

Hornak, A. M. (2009). Ethical issues for community college student affairs professionals. *New Directions for Community Colleges, 2009*(148), 53–62.

Kitchener, K. S. (1985), Ethical principles and ethical decisions in student affairs. *New Directions for Student Services,* 1985: 17–29. doi:10.1002/ss.37119853004

NASPA. (n.d.). Principles of Good Practice for Student Affairs. Retrieved from https://www.naspa.org/images/uploads/main/Principles_of_Good_Practice_in _Student_Affairs.pdf

Sandeen, A., & Barr, M. J. (2014). *Critical issues for student affairs: Challenges and opportunities.* San Francisco: John Wiley & Sons.

U.S. Department of Education. (2012). Family Policy Compliance Office. Retrieved from: http://www2.ed.gov/policy/gen/guid/fpco/index.html (2018 January 8).

Vaccaro, A., McCoy, B., Champagne, D., & Siegel, M. (2013). Decisions Matter: Using a Decision-Making Framework with Contemporary Student Affairs Case Studies. NASPA-Student Affairs Administrators in Higher Education. Washington, DC.

Chapter 10

CONCLUSION: WHAT DOES THIS ALL MEAN?

Anne M. Hornak

If this book were written 20 years ago, would the discussions about ethical issues on college and university campuses be the same? Would we be debating the analysis of ethical issues from the same lenses? The answers are likely yes and no. We live in an incredibly complex and dynamic world; however, we always have. The difference today is how we get our information and how fast information changes. This is largely a result of the 24-news cycle and social media; however, we also have more sophisticated ways of obtaining information, through technology. Our best decisions are made on the information we have at that time. When information changes, we need to go back and reevaluate our decisions often requiring leaders to change outcomes.

The chapters in this book were written to address ways to think about our work in student affairs in the context of the ethical and legal issues we face daily. The chapters offered real-world examples, case studies, theoretical analysis, and decision-making frames to continue to challenge how we think about legal and ethical issues in our work. In July 2015, ACPA-College Student Educators International and NASPA–Student Affairs Administrators in Higher Education adopted a revised version of the Professional Competency Areas for Student Affairs Educators (ACPA & NASPA, 2015). The competencies offer practitioners a framework of skills that are shared across the profession. The professional competencies compliment the ethical standards, and should be used in concert with the ACPA Statement of Ethical Principles and Standards (ACPA, 2006) and the NASPA Standards of Professional Practice (NASPA, 1990). ACPA and NASPA are umbrella organizations within student affairs, the specific functional areas also have ethical codes and standards that guide daily work. In addition, each institution has access to in-house or retained legal counsel, which should be consulted when faced with a legal issue. In regards to ethics, institutions rarely have an ethicist on campus to address ethical issues. Therefore, the development of a professional network to consult with is critical for professionals.

Typically, colleges and universities use discipline-based ethical standards and codes to guide the work of faculty and staff. At some institutions, there is an anonymous line that faculty and staff can call if they need to report or consult on an ethical situation (e.g., EthicsPoint). Students often report their ethical and legal concerns to individuals on campus whom they have a relationship with, such as resident assistants, faculty, academic advisors, counselor, and even the ombudsperson. Our biggest issue with the ethical codes and standards that are focused on the work of higher education and student affairs professionals is the ambiguous nature of the behavior and then the reporting structure. For example, ACPA has an anonymous line for consulting on suspected unethical behavior. However, ACPA has no jurisdiction over the behavior of an individual on campus. The goal is to assist individuals in analyzing the behavior and determining the best course of action. The ability of ACPA or NASPA to discipline or censure professionals is beyond the role and purvey of the committees. The statements are meant as guidance and offer direction to student affairs professionals in their work.

In this section, I will overview the ACPA ethical code and the NASPA standards individually and then explore the ACPA/NASPA professional competency areas to illustrate the collaboration of the codes to the competencies. It is important to distinguish between the provisions in the ethical principles and how they translate to professional behaviors. Another distinction important to note are the principles that offer guidance for ethical behavior and ideal standards set by the profession. The codes are not prescriptive in nature or design. The ACPA Statement of Ethical Principles and Standards (2006) is organized into four sections. Within each section there are elaborations that focus on working with colleagues, students, educational institutions, and society. The four sections are: (1) Professional Responsibility and Competence; (2) Student Learning and Development; (3) Responsibility to the Institution; and (4) Responsibility to Society (ACPA, 2006). The NASPA Standards of Professional Practice (1990) highlights 18 standards to guide practice. The standards highlighted in the document are: (1) Professional Services; (2) Agreement with Institutional Mission and Goals; (3) Management of Institutional Resources; (4) Employment Relationship; (5) Conflict of Interest; (6) Legal Authority; (7) Equal Consideration and Treatment of Others; (8) Student Behavior; (9) Integrity of Information and Research; (10) Confidentiality; (11) Research Involving Human Subjects; (12) Representation of Professional Competence; (13) Selection and Promotion Practices; (14) References; (15) Job Definitions and Performance Evaluations; (16) Campus Community; (17) Professional Development; and (18) Assessment (NASPA, 1990). While each document varies in detail and depth, both offer practitioners guidance on behavior related to professional conduct and many were referenced throughout this book.

The Professional Competency Areas for Student Affairs Educators (2015) is a document that is organized around 10 competencies with discrete outcomes that are categorized as foundational, intermediate, or advanced. The organizations have also developed a rubric to assess competency in the area. While there is significant overlap among the outcomes associated with the competency areas, each of the 10 areas has a distinct central idea that makes it unique. The 10 areas highlighted in the document are: (1) Personal and Ethical Foundations; (2) Values, Philosophy, and History; (3) Assessment, Evaluation, and Research; (4) Law, Policy, and Governance; (5) Organizational and Human Resources; (6) Leadership; (7) Social Justice and Inclusion; (8) Student Learning and Development; (9) Technology; and (10) Advising and Supporting (ACPA/NASPA, 2015). The document explains the competency area and then offers behaviors associated with the three levels of outcomes—foundational, intermediate, and advanced. The accompanying rubric can then be used for assessment of the competency areas.

The analysis of ethical issues in student affairs and higher education is nuanced and complex. This book was designed to help readers understand how complex this work is. Not only do we work with the intersections of ethical and legal standards, we have personal values and morals that can be an asset or a blind spot when doing the work. The most important aspect of ethical and legal practice is to continue to consult the standards, values, polices, and laws that guide our work. Additionally, it is essential that professionals develop a network of other professionals who can serve as consultants. These issues are complex and multifaceted and decisions should not be made in silos and vacuums.

REFERENCES

ACPA—College Student Educators International. (2006). *Statement of ethical principles & standards.* Washington, DC: Authors.

American College Personnel Association & National Association of Student Personnel Administrators. (2015). *ACPA/ NASPA professional competency areas for student affairs practitioners* (2nd ed.). Washington, DC: Authors.

NASPA. (1990). *Standards of professional practice.* Washington, CD: Authors.

INDEX